D0927068

PLATINUM GIRL

PLATINUM GIRL

The Life and Legends of Jean Harlow

EVE GOLDEN

Abbeville Press ▾ Publishers
New York ▾ London ▾ Paris

To my mother, Eleanore Golden

EDITOR: Alan Axelrod
DESIGNER: Patricia Fabricant
PRODUCTION EDITOR: Cristine Mesch
PRODUCTION SUPERVISOR: Hope Koturo

 Inquiries should be addressed to Abbeville Press, 488 Madison Avenue, New York, NY 10022. Printed and bound in Hong Kong. First edition.

Library of Congress Cataloging-in-Publication Data

Golden, Eve.
Platinum girl : the life and legends of Jean Harlow / by Eve Golden.
p. cm.
Includes bibliographical references and index.
ISBN 1-55859-214-8
1. Harlow, Jean, 1911–1937. 2. Motion picture actors and actresses—United States—Biography. I. Title.
PN2287.H24G65 1991
791.43′028′092—dc20
[B] 91-2951

FRONTISPIECE: Portrait still from Red-Headed Woman, *1932*

ABOVE: Portrait still from Libeled Lady, *1936*

PAGE 6: Glamour still, 1931

PAGES 1, 9, 11, 13, 31, 49, 61, 87, 113, 135, 175, 197, 213, 229: British cigarette cards from the collection of Walter J. Wiener, Jr.

CONTENTS

Prologue: 1934 8

ONE *The Girl from Missouri* 12

TWO *Going Hollywood* 30

THREE *A Star Is Born* 48

FOUR *What Price Hollywood?* 60

FIVE *Strange Interlude* 86

SIX *Blonde Bombshell* 112

SEVEN *It's Love I'm After* 134

EIGHT *Lady by Choice* 174

NINE *Night Must Fall* 196

TEN *Libeled Lady* 212

Epilogue 228

Filmography 231

Sources 242

Index 244

Never shall a young man,
Thrown into despair
By those great honey-colored
Ramparts at your ear,
Love you for yourself alone
And not your yellow hair

But I can get a hair-dye
And set such color there,
Brown, or black, or carrot,
That young men in despair
May love me for myself alone
And not my yellow hair

I heard an old religious man
But yesternight declare
That he had found a text to prove
That only God, my dear,
Could love you for yourself alone
And not your yellow hair.

—William Butler Yeats,
"For Anne Gregory" *(1931)*

PROLOGUE: 1934

Director "Woody" Van Dyke was fond of throwing elaborate Hollywood dinner parties to impress out-of-town guests and visiting celebrities; no doubt this was a result of having been christened Woodbridge Strong Van Dyke II. His home had a grand formal dining room, and every so often he'd hire a contingent of servants, cater a multicourse dinner, and invite as many stars as he could to mingle with the guests.

One night late in 1934, Van Dyke hosted a two-hundred-guest dinner for MGM's Louis B. Mayer and other top film executives—as well as a sizable number of top-brass marines. Van Dyke was eager to give the military men a night to remember, so he asked them which star they would most like to meet during their Hollywood visit. They voted unanimously for the screen's reigning sex goddess, Jean Harlow. The object of countless sexual fantasies, she was the epitome of porcelain-hard glamour. With her revealing, skin-tight gowns, garish makeup, and startling platinum hair, she symbolized the American ideal in aggressive, sexually available women.

Harlow generally portrayed good-natured prostitutes or cheerfully amoral working girls. Although beginning to get critical acclaim for her comedic talents, she was still considered a highly sexed vamp—after all, she'd been married three times by the age of twenty-four, her second husband having died under shady circumstances. She wasn't the girl next door, unless you happened to live between a nightclub and a bordello.

On the MGM back lot, 1936 ▼

Van Dyke sent his social secretary, Florence Turner, to the MGM commissary to issue a frantic last-minute invitation to Jean: Would she, please, as a personal favor, come to dinner that evening and display herself to a horde of sex-crazed marines?

Turner located the sex symbol, sitting with her friend and publicity assistant, Kay Mulvey. The darkly attractive Mulvey nearly eclipsed Jean, who was wearing a polo shirt and trousers. With her hair brushed back and no make-up on, Jean appeared all of twelve years old as she attacked her favorite meal: barbequed hot dogs.

Jean politely told Turner she couldn't possibly attend Van Dyke's dinner, that she and Kay had other plans. Van Dyke himself called later and begged her to save his neck and at least make a brief appearance. Jean was still polite, but she was firm in her refusal.

Jean Harlow immediately realized that this was to be a performance, not a dinner; that the director had been asked to parade Jean Harlow, Sex Queen, before his panting guests. She had been fighting for years to overcome her sexy image and play a wider variety of roles. She was tired of being displayed as a high-profile hooker. "She never took herself seriously, she played at being a movie star," Mulvey recalled when explaining Jean's reluctance to make such bread-and-butter appearances. When Turner had approached Jean at the commissary, she'd leaned over to Kay and whispered, with an evil glint in her eyes: "We've got to do something about this."

The two hundred guests assembled at Van Dyke's home. About an hour into dinner, the butler answered the doorbell and found two female beach bums at the entrance. Wearing huge floppy hats and sunglasses, ratty old beach clothes (which looked as though they'd come in with the tide), and bearing several cameras around their necks, they raced through the foyer and made a beeline for the living room. They flopped down on the living-room floor, set up a beach umbrella, and unfurled a tablecloth on the rug. The butler watched aghast as they hauled hard-boiled eggs out of their picnic basket and began cracking them over the furniture—and each other's heads—scattering shells while merrily snapping photos of each other.

W. S. Van Dyke led his guests in from the dining room for after-dinner cocktails and conversation, and found Kay Mulvey and sex goddess Jean Harlow thus employed, still giggling like schoolgirls. The host and guests had a good laugh once they realized the pair were not, after all, crazed tourists. Only Louis B. Mayer failed to see the humor, glaring at the guilty pair and saying coldly, "You two are *not* funny." He hadn't built up years of publicity behind his blonde siren just to have her disport herself like a female Marx brother.

After staying a while to chat with delighted guests, Jean and Kay departed, inviting the whole gang—all two hundred of them—to Jean's for a pool party the next day. The two went back to Kay's and tried to screw up enough courage to call Mama Jean and tell her that her daughter had just invited the marines to invade for a very large luncheon. Jean, her mother, and stepfather all lived in a large white mansion in

Beverly Hills; although Mama Jean loved playing hostess, this was a bit much on short notice.

Mama Jean was not amused, but nothing her Baby did could annoy her for long, and she arranged to have the lunch catered.

The marines arrived to find Jean helping to set up picnic tables, again wearing her signature polo shirt and floppy trousers, hair tied back, and face scrubbed clean. She happily signed autographs and posed for snapshots, alternately splashing about in the pool and "tanning" under a protective beach umbrella. No one who attended that lunch ever forgot their shock at discovering that Hollywood's steamiest dish was actually a tomboyish kid sister, more adept at softball than seduction.

Even the talented Bette Davis marveled at Jean's ability to subvert her own personality and create a totally different screen persona. Journalists laughed off the idea that the screen's sexiest star was really just a good-natured prankster—until they met her. Autograph seekers, expecting to be waved off by a bejeweled hand, were instead invited over for hot dogs and soda, and received years of cheerful postcards from the actress.

But the average moviegoer was not willing to believe that what appeared onscreen was anything but the truth. Charlie Chaplin must be a loveable tramp in real life, Boris Karloff a murderous fiend, and Marilyn Monroe a carefree bubblehead. Jean Harlow hated how her screen image fed upon itself, intruding into her private life and limiting her to one narrowly defined character both on- and off-screen.

Jean's story is one of a naturally happy-go-lucky woman who found it difficult to stand up for herself. Not a hard-headed fighter like Davis or Katharine Hepburn, nor a self-destructive loose cannon like Judy Garland or John Barrymore, Jean spent her brief life trying to assert personal and artistic integrity while still playing ball with the studio. Despite compromise, she somehow managed to emerge from Hollywood's front lines with her sense of humor and career intact. Hers is a short story, but it is also—on balance—a success story.

WHOSE BEAUTY IS FRAMED BY THIS LOVELY HAIR!

ONE

THE GIRL FROM MISSOURI

Teenaged Harlean Carpenter, ca. 1925

▼

Jean Harlow was born into a singularly ordinary world. No inner-city poverty or elegant foreign schooling; she was born neither in a trunk nor a palace. Jean's childhood was straight out of a Booth Tarkington novel: the idyllic small-town America we long for when speaking of The Good Old Days.

Turn-of-the-century Kansas City, Missouri, could be described charitably as picturesque or quaint, with its cozy, prosaic architecture and tree-lined streets. Many of its citizens, however, found it stifling and uninspiring. Nevertheless, Kansas City was safe, calm, and nurturing; from the perspective of a hectic adulthood, youth spent there might seem one long Sunday School picnic.

The future actress was born into this world on March 3, 1911. Her parents were dentist Mont Clair Carpenter and his young wife, Jean Poe Harlow Carpenter (studio publicity agents later used the ritzier-sounding "Carpentier" in their press releases). Had the baby been a boy, he would have been called Harlow Carpenter, diplomatically honoring both sides of the family. A compromise was reached, and the girl was named Harlean. Even after the christening, though, her family called her "The Baby," a nickname that stuck for life. Her mother (thereafter known as Mama Jean) described her only child as "very red in the face, with an amazing growth of cotton-white hair." That Harlean was born a platinum blonde is substantiated by photographs and by her maternal grandmother, who recalled that "at school the children would call her 'cotton top.' It made her furious." Harlean herself shrugged, "I must have been a knockout, but it's a little difficult to remember."

Harlean's father came from old Pennsylvania stock; George Carpenter had fought in both the American Revolution and the War of 1812. Abraham, Harlean's grandfather, enlisted in the Civil War at twenty and was wounded two years later. He returned to active duty with the Pennsylvania Volunteers until the end of the war, then went home to marry Dianna Beale. The Beales themselves were of impressive lineage, having emigrated from Germany in 1752 and fought in the American Revolution. (Among Jean's Beale ancestors was a woman with the delightful name Delilah Devore, sounding much more like a sex bomb than "Jean Harlow.")

In 1872 Abraham and Dianna Carpenter followed the mass of pioneers to the vast, lonely Midwest hoping to carve out a new home and future. Through eight years of killing drought, Carpenter stubbornly refused any government aid, exhibiting a hardheadedness unusual even in pioneering days. Somehow, he, his wife, and their three sons managed to make their Marshalltown, Iowa, farm a going concern. Eventually they set out for the still newer frontiers of Kansas.

Mont Clair was born in 1877. A quiet, studious young man, he was not cut out for the life of the pioneer. He left his rather intimidating family behind and moved to Missouri, graduating from the Kansas City Dental College in 1902. From this point on, the Carpenters fade from view. They were not given to public statements or enthusiastic interviews about their famous granddaughter. One pictures them looking like Grant Wood's *American Gothic:* good, kindly people made out of sandpaper and granite, hardly the kind to pour out their hearts to *Photoplay* or *Modern Screen.*

The Harlow side of the family, however, was as colorful as the Carpenters were dour. S. D. Harlow and his wife, the former Ellen Williams, were upper-middle-class Iowans residing in the boom town of Denver when their daughter Jean Poe was born in 1891. Family legend connects them to writer Edgar Allan Poe, although no real genealogical evidence can be found to back this up.

S. D. was a prominent real estate broker and respected citizen of Denver; of Kentucky heritage, he came to Iowa when he was still a child. A hearty, opinionated man, he treated his wife and child as a kindly monarch treats his subjects, pampering them shamelessly but disciplining them firmly. Ellen Harlow, as the wife of a self-made hustler, was able to keep her feet on the ground. She knew exactly how their fortune had been made, and how it could be lost in a boom-and-bust economy. No doubt she followed with a worried eye the rise and fall of Horace and "Baby Doe" Tabor, the silver magnate and his youthful bride whose sudden fall from grace epitomized the dangers of becoming too complacent. Her surviving letters suggest Ellen Harlow was an intelligent, incisive woman, not as garrulous as her husband, but fully able to enjoy what fate and the Gold Rush had given her.

Unfortunately, the Harlows' daughter Jean never developed an ounce of common sense. As the child of a wealthy, indulgent man, she grew up to be vague, imperious, and self-centered, spoiled by her par-

ABOVE: The Baby, 1911; RIGHT: Mama Jean, early 1930s

▼

ents and aunts Jetta and Lillian. But she had the kind of buxom blonde looks popular in the early 1900s and mastered the helpless, kittenish charm of a spoiled darling. This was sufficient to overwhelm the sheltered young Dr. Carpenter; it wasn't until years later that he learned how the fluttery exterior hid a woman determined to have her own way. The blonde heiress and the aristocratically handsome dentist were married in 1908.

The following year they moved into a modest gray stone house at 3344 Olive Street in Kansas City (the building was demolished in the late 1930s to make way for highway alterations). Dr. Carpenter opened a dental office on the ground floor, and the family lived upstairs. Significantly, the house was owned by Mrs. Carpenter's father, who used it as a Missouri-based address for his real estate firm. It wasn't long before the good dentist realized he'd not only married Jean, he'd married the entire Harlow clan, and life under his father-in-law's roof was not conducive to marital happiness, especially as his wife was still acting like a spoiled daughter.

When Mama Jean wanted her own way, she was not above pitching a fit; for most of her life, she was subject to emotional outbursts and crying jags. This was more than Mont Clair could handle. A reserved, almost reclusive man, he left his wife to the ministrations of her parents and retreated into his work. He began volunteering all of his free time to the Children's Mercy Hospital and was eventually made a member of its board of directors. Through the years local papers took note of the awards and citations with which he was showered, while his marriage settled into a convenient but unsatisfying routine.

Harlean was probably born at home. Most people were in 1911, and the availability of medical equipment in the Olive Street house made it especially suitable for lying-in. Mrs. Carpenter was attended by Dr. W. J. Clemmons, and a Miss Goudy was employed to look after mother and child. Even after Mama Jean was back on her feet and Nurse Goudy dismissed, she and Harlean were looked after by Ellen Harlow, with S. D. hovering in the background. The real estate mogul fell instantly in love with his new granddaughter and began spending more and more time at "his" Olive Street house. Mont Clair began spending more of *his* time at the office.

"My grandparents were about two of the most doting . . . who ever lived," Harlean remembered. "As a result I became a small, pampered tyrant who, at two years old, was in complete control of the house. All throughout my childhood Grandfather and I were boon companions. I believe he had more influence in molding my thoughts and ideas than any other person." Fortunately, he had better luck with his granddaughter than he'd had with his daughter. Perhaps Harlean was made of sterner stuff, or perhaps S. D. simply didn't make the same mistakes twice. Whatever the reason, it was soon obvious that little Harlean had a lot more on the ball than did her mother.

When Harlean was three, she was presented with a nineteenth-century porcelain doll named Isabelle, which had been Mama Jean's favorite toy. It soon met an unhappy end. In one version of the story, Harlean flung Isabelle to the floor and burst into dramatic tears (her "first public performance"). In a later interview, she recalled proudly handing the doll around at a social gathering and looking on in horror when a local matron inadvertently dropped Isabelle, dispatching her to Doll Heaven. Whatever the truth in this story, Harlean soon lost all interest in dolls and became a confirmed tomboy. Isabelle's remains were wrapped in tissue paper, later to be repaired; these shrouded bits of porcelain eventually returned to Mama Jean as part of her daughter's estate.

By 1915 Dr. Carpenter felt so smothered by his in-laws that he moved his family to a separate address, 4409 Gillham Road. Harlean's room overlooked a small park, and she was given an Airedale named Tigalaff, the first in an endless array of pets. If she couldn't see quite as much of her grandparents, at least she and Mama Jean had plenty of time and room to play. Dr. Carpenter no longer worked at home, having moved his offices to the Waldheim Building in downtown Kansas City, where he maintained his practice for the next thirty-six years.

The "small, pampered tyrant" at five, 1916 (Bettmann/UPI)

Harlean's summers were spent at the Harlows' estate, Red Gables, overlooking the Kaw River near Bonner Springs, Missouri. Much of her growing menagerie was boarded there, including a pony. "This is where I grew to know what kind of child my granddaughter was," wrote Ellen Harlow. "You could never imagine Harlean the child and Jean Harlow the actress as being one and the same person."

Harlean was bright and affectionate, "really a serious girl at heart, and a good girl." Also sentimental: Harlean presented her grandmother with her outgrown baby ring and bracelet, asking her to keep them safe where they wouldn't be lost (this was the kind of starry-eyed behavior she inherited from her mother). Ellen Harlow recalled that Harlean sometimes spent winter days meditating in the unheated attic while gazing out at the Kaw River below: "There are a million stars on the river when the suns shines," Mrs. Harlow quoted her granddaughter.

S. D. continued spoiling and doting on the girl, giving her an ermine bedspread for her fifth birthday (which no doubt would have appalled the hard-working Carpenters back in Kansas). As an adult, even Harlean laughed at the extravagance of ermine for a rowdy five-year-old. Both Red Gables and the Carpenters' Gillham Road house overflowed with servants, no doubt paid in part by the Harlow grandparents. Harlean and the chauffeur's son became playmates, and passersby in the park often saw the pale, white-blonde girl and the black teenager tending her flock of pets on the front lawn.

When she was old enough, Harlean was enrolled in Miss Barstow's School. Barstow's (founded in 1884 and still operating today) was an elite prep school catering to the daughters of the upper middle class. A Barstow's certificate was recognized for admission to Vassar, Smith, Radcliffe, and Wellesley. Harlean attended as part of a coeducational day program, along with two other girls and one boy of her own age.

In 1916, when Harlean first began attending classes, Barstow's was housed in a large white colonial building on Westport Avenue (looking very much like the mansion she herself would later build in Hollywood). Barstow's was, at the time, not the venerable seat of learning that it later became, still having one foot planted firmly in the nineteenth century. Gaslight was used well into the 1920s, and Harlean's contemporaries recall that discipline and workload varied wildly according to the whims of individual teachers. Class trips and special events often intruded on lessons; in 1922, the entire school spent one day avidly watching a nearby house towed by horses to another location. A local estate provided an abandoned cottage for picnics. Accommodating teachers would pile the children onto the 83rd Street and Wornall Road trolley, and classes that day took place in "the shack."

The kids patronized Morton's Hall and Confectionary, a nearby ice cream shop where Harlean discovered both a weakness for chocolate sodas and an unfortunate tendency to put on weight. For the rest of her life, she had to temper her healthy appetite with bouts of fasting and vigorous exercise. This sometimes brought on fainting spells, as one childhood friend remembers. Harlean had decided she was getting a bit round and simply gave up all forms of food for a few days. Not surprisingly, she passed out cold while visiting this friend and had to be laid out on the living-room sofa and fed hot soup until she'd recovered. The Harlows strongly disapproved of dieting (Mama Jean was no sylph), so Harlean's fasts had to be conducted in secret.

One of the teachers at Barstow's, Miss Babbitt, instituted a variation of Show and Tell, in which her students were encouraged to bring a favorite pet to class (either Miss Babbitt had been unduly influenced by Mary and her Little Lamb, or she was just prone to bouts of whimsy). Her niece recalled that "most [children] came with cats and dogs, but Jean brought in a basket, and when she presented it to the class, a big white head popped out of it." Harlean had decided that Tigalaff was entirely too mundane to display, so she'd coerced a live goose into her basket. She was already beginning to learn how much fun it was to be a show-off, to be just different enough to make a splash.

Every day at noon, Mama Jean showed up to take Harlean to the Muehlbach Hotel for lunch. "Throughout my school years mother never had a luncheon engagement with anyone else," she later said. "I recall that the headwaiter and the chef became interested in the little girl who sat on the telephone books, and how almost daily the chef prepared a special treat for me." Mama Jean's coddling was contagious, and soon it seemed the entire world was dedicated to Harlean's happiness and comfort. She was becoming the Golden Girl even more so than most only children, and Mama Jean began exhibiting an extraordinary attachment to her daughter.

If Harlean's father and paternal grandparents were somewhat detached and distant, the Harlow branch made up for it. Their attentions to their granddaughter were warm and nurturing, a much-needed healthy influence; but Mama Jean displayed a neurotic possessiveness. Even the charming ritual of the good-morning kiss was carried to extremes: "I started when 'Baby' was a tiny infant and I have never let anything interfere with my kissing her good morning as soon as she opened her eyes. Sometimes I sit for an hour watching her in her sleep." One can only assume that these predawn visitations were suspended during her daughter's marriages.

An active, healthy girl who loved climbing trees and riding horseback, Harlean never had much patience for high fashion. She was dolled up in white pinafores until her rambunctiousness proved this to be a waste of money; the dresses never lasted a week. Finally, Mama Jean realized that little jersey dresses in pastel colors could be repaired and laundered much more easily. Harlean was free of the Little Lord Fauntleroy look, though her closets were always stuffed full of new, frilly dresses. As soon as she was old enough, Harlean took to sweaters and loose slacks, before most women would be caught dead in them.

Like most little girls, though, Harlean had her sticky-sweet, sentimental side. She developed a passion for writing, which she never outgrew. Her mother saved these literary efforts, most of which were faux-medieval poetry heavily influenced by Tennyson. One typical work shows unusual introspection for a child:

The sun is dying as my hopes have died before
In its vanishing glory I see my past
A past of pomp and splendor
And yet now I have scarce enough to clothe myself
And still I am rich
For I have found peace of mind and friendship
In fewer words I have found God.

When Harlean was eight, the Carpenters moved again, into an impressive eighteen-room red brick house at 79th and Tracy Avenue. This home was situated a considerable distance from downtown Kansas City, on five acres of land—a large estate for a three-member family. Mama Jean was given a bright blue Packard to help her in her daily social rounds. Dr. Carpenter made sure his family was amply provided for and lacked nothing, except his presence.

Harlean found the Packard irresistible and began charming the chauffeur's son into giving her driving lessons. After she'd learned to put the car in gear, she figured braking and steering would come naturally, so she set off on a joy ride. Although Harlean escaped the ensuing collision unscathed, Mama Jean's new (uninsured) car was put out of commission for some time. Harlean agreed to wait a few more years before attempting to drive again, but the lure of the open road was so great that she'd become an expert behind the wheel by the age of twelve. She paid Mama Jean back for that Packard, though it took more than a decade. On her own twenty-third birthday, she bought her mother a new roadster.

The red brick home finally provided ample room for Harlean's pets. One fan magazine stated that the Carpenters maintained (in addition to Tigalaff) "six saddle horses, two cows, chickens, twenty ducks, two lambs, two pigs, four dogs and a pony named Beauty." This was no doubt a gross exaggeration, but the family did possess an unusually large menagerie for one small girl.

As she grew, Harlean developed into a rather nonchalant student: bright, but lazy. Since everything came easily to her, she never learned the knack of putting herself out for a goal. Why knock herself out for an A in spelling, which meant nothing to her, when she could spend her time with a foreign language or literature? She continued to write, and

Harlean outside the family's new Tracy Avenue house, 1919 (Bettmann/UPI)

one of her short stories was published in the 1920–21 yearbook. "An Elf's Adventures" was typical of the cloying fairy tales still popular at the time, involving a fun-loving elf named Mischi who runs away from school and is nearly captured by "a fat little girl." It was hardly an impressive work, even for a ten-year-old, but Harlean's ambitions ran deep and she persevered.

In 1922 she made her first stage appearance, as one of the Merry Men in a school production of *Robin Hood.* Grade-school plays are rarely reviewed, so the quality and enthusiasm of her performance has been lost to posterity; photographs show her as rather chubby but sufficiently merry in her costume. Harlean loved all the attention and excitement of appearing before an audience and became an instant ham. During one of Mama Jean's afternoon teas, Harlean decided to put on an impromptu circus for her mother's friends. She led her menagerie up onto the porch and began parading around like a junior Barnum. Plates were broken, tea spilled, and the ladies were not amused.

But Mama Jean couldn't bear to punish The Baby, not even when she bought a pack of Clown brand cigarettes and polished them all off in one sitting. Not only wasn't she taken ill, she decided she enjoyed smoking and had to be firmly talked out of it by her parents, who raised the specter of yellow teeth and stunted growth. This persuaded her to put off smoking until she was older. By the age of fourteen Harlean decided that she'd reached her adult height anyway and took up cigarettes again. She remained a chain smoker for the rest of her life, although she switched from Clown to the more adult Lucky Strikes.

Harlean's childhood wasn't one long round of picnics and pony rides, however; the Carpenters had been growing apart for years and decided to divorce in 1921. Mont Clair was increasingly unable and unwilling to deal with his wife's temper, and withdrew into himself and his work, leaving their ten-year-old daughter to play nursemaid and companion.

The divorce itself wasn't a bad thing for Harlean; happily divorced parents are far healthier for a child than unhappily married ones. But the question of custody was another matter. It was unheard of in 1921 for a father to win a custody battle, and there's no indication that any battle was waged in this case. Harlean went to live with her harebrained, volatile mother, although she'd have been much better off with her emotionally and financially secure father. The girl remained close to the Harlow side of the family, visiting them often; but she and Mama Jean became more dependent on each other. It was "us against the world."

Harlean loved her father and never got over the separation from him. Although she continued to write and visit him in her adult years, her romantic life became a search for another Dr. Carpenter. Even people who don't set much store by psychology cannot deny that the majority of men she dated (and married) both looked and acted like her father: intellectual, somber, reclusive.

Mama Jean packed up The Baby and moved to Los Angeles soon after the divorce, finally able to pursue her lifelong dream of becoming an actress. The ex–Mrs. Carpenter was only thirty, still attractive in a bovine sort of way, and was possessed of a driving ambition. It's not fair to presume she was untalented; indeed, many untalented actresses made headway with nothing more than the proper "push." And Mama Jean was not lacking in push. She began haunting the studios, registering with casting directors, getting photos taken to drop off at agents.

She got exactly nowhere.

Mama Jean took rooms at the La Brea Apartments and registered Harlean at the only private school in town, the Hollywood School for Girls. Although it boasted some influential students, Louis B. Mayer's daughter Irene remembered the school as "a jerry-built place run on a shoestring . . . [with] no pretensions whatsoever"—clearly the perfect school for Los Angeles, which in 1921 was a boom town filled with recent immigrants and new money. The Hollywood School for Girls (not to be confused with the more famous Hollywood High) looked like something out of a Marx Brothers movie. Advertised as an "outdoor" institution, one entire wall of the huge one-room schoolhouse actually folded back to look out on the sidewalk. (The building, at 1749 La Brea, is abandoned and boarded up today.) Emphasis was on sports rather than academics, which suited Harlean.

Despite the school's name, it also catered to several male students, including Douglas Fairbanks, Jr., and Joel McCrea. McCrea was six years Harlean's senior, but the two became friendly after bumping into each other at casting offices (Mama Jean took The Baby along on weekends). McCrea was a hopeful young actor who made good and became a major star by the late 1920s. He recalled the sullen young Harlean dragged into these offices by her mother; the little girl was plump, unremarkable, and unenthusiastic. Both McCrea and Harlean were told they had "funny noses" and would never get anywhere in films.

The girl tried to fit in at school, but being one of the few boarding students didn't help. The late Irene Mayer Selznick recalled that students had to wear severe navy-blue uniforms, but that Harlean stood out, possessing a noticeable pizzazz even at that age. Her classmates began calling her "The Baby Jeritza," for her startling resemblance to opera diva Marie Jeritza, and Harlean played to her audience. She began developing attitude; the more films she watched, the more she emoted. She learned to smoke like Nita Naldi, throw back her head imperiously like Gloria Swanson, to laugh and shimmy like jazz-mad Mae Murray. Mama Jean might become an actress in real life, but Harlean was discovering the joy of acting her way through a boring school day. Even history was easier to take if you pretended you were Lillian Gish.

And she became as movie-crazed as any of her classmates. Her family had curtailed her film-going in Kansas City, but now Harlean was free to race to any of the local theaters whenever she could scrounge up the admission. She enjoyed Charlie Chaplin (whom she even spotted once on Hollywood Boulevard) and Charles Ray, but her real love was reserved for cowboy star Buck Jones, and this gave added impetus to her horseback riding lessons.

Weekends were spent with Mama Jean, and Harlean's departure on Fridays was watched avidly by her classmates. Mama Jean would breeze up in a chauffeured limousine, "looking very much the merry widow," as Irene Mayer recalled. A terribly attractive, foreign-looking man ("very masculine, a big bruiser") would alight from the car as Harlean ran down the school steps to be swept up and away by this colorful pair. The schoolgirls watched from behind a nearby clump of bushes, sighing enviously.

The handsome foreigner who swept Harlean away on weekends had also swept Mama Jean off her feet. Marino Bello, a native Italian in

"The Baby Jeritza" at Hollywood School for Girls, 1923 (Bettmann/UPI)

▼

his late thirties, was every bored housewife's dream: sexy, handsome, and Continental. He was also the worst thing that could have happened to the ex–Mrs. Carpenter and her daughter. Marino was the epitome of an image Italian-Americans have battled for years: oily, slick-talking, and more than a little crooked. After more than a decade of the sedate, considerate, and very tedious Mont Clair Carpenter, it's no wonder Mama Jean fell for this romantic rogue.

Marino never seemed to have enough money, or current employment. He was not involved in organized crime, but he was a big-mouthed, fast-talking scalawag. Harlean, friendly puppy that she was, grew to like him and accepted him as her stepfather. Much to the

Harlows' despair and Mont Clair's disapproval, Mama Jean and Marino married in 1922, drawing Harlean ever farther from the more stable and intellectual side of her family. Mont Clair himself remarried in 1928; his was a lifelong and happy marriage, and Harlean got along famously with her new stepmother, the former Maude Seth.

The next few years were fairly uneventful for the preteen girl, but Mama Jean was kept hopping. Marino was incapable of holding down a job, and the new Mrs. Bello was no longer receiving support from her ex-husband. The few extra dollars from her parents didn't stretch very far, so poor Mama Jean was actually compelled to work for a living. Not the acting that she longed for, but waitressing and salesclerking. This was not what she'd come to California for, and soon the Midwest was looking more and more glamorous; a vacation really *was* a vacation, as she put up her tired feet in the Harlows' guest room while her husband gallivanted around Chicago and her daughter rode horseback through the park. Mama Jean's acting career was getting nowhere fast; she was in her mid-thirties, and her parents tried once again to pound some sense into her head. Move back home, they told her, California just isn't working out, and maybe you and Marino can find jobs closer to your hometown. Besides, the Harlows missed their granddaughter.

Much to Harlean's distress, the Bellos elected to return to the Midwest late in 1925. The girl had come to love California, with its free-and-easy atmosphere, beaches, warm breezes, and long, hot summers. A return to the frigid and strait-laced home of her childhood threw Harlean into an adolescent sulk.

She was enrolled in a French Catholic girls school for the winter–spring semester of 1926, an arrangement that lasted about five minutes. The "Baby Jeritza" of Hollywood was just about as fond of the nuns as they were of her, and she started a campaign to get transferred to a more congenial school. She was temporarily dumped into Miss Bigelow's Girl's School while her contingent of parents, stepparents, and grandparents submitted her for acceptance into Lake Forest Academy's Ferry Hall. Harlean easily passed the entrance exams and was accepted at the well-established prep school for the fall semester.

When Harlean entered Ferry Hall at fifteen, the Roaring Twenties were just beginning to roar.

The smock dresses and pinned-up hair of Harlean's youth were fast becoming passé (she'd spent most of those years in school uniforms, anyway). Her bobbed hair, which had deepened to a honey blonde as she entered her teens, was the latest style, and she was able to indulge in all the modern fashions: just-below-the-knee pleated skirts, drop-waisted sweaters, and T-strap shoes. Fresh from her brief bout with Catholic school, Harlean once again became the local flaming youth. Her fellow coeds quickly realized that here was a force to be reckoned with.

She'd smuggled her Victrola into her room and crowded into the closet with friends and their records (most machines at the time had no volume control, making it tough to play records surreptitiously). The girls also hoarded illegal hot plates for illicit treats; night after night they plugged up the transoms after lights-out and read Elinor Glyn novels till all hours. Mama Jean and Marino had taken rooms at the Highland Park Inn nearby, but school visiting hours were very strict and Harlean spent less and less time with her mother. Under the influence of her classmates, she was swiftly turning into a Preppie Princess, uppity in her bearing, but basically a wholesome, mischievous teenager.

She went on hayrides, attended costume parties (she and a friend donned raincoats, galoshes, and bathing caps, attending as "The Slicker Twins, a Lot of Good, Clean Fun"), and managed a mention in the yearbook as having Best Figure. For all the press about the red-hot, jazz-crazed youth of the twenties, Harlean's school years seem, from a modern perspective, incredibly innocent. In the late twenties, "good" girls didn't go unchaperoned on dates, and petting parties were the height of naughtiness. Girls who lost their virginity were beyond the pale—more to be pitied than envied. Smoking (which Harlean did) was considered ill-bred, as was drinking (which Harlean did not do). Drugs were unheard of, except in music circles, where some jazz musicians were reported to smoke reefers. Certainly, no Ferry Hall girl would admit even to knowing what marijuana was.

Harlean became friends with Adaline Morrison when the girls discovered they wore the same dress size and started raiding each other's closets. Adaline recalled that Harlean was disciplined for wearing an ankle bracelet given to her by a male admirer. "Several of us wore them, but exception had been taken" to Harlean's, and the dean threatened her with exclusion from the concert program unless it was removed. Harlean went off in a huff, called a cab, and was packing her suitcase before Adaline managed to cool her down. A later biographer claimed that Harlean was disciplined for refusing to wear a brassiere, but Ferry Hall officials deny that any such disciplinary record exists; the episode is surely based on the less-exciting bracelet story told by Adaline.

Harlean had to go through the hazing process still typical of colleges and prep schools, and Adaline recalled that "we were very hard on 'The Blonde.' Could she take it? Was she a sport?" Fortunately, Los Angeles had hardened Harlean socially, and she was more than a match for the Ferry Hall girls. She was ordered by the hazing committee to appear at breakfast with a bath towel around her head and an alarm clock suspended from her neck; she had to wear her clothing backwards and salute seniors on bended knee. Harlean really got into the spirit of things and began making up her own hazing rituals, roaming into the cafeteria with cold cream smeared on her face and eating all her food using just knives. She'd beaten the committee at their own game and was readily admitted into the clique of Popular Girls.

Despite her lack of interest in higher education, Harlean had a good enough mind to get by in classes without straining. She excelled in English and French, and was very interested in dramatics. She began taking breathing exercises, lying on the floor with books piled atop her while reciting poetry, much to the amusement of her dorm mates. Winning the lead in the school production of *The Winter's Tale* proved to be her first and last brush with Shakespeare. One class at which Harlean did not excel was gym. Although she loved open-air sports, much of this class consisted of donning hideous bloomers and doing endless hours of calisthenics (long before Jane Fonda popularized them as aerobics). Harlean claimed the flat sneakers absolutely ruined her feet for high heels and managed somehow to obtain a doctor's certificate excusing her from gym class.

All this time, of course, she was watching the boys, and the boys were watching her. While Ferry Hall was a girl's school, there were both boys' prep schools and Lake Forest College nearby, and plenty of opportunity for flirting. Harlean dated and teased as much as the next girl, but she never fell prey to any serious crushes until she met Charles Fremont McGrew II, in May of 1927. Chuck McGrew was a moderately wealthy twenty-one-year-old orphan who lived with his grandparents. He'd seen Harlean around town and was drawn to her; she looked older

Harlean (arrow) in a Ferry Hall production of The Winter's Tale, *1926*

than her sixteen years and was the center of an admiring crowd at all times, sure bait for any competitive college boy.

Chuck tried several times to bump into Harlean, without success. He met her at a spring dance, but no sparks flew, and he began to despair. So Chuck followed the lead of Cyrano de Bergerac and had a friend beg Harlean for a date on his behalf; he was luckier than Cyrano, and the two soon became an "item" around school.

That summer, love was in bloom. Chuck and Harlean fell for each other with all the force of teenaged hearts and hormones. They began talking of marriage, much to the alarm of their families. The McGrews had no objection to Harlean per se, with her impressive ancestry and Ferry Hall enrollment, but they weren't about to see their grandson and heir entangled with a schoolgirl at this stage of life.

Even the romantic Mama Jean didn't want to lose her Baby at sixteen. She, Marino, and the family in Kansas City strictly forbade any talk of marriage until Harlean had turned eighteen. By that time, they figured, the bloom would be off the romance. The kids, however, ran out of patience; since they had their families' approval for an eventual wedding, there was no sense waiting.

On September 20, 1927, when their friends were occupied with thoughts of the following day's Dempsey-Tunney fight, Harlean and Chuck got into his green roadster and took off for Waukegan. They located Justice of the Peace Louis Ekstrand and were married shortly after midnight, Harlean giving her age as nineteen to avoid any unpleasantries.

A little shocked and sobered, the newlyweds drove slowly back down Lake Shore Drive and into Highland Park to confront the Bellos. Mama Jean, as expected, dissolved into tears while Marino phoned the McGrews, Harlows, and Carpenters for a family powwow. Not surprisingly, there was a lot of yelling and crying, while Harlean and Chuck huddled in the corner wishing they'd kept on driving north toward Canada that night.

No attempt was made to annul the marriage, indicating that the kids admitted to sleeping together. This was perfectly normal for an engaged couple, even in 1927; it's entirely possible they'd been having sex for weeks, and certainly their wedding night must have continued after "you may now kiss the bride."

This threw the whole affair into a new light. What if The Baby were pregnant? Being a child bride was bad enough, but the thought of single motherhood, divorced or not, made up the minds of her family. For better or for worse, Harlean would stay married. The McGrews were even less happy, but they agreed to make the best of a bad situation. Of course, Harlean would have to drop out of school, as Ferry Hall did not admit married women. Chuck had little interest in education himself, and was raring to begin his life as a grown-up, married man of the world.

Above: Charles Fremont McGrew II; RIGHT: newlyweds Chuck and Harlean McGrew on their honeymoon cruise, autumn 1927

▼

His grandparents were planning an excursion to California by ship. It was popular at the time to cruise via ocean liner through the Panama Canal from coast to coast—a lengthy undertaking, but in those pre-jet days, a romantic and languid one. The junior McGrews took a train to New York, where they met up with the elder McGrews and boarded their ship. Harlean was on her way back to California, this time for good. Once they arrived in Los Angeles, Harlean realized she was home at last. The thrill of her younger days on the West Coast came back to her, and she easily persuaded her husband that it would be wise to start their new life in a new town, to make their California honeymoon a permanent one.

The McGrews wired their families that they'd decided to settle in California. Pooling their considerable resources, they rented a Spanish-style bungalow in fashionable Beverly Hills, just two doors from Clara Bow. Harlean bought herself a pomeranian named Oscar, and they set out to enjoy the good life.

No sooner had their wire arrived than Mama Jean was upstairs packing. She was still smarting from her last bout with California, but there was no way this woman was letting her Baby start married life without a shoulder to lean on, without her mother to look after her. Marino himself was chafing under the eagle eyes of the Harlows, as had Mont Clair before him. So the newlywed McGrews had barely settled into their home when the Bellos showed up on their doorstep, having just moved in down the street. Harlean happily threw herself into Mama Jean's arms as Bello and McGrew sized each other up. Now that Harlean was Mrs. Charles McGrew, Mama Jean could shuck any appearances of motherhood; the two became "pals." And just as often, Harlean found that her's was the shoulder being leaned upon. She was looking after Mama Jean.

TWO

GOING HOLLYWOOD

Glamour still, 1931

The Hollywood that the young McGrews encountered in late 1927 was different from what Harlean had known several years earlier. Los Angeles was a one-industry town, and that industry had been thrown into turmoil by the sudden and unexpected success of talking pictures.

Talkies were nothing new in the autumn of 1927, when Warner Bros. premiered *The Jazz Singer,* and why that particular film turned the industry on its ear is a mystery still. The story was hopelessly outdated and sentimental; viewed today, *The Jazz Singer* is stilted and racially offensive, although Al Jolson's magnetism still attracts. Reviews even at the premiere were mixed, and most people thought talkies were a fad. But by the end of the 1920s, the thirty-year-old art of the silent film was a dead one. Hopes that talking and silent pictures might co-exist as parallel art forms, like painting and photography, proved vain.

An enterprising actress couldn't have picked a better time to move to Los Angeles. Change was in the air. Primarily, the new screen actors came from the theater. Nearly all of the major stars of the 1930s were discovered on Broadway: James Cagney, Ruby Keeler, Joan Blondell, Barbara Stanwyck, the Marx Brothers, Bette Davis, Katharine Hepburn, Irene Dunne, Mae West, Kay Francis, Claudette Colbert, Fred Astaire, Ginger Rogers, Jeanette MacDonald, Humphrey Bogart, Spencer Tracy, Edward G. Robinson, Miriam Hopkins, Paul Muni. Although Clark Gable had worked as a film extra, it was onstage he first attracted notice. Another group to get a boost from talkies were performers who had been on the fringe of success—extras, bit players, and supporting actors whose careers were dying on the vine. Myrna Loy, Carole Lombard, Norma Shearer, Gary Cooper, Loretta Young, and W. C. Fields found their careers reenergized by the advent of sound.

This was the situation that greeted sixteen-year-old Harlean McGrew, who had learned from her mother the frustrations awaiting any hopeful actress. McGrew must have known of his mother-in-law's attempts to break into films, but naturally assumed that her failure would discourage Harlean.

On the whole, the marriage was an idyllic one. The McGrews were young, beautiful, and wealthy. Both were just out of school and suddenly found themselves living in the adult world, but without the worries and responsibilities normally inherent in growing up. McGrew expected to enter the real estate field like his grandfather, but was in no great hurry to do so. He and Harlean were very much in love with each other, with California, and with their lot in life.

Harlean wrote regularly to Mont Clair and her new stepmother; Maude remembered years later that the letters showed no indication that the elopement may have been a mistake.

The McGrews spent their first few months in Beverly Hills furnishing their bungalow; Harlean played housewife while Chuck began a desultory search for work. His inheritance was enough to keep the couple comfortable, but in order to compete with their wealthy friends, a steady supplementary income was necessary. They were to be respectable middle-class youngsters: the husband would work to support his family, while the wife stayed home to raise children.

It wasn't long before Harlean, a high-spirited teenager, started getting restless. The life of a suburban housewife soon lost its charm, and she began trying to make friends and see the town. McGrew was not unusual in his assumption that a prep-school girl, even an impetuous one, would expect to settle down and start a family after marriage. But Harlean was quite capable of finding diversion while her husband was otherwise occupied, and this did not sit well with him.

She began looking up her old classmates and going on shopping expeditions, luncheons, and sightseeing trips. She and Chuck became part of the "trust fund" set in Los Angeles, and began entertaining friends at home. One of these was Lucille Lee, a girl about Harlean's age who spent some of her leisure time working as a film extra.

Harlean already knew her way around the studios from her high school days. She remembered how exciting the atmosphere was, but how impossible it was to find work. So it was with no great expectations that she gave Lucille a ride to Fox Studios one day in mid-1928. The job market hadn't changed much since 1925, but Harlean had. When she'd first attended casting calls with Mama Jean, she'd been a chubby, unremarkable kid. But by the time she returned in 1928, Harlean had acquired a marketable form and face.

Hollywood was overflowing with beauties, all looking as though they'd issued from the same cookie cutter. Each era produces its own popular "look," and the look of that time was still the plump, Kewpie-doll cuteness of the early twentieth century. Dozens of starlets rose to a minor fame and faded away, not possessing that off-kilter something to set them apart. The real successes were those with memorable features: "we had *faces,*" as Norma Desmond put it in *Sunset Boulevard.*

Harlean, too, had a "face." She was no breathtaking beauty, but she did have a quirkily compelling look. She was small: 5′3″, a little over a hundred pounds. Her most arresting features were her blue-gray eyes; large, round, and deep-set, they seemed made for the movie camera. She had good "camera bones," as well, with the essential strong, high cheekbones. Her forehead was perhaps too broad, and her chin receding, but that was offset by a lucky cleft. Her mouth was terrific—a fashionable cupid's bow, which broke into an infectious and genuinely beautiful smile. Her nose seemed to have been designed with an architect's T-square, being entirely composed of sharp 45-degree angles. Her flawless ivory skin seemed to glow with health.

This isn't quite the picture Harlean herself got when she looked in the mirror. She, like many people, lost all sense of reality when it came to her own appearance. "There is, first of all, the little matter of my face not matching," she told reporter Carolyn Hoyt in 1936. "I have no chin to speak of. My eyes are set too deep in their sockets. My nose doesn't belong to my face at all. When noses were shuffled and dealt out, I drew somebody else's . . . and my figure is just one of those things . . . my shoulders are too broad and too square. My hips are too broad . . . my legs are—well, all right, I suppose, as legs go. You may have observed, though, that I never wear short skirts."

Harlean even thought her smile was foolish. "Poor child," remarked Hoyt, "she believes all this." In photos, Harlean's appearance varies, as does everyone's. In a flattering light, with the right makeup and photographer, she was one of the great beauties of the twentieth century. On a bad day in harsh sunlight, she could be downright plain.

But she had more than a pretty face and shapely figure. She had that indefinable something that registers on film, that oddity of personality or talent that sets the star apart from the mere actress. It still hits audiences today, and it hit Fox casting director Joe Egli. Right between the eyes.

He approached Harlean and asked if she were registered with Central Casting, the recently formed "clearing house" for extras. No matter how much she impressed Egli, he couldn't help her unless she was properly registered. He gave Harlean a note directing her to the casting organization; she pocketed it and went home to think it over.

When she mentioned the letter to her friends, they told her she was crazy not to follow up on it—after all, she'd been noticed on her very first day at a studio, whereas some of them had been attending casting calls for months with no reaction. Mama Jean was particularly excited and offered to accompany her daughter to Central Casting.

Harlean now took her future into her own hands. The process of registration and endless follow ups was, and still is, time-consuming and disheartening. Harlean knew this and must have been serious about her chances to take this step. It was not something she would have done on the spur of the moment.

Mama Jean was thrilled that Harlean wanted to take up the standard again. She and Marino had been acclimating themselves to California, but neither had settled into any pretense of job-hunting. The blonde mother and daughter, both wearing the unflattering, severely bobbed hair so popular at the time, arrived at Central Casting some time during the closing months of 1928. Mama Jean registered herself as Jean Bello. Harlean, whether out of sentimental loyalty to her mother or second thoughts about her husband's reaction, registered under Mama Jean's maiden name: Jean Harlow.

The newly named actress waited barely a week for her first call. She nearly directed the phone call—for "Jean Harlow"—to her mother before remembering that *she* was Harlow. Indeed, it would take Jean years before she legally changed her name.

She was told to report to Paramount Studios the following morning, to bring her best evening gown, and to be prepared to spend the day. Jean was flustered; registering for film work was one thing, but actually to appear in films was something else again. She knew her husband and her family would disapprove. They had never been happy with Mama Jean's attempts to break into the profession, and there was no reason to believe they would feel any differently about The Baby. Then there was the matter of Mama Jean, who had struggled for years to become an actress, with nothing but rejections to show for it. Jean's getting a call so quickly (and under her mother's maiden name!) might rub salt into old wounds.

As much as she loved her mother, her family, and her husband, Jean decided not to let any of them stand in her way. She suspected by now that even if her marriage was to last, she would never be happy as a homemaker. Untrained for any profession but more familiar with acting than anything else, she reported to the studio.

She and her black gown were selected from the mob of extras and assigned to *Moran of the Marines,* starring Richard Dix and Ruth Elder. Jean was directed to the sound stage and spent the next few days sitting around a restaurant set, waiting for the cameras and lights to be adjusted and getting acquainted with her fellow extras. She was paid $7.00 a day, standard for extra work.

Jean's new job threw her in with a different crowd than what she was accustomed to. Despite her sometimes tough demeanor, she was an extremely sheltered young woman; she'd been under her mother's wing since birth, and her very proper grandparents tried their best to shield

An extra in her first film, Moran of the Marines *(1928); Jean can be seen with elbows on table just left of center.*

▼

her from the harsher realities of life. She'd gone to school with upper-middle-class neighbors, associated with Mama Jean's "women's club" friends, and dated only socially acceptable young men. Any contact with the theatrical set or rowdier children had been discouraged. As much as Jean may have wanted to broaden her horizons, it was impossible to escape her family's chaperonage.

Suddenly, she was in the midst not only of slumming society folk, but the down-and-out actors, small-time hoods, struggling geniuses, has-beens, and opportunists who flock around film studios. And it was in precisely this creative, stimulating atmosphere that Jean blossomed. She began to develop a latent gift for making friends. As a child, she'd been somewhat of a loner, content to spend her time with her pets and her mother. Now she was able to relax among people who knew nothing of her background and accepted her as one of themselves. Her youth and beauty stood out, but it was her sense of humor and mischief that endeared her to her coworkers.

As the casting calls began coming in with some regularity, Jean realized that she would have to inform her husband and family that this was not just a lark, but a full-time career. Mont Clair, having long ago relinquished parental responsibility, sighed in resignation and offered no objections. S. D. Harlow was more of a problem. He'd derided Mama Jean's theatrical ambitions as a "phase" and felt that his granddaughter was passing through a similar period—annoying, but fairly harmless. He gave his consent, but with reservations. McGrew sulked and stormed, but didn't go so far as to put his foot down—yet.

Throughout late 1928 and early 1929, Jean jumped at every assignment she was offered. It's impossible to say exactly how many films she appeared in at this time, as Central Casting has discarded all their old files, but sharp-eyed observers with pause buttons on their VCR remote controls may be able to spot her in previously uncatalogued films within this period.

In 1935, Jean recalled her early work and made up a list of necessities for anyone planning to earn a living as a film extra. This list is as pertinent today as it was sixty years ago and shows how serious Jean was about her work, how quickly she caught on to the intricacies of her trade. Working in films, even as an extra, required more than a pretty face and ambition, according to Jean; one also needed to pay attention to:

> *Shoes.* Assistant Directors always look at your feet first.
>
> *Hair.* No matter how simple a coiffure you evolve, the beauty shop cannot be dodged forever.
>
> *Makeup.* You'll never get a close-up unless your makeup is satin-smooth with the very best grease and powder and shading.
>
> *Telephone calls.* Not only the daily routine to Central Casting, but the three or four calls every day to Marcella or Red, or Tommy, the several various persons in different studios who had manifested a degree of friendliness sufficient to warrant a call to remind them of your existence.
>
> *Hats.* You can't fake hats the way you can fake clothes. Hats CHANGE—irrevokably.
>
> *Transportation.* The cruelest burden of all the burdens. First National, way over in the valley. Metro, far out in Culver City. Fox, in Westwood. Funny the way Easterners came out here and expected to find all the studios cuddled up in one handy group in the heart of Hollywood.

After *Moran of the Marines* and *This Thing Called Love,* Joe Egli at Fox used Jean in *Fugitives.* She appeared at Paramount in *Close Harmony,* a musical starring Nancy Carroll and Charles "Buddy" Rogers; *Weak But Willing,* a short comedy directed by Al Christie; and the Ernst Lubistch operetta *The Love Parade,* starring Maurice Chevalier and Jeanette MacDonald. In this last film, Jean appears in the audience of a climactic opera scene. One of four young society women in a box seat, she stands and demurely applauds as Chevalier joins MacDonald in the Royal Box. Dressed in matronly black and looking slightly plump, Jean smiles and bows toward the camera. This and her platinum hair are all that set her apart from her fellow extras.

The hair was something new. About the same time Jean entered films and changed her name, she decided to change her appearance as well. The California sunshine had begun to lighten her hair a shade or two from its natural honey blonde, and Jean realized that the "cotton top" she'd so despised as a child could be a valuable asset, a way to set her apart from the hordes of hopefuls at the cattle calls.

There were many blondes onscreen in the late 1920s, including such major stars as Marion Davies, Mae Murray, and Blanche Sweet. But these women were golden blondes, nearly brunette in some lighting. Jean decided to go one step beyond and become a platinum blonde. She certainly wasn't the first; there were a good number of platinum heads visible in crowd scenes. Indeed, it was the very visibility of those heads that spurred Jean on. Nevertheless, it was quite a daring step to take, even for an actress. She knew, however, that her pale coloring would lend itself well to the extravagant shade, and her white-haired baby pictures reassured her that, after all, she was only returning to her original color.

Not that achieving platinum was an easy task. There were no one-step formulas at that time. First, the color had to be stripped with a combination of hydrogen peroxide and ammonia, a process that took one or two treatments in Jean's case, since her hair was already light; a brunette might have to endure several hours of repeated bleachings before all the color was gone. The mixture was irritating to the scalp, and the fumes were overwhelming. Once the color was completely stripped, a platinum rinse was applied, resulting in a head of shining white hair with an almost imperceptible blue-lavender glow.

The process took quite a toll even on the healthiest hair. Along with the color, most of the natural moisture and wave were removed, leaving the hair dry, brittle, and difficult to manage. Platinum hair could not hold a permanent wave, and since most of the original curl had drooped in the bleaching process, Jean had to pin-curl or finger-wave her hair every night. She also had to treat it with oils and moisturizers and shield it from the sun to prevent further damage. In addition, Jean had to have her roots touched up every week or two. Most blondes could get away with putting this off, but Jean had close-ups to think of and couldn't risk even a half-inch of roots, which might cost a potential part. These touch-ups were accomplished with a "white henna" paste made up of more peroxide and ammonia, thickened with magnesium, and applied to the hairline. The initial process, including the follow-up shampoo and set, cost anywhere from $7.50 to $50.00, depending on hair length and color, and the beauty shop's own price scale. The weekly touch-ups added another $10.00, a tremendous expense for a $7.00-a-day extra.

Most beauty shops refused point-blank to work on platinum hair, but Jean found a Los Angeles establishment, called Jim's, which she patronized for years. In New York, she used R. Louis, who would tell the press in 1931 that bleaching "is absolutely ruinous to the hair of the average person," that the hair would dry up and break off within six months. Helena Rubenstein sniffed that "truly elegant women . . . will not subject their hair to it." Paul of Fifth Avenue turned away hopeful platinum blondes, and Elizabeth Arden would treat these ladies only if they had already dyed their hair and only needed a touch-up.

Jean's impetuous action was destined to have an amazing impact on both the film and beauty industries. In the wake of her remarkable success, nearly every major star went platinum for a time. Clara Bow bleached her hair after eloping with cowboy star Rex Bell; Greta Garbo glumly submitted to a platinum wig in *As You Desire Me,* Joan Crawford tried the shade in *This Modern Age,* Bette Davis in *Fashions of 1934,* and rising contract players Alice Faye, Carole Lombard, Anita Louise, Lola Lane, and Lyda Roberti found themselves turned into Harlow clones. Golden-blonde Mae West lightened her hair in 1932; in *Go West, Young Man,* character actress Elizabeth Patterson looks askance at West's platinum locks and huffs, "When *I* was a girl, people with hair like that didn't go out in the sunlight!" Even *actor* Gene Raymond found himself with platinum blonde, marcelled hair. By 1931, beauty parlors in every major city were overwhelmed, as tens of thousands of women demanded platinum.

Besides dyeing her hair, Jean invested in her first theatrical agent, a second-rate shyster named Arthur Landau, whom writer Anita Loos described as "one of those fringe characters in the early days latching on to people to try and make money." Jean, always a soft touch and a dreadful judge of character, was impressed by his faith in her and agreed to pay him a 10 percent commission on any jobs he might find. She thought him an endearing character, calling him "Pops" and even loaning *him* money.

With or without Landau's help, Mama Jean landed an extra part as a cafe customer in *Masquerade.* There is no record of her ever appearing on-screen again, though not for lack of trying.

Jean's luck began to improve when short-comedy producer Hal Roach cast her in *Liberty,* with Laurel and Hardy. Her part wasn't much—she looks on in horror as the comics tumble out of a cab with their pants around their ankles—but she was noticed and appreciated by the cast and crew. Roach called her back for a featured bit in *The Unkissed Man* as a doctor's patient, small bits in such oddly titled shorts as *Why Is a Plumber, Bacon Grabbers,* and *Thundering Toupees;* and in May 1929 she appeared again with Laurel and Hardy in *Double Whoopee.*

In the wake of Jean's first success, stars and starlets were plucked, bleached, and marcelled into Harlow clones. TOP (LEFT TO RIGHT): *Marion Davies, Joan Crawford, Carole Lombard;* MIDDLE (LEFT TO RIGHT): *Greta Garbo, Betty Grable, Constance Bennett;* BOTTOM (LEFT TO RIGHT): *Lyda Roberti, Alice Faye, Joan Blondell*

▼

CBS

"I wouldn't trade my experience in those comedies for anything," she said later. "There was a friendliness and camaraderie about that small studio that was vastly different from the impersonality of the larger studios." The Roach lot had been nicknamed "A Lot of Fun," an opinion Jean heartily seconded.

The affection was reciprocated: in their 1930 short comedy, *Brats,* Laurel and Hardy played mischievous children, and on an oversized mantelpiece seen in the film was a framed photo of Jean, representing the brats' mother, who has no other "part" in the film. In their Foreign Legion comedy, *Beau Chumps* (1931), another photo of Jean (this one signed "Jeanie-Weenie") represented the vamp who'd broken the hearts of the entire cast.

Double Whoopee was the closest thing to a big break that had come Jean's way. At one point in the film, she pulls up in a limousine at the hotel where Laurel and Hardy work as doormen. Wearing a black chiffon gown and mustering an appropriately snooty attitude, she saunters into the lobby, unaware that her gown has been caught in the car door. In nothing but her black lace step-ins, she signs in at the desk, discovers her predicament, and rushes madly off in Stan Laurel's coat. Jean enthusiastically sought coaching from her director and costars, playing this scene in an effective deadpan. "No one was too busy to help or advise," she recalled. "Stan and 'Babe' [Hardy] realized my ignorance and did everything in their power to make me feel at ease." She was

With Bryant Washburn in The Unkissed Man *(1929)*

▼

The infamous lingerie scene in Double Whoopee *(1929), with Laurel and Hardy*

▼

beginning to realize that comedy was her forte—not only did she have the knack for it, but the rollicking atmosphere of the Roach lot appealed to her.

When *Double Whoopee* was released in mid-May, Jean called home to brag to her friends and relatives. Spending her entire paycheck on long-distance phone calls, she relayed the most exciting news yet: Hal Roach, impressed with her striking looks and her talent, had signed her to a five-year contract at $100 per week. Roach's assistant director, Bobby Short, had earlier signed her to a short-term contract, but her showing in *Double Whoopee* was so promising that Roach had upped the terms and took her on as a stock-company player. This was a considerable accomplishment for a teenager who had been in the business only six months. She was now the chief moneymaker in the McGrew household, and frequent handouts were given to the Bellos, as well. Mama Jean had no income, and Marino invested what little money he had in get-rich-quick schemes. More importantly, the Roach contract dispelled any doubts Jean may have had about her career.

S. D. Harlow dutifully trouped down to the local theater to see his granddaughter in *Double Whoopee.* He was proud of her in spite of him-

self; the Harlow determination and ambition had apparently skipped a generation. If Jean was able to succeed where her mother had failed, S. D. was prepared to make the best of it. Yet he was not amused by what he saw on-screen and telephoned Jean that night to give her holy hell for appearing in her underwear. Acting was one thing; after all, Maude Adams and Lillian Gish were beyond reproach. But Adams and Gish did not flaunt themselves in black lace step-ins.

He had never used harsh language with her before, according to Jean, "but he hit a pretty good average in those five minutes." Bulldozed by her husband and now her grandfather, she reluctantly agreed to give up her budding career. She had never before defied her family, and now she bowed before this unified onslaught. Hal Roach was disappointed to lose the services of such an agreeable and hardworking actress, but he had no desire to make trouble between Jean and her family. He tore up the contract and signed Thelma Todd, another blonde comedienne, to replace her. Jean told Central Casting to remove her name from the rolls.

It was with no good grace that she returned home that day. She blamed McGrew as well as her grandfather for the loss of her career, and she blamed him for every boring moment of each unfulfilling day. As she and her husband grew up, they were growing apart. The marriage was beginning to crumble. Long afternoons spent listening to Mama Jean whine about what a waste it all was didn't help, either.

Early in that summer of her discontent, Jean made the acquaintance of Edwin Bower Hesser, a well-known photographer. Hesser wasn't affiliated with any one studio, but he had made a considerable name for himself photographing society women and actresses. Adela Rogers St. Johns described him as "a pleasant plump little man, artistic to his fingertips and harmless as a kitten." His specialty was seminude "artistic" studies of such well-known stars as Gloria Swanson, Bessie Love, and Corinne Griffith—not to mention Miss St. Johns herself. Jean managed to arrange a session with Hesser in Griffith Park, his favorite setting. The results are quite bucolic, reminiscent of Isadora Duncan studies. Jean, draped in flowing chiffon, disports herself in various nymphlike attitudes on a rock ledge. The ankle bracelet, which had caused her such grief at Ferry Hall, is her only apparel aside from the chiffon. Laughing and a little self conscious, she is very much the healthy, curvacious teenager—and quite obviously naked under the diaphanous scarves.

No use was made of the Hesser photos during Jean's lifetime. MGM never had to mount a cover-up, and the pictures never resurfaced to threaten Jean's career, as Marilyn Monroe's nude calendar did during her starlet days. (A nude photo purporting to be of Jean surfaced years later in Kenneth Anger's vicious *Hollywood Babylon.* It shows a woman, who bears no resemblance to Jean, reclining among brocade shawls. The bone structure is all wrong, the platinum hair appears to have been

From the Edwin Bower Hesser session in Griffith Park, 1929

▼

airbrushed in, and the photo is certainly not in Hesser's style. This didn't stop Anger from printing it and *Newsweek* from featuring it in its "Newsmakers" section.) In any case, Hesser's work was so well known in Hollywood that a sitting with him was considered an honor, not a scandal. But the photos proved to be the final breaking point in Jean's marriage. As could be expected, McGrew was furious when he saw the prints Jean took home.

Jean later denied the existence of these photos, and the question remains as to why she posed for them in the first place. The sun was bright, the scarves tissue-thin; she had to know how naked she would appear. The answer lay in Jean's love affair with the camera, and her delight in shocking people. All her life she had an irresistible urge to puncture stuffiness. She was a pliable, agreeable girl who allowed herself to be pushed around—up to a point. But anyone who pushed too far—parents, husband, or employers—found that when she felt trapped or put-upon, she acted rashly (her elopement) or played unconventional pranks (the Hesser photos).

From the beginning, Charles McGrew had been trying to discourage Jean from working in films. He knew full well that she and her mother had little chance of success, and cited Mama Jean's failures to back him up. The sabbatical Jean's grandfather forced on her was all the more galling as supplemented by McGrew's I-told-you-so attitude and served only to strengthen Jean's resolve to prove her husband wrong by a return to the screen.

Her desire to work contrasted sharply with McGrew's own reluctance to find a job. The little money she brought in was more than he was earning. While the couple didn't have to worry about paying the bills, their income was worse than halved when Jean left films. McGrew was forced to begin serious job hunting, and resented this mightily.

Quarrels became more frequent, McGrew reportedly took to drink, and Jean spent more time with her mother and Marino. Then McGrew found the Hesser pictures. It's not certain if Jean deliberately left them out to be discovered, or if it was all an accident. The result was the same: on June 11, 1929, Jean packed up and went home to mother.

Although McGrew no longer had any say in her acting career, Jean would still have to deal with her grandfather. Mama Jean realized that the old man would have to be confronted in person; for both mother and daughter were experts at wrapping him around their little fingers.

When S. D. Harlow received a call that Jean would be arriving for an unscheduled visit, he knew something was up. He had mixed feelings about her recent separation, and he thought she might want to discuss it with him. It's not known if the subject of Charles McGrew II was ever broached, but by the time she returned to Los Angeles Jean had her grandfather's reluctant consent to return to films. She also had an ul-

The Saturday Night Kid *(1929), with (left to right) Jean Arthur, Clara Bow, and Leone Lane*

▼

timatum: S. D. would no longer foot the bills. If Jean wanted to survive as an actress, she would do it without his financial support. As she later recalled the confrontation, her grandfather said, "The only way that you will grow hard enough to succeed is to be driven by necessity."

Jean told Central Casting to reactivate her name on the "at liberty" list and sat back to see what would happen. As it turned out, she had picked up her career at the perfect moment. Someone at Paramount remembered her and requested her for a role in *The Saturday Night Kid,* a comedy-drama starring Clara Bow as Mayme, a salesgirl at Ginzberg's Department Store. During the course of the film, Mayme must contend with a reluctant boyfriend (James Hall), a thoroughly rotten sister (young Jean Arthur, still some seven years away from stardom), and an overbearing supervisor (Edna Mae Oliver, who nearly stole the picture). A typical Bow vehicle, the script depicts her as hot-headed but kindhearted, giving her the opportunity to crack wise, throw tantrums, and generally kick up her heels.

Bow went out of her way to make Jean feel welcome, and, in return, Jean idolized Bow. Although Jean was little more than a bit player, Bow made sure she was included in more publicity than was customary. Assigned the role of Pearl Carroll, a Ginzberg salesgirl, she appeared in perhaps half a dozen scenes and had as many lines. This was Jean's first speaking part, as all of her slapstick comedy shorts had been silent. She's quite visible in the film, dressed in black at her perfume counter, and is given a bit of business early in the action. She looks slim and very young, wearing almost no makeup. (Although her name did not appear

With star Clara Bow and fellow extras in The Saturday Night Kid

in the film's opening credits, Jean was listed eleventh at the close—though credited with the part of Hazel, actually played by Leone Lane.)

Her few lines are delivered with authority and good comic timing. In the film's closing moments, Jean appears backstage at a Ginzberg allegorical revue, complaining about her costume, an outlandish brocade evening gown. She is quite effective and manages to milk a few laughs out of her brief time on-screen.

Jean became friendly with James Hall, the male lead. Hall and Ben Lyon had been working on the silent film *Hell's Angels* since late 1928, but were currently at loose ends. *Hell's Angels* was being reshot as a talkie by producer Howard Hughes, so the cast was temporarily at liberty and carrying out other assignments. Hall took Jean to lunch several times and to dinner dances at the Montmartre. No romance developed, but the two became good friends and sometimes double-dated with Ben Lyon and his fiancée, actress Bebe Daniels.

Jean's role in *The Saturday Night Kid* didn't take long to shoot, and soon she began getting more calls. She worked on two projects at United Artists, the first of which was *New York Nights,* Norma Talmadge's first talking film. According to costar Gilbert Roland, Jean stood out amid the crowd of extras, leading those present to wonder why she was stuck in minor roles (in this case, a shocked party-goer who witnesses a shooting). Roland claims to have pegged Jean instantly as star material.

Hopeful young starlet Jean Harlow, 1929

▼

Her next UA film *was* big—Charlie Chaplin's *City Lights*—but her own participation fell short of Roland's prediction. *City Lights* (which had been shooting for more than a year, but wasn't released until 1931) is regarded as a classic, but Jean's contribution was a step down. As an extra in a nightclub scene, she is impossible to spot in the actual film, although she is clearly present in still photos. It's almost certain that, with Chaplin's penchant for endless retakes, Jean's footage wound up on the cutting room floor.

As 1929 drew to a close, she remained on the fringes of success; still doing bit parts and extra work, wondering if Gilbert Roland might have overestimated her potential, and hoping that Charles McGrew wasn't the one who had been on target.

THREE

A STAR IS BORN

Portrait still, 1931

▼

While Jean was providing background color at United Artists, trouble was brewing across the lot at the studio's offshoot, The Caddo Company, Inc. Caddo's head, the eccentric young millionaire Howard Hughes, was embroiled in his production of *Hell's Angels;* Jean's friends James Hall and Ben Lyon were still marking time while the film went through one crisis after another.

Hughes, an aviator, had decided to leap into the film business with a breathtaking, heart-stopping tribute to the Royal Flying Corps of WWI. He hammered out a plot line with director Marshall ("Mickey") Neilan and writer Joseph Moncure March, then tackled the more intimidating technical problems: this was not just any film, this was to be a Howard Hughes film.

He toured Europe and returned with a fleet of period aircraft that would have been the envy of many a small nation's airforce, he signed up every ex-fighter and stunt pilot he could locate, and he constructed his own airfield in the San Fernando Valley. Sets went up, a cast was hired, and filming began on Halloween 1927—the same season that Harlean had arrived for her California honeymoon.

Hall and Lyon portrayed brothers Roy and Monte Rutledge, Oxford students caught up in the war. Roy (Hall) is a stolid, patriotic youth determined to fight for God and country; Monte (Lyon) a ne'er-do-well not at all cut out for military life. Swedish actress Greta Nissen was cast as Helen, a society girl no better than she should be, flirting with both brothers in turn as well as every other man who crosses her path. The plot veered from drawing-room romance to aerial adventure, as the Rutledge brothers battle German dirigibles, shoot down enemy planes, and come to terms with the faithless Helen. Eventually, on a suicide mission, they are captured, and Roy is forced to kill Monte, who threatens to turn traitor. Roy goes to the firing squad, knowing that he has sacrificed his brother's life for the greater good.

Hell's Angels took more than a year to complete, both because of the complicated technical problems and Hughes's perfectionism. He insisted on waiting for real rainstorms to film in, not wanting to pawn off phony storms on his public. The dogfights took forever to plot out and choreograph, and could only be shot during picturesque days: sunny, but with enough clouds for the planes to dart attractively in and out of. There were plenty of crashes, many injuries (including Hughes himself, who pancaked his own plane en route to the studio), and several deaths. A mechanic responsible for sending smoke out of a "hit" plane was unable to escape when an actual accident occurred; one pilot was electrocuted when he hit a high-tension wire; another died during storm filming. But the major expense involved a sequence taking place at a garden party, far from the flying fields.

Hughes was experimenting with a process called Multi-Color. Experiments with color had been taking place since the dawn of film; a few silents had even been laboriously hand-painted frame by frame. Many early films used overall tinting (red for fire, blue for evening, and so on), which is why modern audiences, who see untinted prints of the early films, are often baffled by "night" scenes obviously shot in broad daylight. But Multi-Color was proving to be both expensive and more difficult than Hughes had imagined.

Throughout 1928 and into 1929, while Jean's own career waxed and waned, *Hell's Angels* ground on at a then incredible cost of $5,000 a day. Hall, Lyon, and Nissen were becoming forgotten figures in Hollywood, and even Lyon's busboy was getting suspicious: "Every day you go studio, paint on face for picture. You do this long time now, but I no see any picture. You got money. You bootlegger?"

Finally, the film was in the can and ready for its preview. The Los Angeles audience made clear what Hughes, obsessed to the exclusion of the outside world, hadn't noticed: *Hell's Angels* was a silent movie. In the time it had taken to shoot the film, the talkie revolution had pulled the rug out from under Hughes. Instead of a buoyant, stirring air saga, he had himself a $2 million lead balloon. But Howard Hughes was not the type to admit defeat. He was young, wealthy, and, some thought, insane. He would reshoot *Hell's Angels* as a talking picture if it took him the rest of his life. Joseph Moncure March was reenlisted to turn the shooting notes into a dialogue script, and the demanding, brilliant, and difficult James Whale was hired as "dialogue director." Hughes realized that he himself would be unable to guide the cast through a talking performance, and Whale was an intimidating enough person to whip them into shape. He had recently worked on *All Quiet on the Western Front* and was later responsible for such films as *Frankenstein, The Invisible Man,* and the 1936 version of *Show Boat.*

Hell's Angels *poster art (1930)*

▼

HELL'S ANGELS
Howard Hughes'
Thrilling
Multi-Million
Dollar-Air
Spectacle
with
JEAN
HARLOW
Ben Lyon
James Hall
UNITED
ARTISTS
PICTURE
'Hap' Hadley

James Hall and Ben Lyon were signed by Caddo for their second bout with *Hell's Angels,* but Greta Nissen was unable to rejoin the cast. Popular legend has it that her Swedish accent ruled her out for the role of the English Helen, and this seems to make sense—although none of the other cast members sounded remotely British. But Nissen herself claimed that prior contractual obligations forced her to turn down the role. (Her film career eventually foundered, and she settled for a long, happy retirement and marriage to a wealthy California businessman.) Hughes was forced to film around Helen until another leading lady could be found. This posed no problems for the first few months, as Helen appeared in only a half-dozen scenes and there was plenty of other work to do. In the meantime, Hughes and his people began to hunt for a new leading lady. She had to be blonde, and she had to be sexy—after all, not everyone in the audience would be fascinated with the war story. Hughes didn't want to hire a well-known actress, as he had decided to create his own star and place her under long-term contract. He was convinced that the part would make any competent actress into an overnight success, and he wanted full control over her. Whale also wanted control and knew that a terrified starlet would be putty in his hands.

Dozens of blonde starlets were dusted off and tested for the role, including Ann Harding, June Collyer, Carole Lombard, Marion Marsh (who eventually did play a bit part in the film), and Thelma Todd. Todd seemed to be dogging Jean's footsteps, having just replaced her at the Hal Roach "Lot of Fun" in mid-1929, but neither she nor any of the other hopefuls pleased Hughes, who was looking for someone startlingly different.

Finally, Hall and Lyon recalled the blonde bit player from *The Saturday Night Kid,* the one who had been so much fun to work and play with. Lyon located Jean at a nearby studio and asked her, "How would you like to play the lead in *Hell's Angels*?" Well aware of his penchant for practical jokes, Jean gave him a Bronx cheer. But Lyon continued: "I mean it. What time do you break for lunch?"

Her lunch hour started at 12:30, and by 12:40 she found herself being dragged bodily into Howard Hughes's office. The mogul was hardly bowled over when Jean walked in, but sighed to Lyon, "Let her have a voice test. You've made tests with everyone else, so you make it with her. . . . Make it tonight."

James Hall later said that he had brought Jean to Hughes's attention. The shadowy Arthur Landau also claimed credit, saying he'd brought her directly from *Double Whoopee,* which had been filmed nearly a year before—quite a walk between sets. Nor does Landau's record as an agent lend credence to his claim.

That night, Jean and Lyon rehearsed until the camera and sound crew showed up around ten. Writer March, who was present at the test, took one look at Jean and made the famous remark, "My God, she's got a shape like a dust pan!" Looking at the test, one can only wonder where March bought his dust pans. Jean appears slim, girlish, and quite photogenic. Hughes viewed the three-minute screen test the next day and reluctantly signed Jean Harlow for the female lead in *Hell's Angels.* Whale, March, and Hughes himself expressed doubts about her abilities, giving the lie to later stories that her beauty, talent, and sex appeal had stamped her as an instant star. Jean herself was realistic about it: "I don't know how I got the part," she said. "I suppose Howard Hughes was just so sick of looking at blondes, he was in the mood to give up!"

After two years of bit parts, Jean was finally in the big leagues. On October 24, 1929, Hughes signed her to a three-year contract at $1,500 for the eight weeks of work on *Hell's Angels;* thereafter, she would earn $250 a week when she worked and $200 a week between films. Jean was finally able to write home with some certainty that she'd make Grandfather Harlow and Mont Clair proud of her yet. Nor did the contract come any too soon, as she was supporting both of the Bellos, who seemed quite incapable of holding down paying jobs.

From the Multi-Color sequence in Hell's Angels *(1930), with Ben Lyon, James Hall, and Evelyn Hall*

▼

Hell's Angels: *Helen shows her true colors; with Douglas Gilmore, James Hall, and Ben Lyon.*

▼

Jean plummeted from these heights to new depths of terror and despair on her first working day. She was nervous, of course, but she was young and ambitious. Things had been going along quite well; she'd been the darling of the Roach lot, and even big stars like Clara Bow and Gilbert Roland had been kind to her. But Jean had never dealt with James Whale. He was an irresistible force, and she was a terrified, vulnerable nineteen-year-old.

Although the character of Helen appeared in a mere half-dozen scenes, they were of the utmost importance to the film, as Helen was the only major female character. Most of Jean's scenes were opposite her friends Lyon and Hall. She needed all the moral support they could offer; she was getting nothing but grief and insults from her director.

"Harlow was quite aware of her deficiencies," recalled writer March, "and a lot of the time it must have seemed like a nightmare to her." For the first time, it was brought to Jean's startled attention that acting consisted of more than hitting your marks and prettily saying your lines. She was called upon to create a character, a mood; she had to carry most of the film on her barely clad shoulders. Whale was not known for his patience under the best of circumstances, and he quickly broke Jean with his constant tirades.

As to Hughes, he was polite in his shy way, and friends later asked Jean if she'd made a play for this very eligible bachelor. But Hughes had his plane sequences (and his current flame, actress Billie Dove) on his mind. Jean was too close to nervous collapse to do any serious flirting, and claimed the boss was all business. "As far as I'm concerned, I might be another airplane," she told Anita Loos. "He expects you to . . . never get tired, give your best performance at any hour of the day or night, and never think about anything else." He did, she added, offer her a bite of his cookie, which was tantamount to a proposal from this man who had a chronic phobia about germs.

But he absented himself from most of the non-aerial scenes, being a little terrified himself of director Whale. Jean was getting shakier by the day. After filming, she would crawl home to a quick dinner and a long cry. Her usually cheerful on-set demeanor changed. Lyon remembered her as quiet and reclusive: "She used to carry with her around the studios a little satchel containing four or five books of poetry, famous prose, or some special branch of the classics she was studying at the time." Not for her the sophomoric pranks of her costars, who, as Lyon recalled with a great deal of shame, teased the hard-of-hearing Hughes by "pretend[ing] we were talking about him when we were actually only moving our lips. . . . He took it very well, but it really wasn't funny when I look back at it."

As shooting continued into 1930, Whale became more and more of a tyrant. During one seduction scene, Jean was unable to exude the lurid sexuality Whale wanted. She turned desperately to her director and pleaded, "*tell* me—tell me exactly how you want me to do it!" Whale drew himself up and snarled, "My dear girl, I can tell you how to be an actress, but I cannot tell you how to be a woman." Jean broke down completely and rushed off the set in tears.

In addition to her emotional trauma, she was also suffering from a severe case of "klieg eyes," caused by the strong floodlighting (with klieg lights) required for the Multi-Color segments. "We worked for two successive days on my close-ups and each night I went home with inflamed eyes and a headache," she later said. When the pounding headaches got worse, Jean went to a doctor and was told that her conjunctiva had been burned. While not a dangerous condition, it was horribly painful.

Nevertheless, somehow, Jean got through the picture physically, but she was broken emotionally. Up till now, she'd breezed through her assignments with gay assurance and confidence. Now Jean was convinced she was "an awful actress" (her own words), that she'd be hooted off the screen. Indeed, she would never fully recover from *Hell's Angels,* never really regain her youthful self-assurance. Her sense of humor returned, but it was cynical and self-mocking. James Whale and *Hell's Angels* had killed the carefree Hal Roach extra.

The Caddo Company set about publicizing the film and its new star with all the forces at its disposal, making sure the public would be breathless with anticipation by the time *Hell's Angels* was released. Jean was certain that her performance would shatter all those expectations, and found it difficult to get excited about touting her own Waterloo. Hughes's press agent Lincoln Quarberg was turned loose on Jean and zeroed in on her hair. Until now, the shade had been pretty much anonymous, each beauty parlor assigning it their own name or, more often, number. Quarberg came up with the tag "platinum blonde."

Hell's Angels had its talking premiere in June of 1930. Hughes spared no expense, hoping to dazzle the audience into forgetting the film's disastrous silent debut the year before. Grauman's Chinese Theatre was hired for the event, the biggest Hollywood premiere yet. Jean grew increasingly nervous. "I couldn't read a paper, pass a billboard, sit down in a restaurant but what my own face would be staring at me." Ordinarily, this would be any actress's dream come true, but Jean was still suffering from her Whale-induced paranoia.

Half a million fans lined Hollywood Boulevard the night of the opening; life-sized World War I planes dangled precariously from overhead wires; the spectacle and hysteria so impressed author Nathaniel West that he used it in his novel *The Day of the Locust.* Jean appeared in white fur and a huge corsage, looking surprisingly calm (semiconscious with fear, she later claimed). She entered the theater and slipped out of the audience to wait backstage. She was determined not to sit through that film and see herself publicly humiliated. Much to her shock, the expected boos and hisses never materialized, and she and her costars were pushed onstage to acknowledge enthusiastic cheers. It never occurred to Jean that she deserved the applause. She merely assumed she fooled everyone into thinking she could act.

"The most sensuous figure to get in front of a camera," was how *Variety* described her, though it added ominously that "she'll probably always have to play these kinds of roles." Bland Johaneson in the *New York Daily Mirror* praised her as "a beauty with plenty of lure," but the prestigious *New York Times*'s Mordaunt Hall dismissed Jean as "mediocre." Most critics loved the visual effects of the film but panned all three leading players as unconvincing. Their opinion, however, had little effect on the film-going public. *Hell's Angels* became the biggest hit of the season and Jean the girl of the moment.

Today, Jean's performance stands up much better than does the film as a whole. She and Ben Lyon are sparkling, attractive, and alive. James Hall (wearing more make-up than Jean) comes across as wooden and uninteresting, though it must be remembered that he was playing a wooden and uninteresting character. If Hughes wanted to make a war film to stand up against *The Big Parade* or *All Quiet on the Western Front,* he failed. *Hell's Angels* simply doesn't have the emotional pull, the excitement that the other films still have after all these years. The aerial dogfights are baffling, as the pilots' faces are hidden under their helmets; a night-time zeppelin raid is the only stirring and outstanding action sequence. Multi-Color hardly proved worth all the added expense and trouble. A color-restored version was recently released by American Movie Classics. The somewhat faded results look uncomfortably similar to Colorization—flat browns and startling greens—but it does provide the one and only glimpse of Jean in color.

James Whale once described Helen as a "pig," and people who haven't seen *Hell's Angels* assume that she is a heavy-breathing, glowering vamp. Nothing could be further from the truth. Jean's Helen is a bright young thing straight out of an Evelyn Waugh novel. Thoughtless and self-centered, yes, but without a mean bone in her body. "When I'm with Roy," she tells Monte, "I'm the way Roy wants me to be—that's caddish, isn't it? But I can't help it. . . . I want to be free—I want to be gay and have fun! Life's short, and I want to live while I'm alive!" Hardly an unsympathetic viewpoint, in 1930 or today. Helen does sleep around, but she also volunteers to work in a canteen on the front lines, not the action of a heartless tramp. When she calls Roy a stupid prig, we are supposed to hiss her as a villainess, but she's right; Roy *is* a stupid prig. While Jean doesn't bring the force to the role that Bette Davis or Vivien Leigh might have in later years, she had nothing to be ashamed of.

Everyone was talking about Jean, and Hughes wanted to capitalize on that. Not all the talk was favorable, but her name was on everyone's lips and must be kept there. So he sent her on a series of nationwide publicity tours. In those days, it took six months or more for films to be distributed from coast to coast, and sometimes it was two years before they reached the hinterlands. So in August, Jean and the Bellos boarded the Santa Fe Chief en route to the New York premiere, making whistle stops along the way. By the time she'd arrived in her hometown for a quick interview, the news was out that the new star was suing her husband for divorce and that McGrew was countersuing, citing the "indecent" photos Jean had posed for.

Amazingly, Jean denied that such photos existed. "They were never taken," she told reporters in Kansas City. "It is the one unforgivable thing he has done—to attempt to blacken my character in an effort to avoid a property settlement." Jean was playing a dangerous game. If the photos did surface, she could be open to perjury charges at worst, and would certainly appear foolish and dishonest. She was lucky. The photos remained a secret until she was famous enough to laugh them off.

The divorce dragged on until January 1931, with suits and countersuits flying fast and furious. McGrew denied Jean's charges of excessive drinking (this was during Prohibition, when such charges were indeed serious), and Jean huffed that "I was compelled by him to make my own living, due to his refusal to support me." Her divorce was finally granted, along with a $100,000 trust fund, $375 a month in alimony, and several of the couple's possessions. Jean haughtily turned it all down (although later press leaks indicated that McGrew's family would never have coughed up the money anyway). "I'd rather have his good will," Jean stated publicly. "I can make it on my own, anyway."

Charles McGrew sank from sight. He resurfaced sadly in 1938 when he declared bankruptcy, unable to meet his second wife's alimony demands. His whereabouts after that remain a mystery.

Jean spent the remainder of 1930 touring with *Hell's Angels*. In New York, she and Mama Jean went on a thirty-one-dress shopping spree costing $1,500. Hughes refused to foot the bill, and Jean's attempts to charm his New York aide, Noah Dietrich, out of the money failed. She wore the dresses onstage and tried to claim them as a business expense, but Dietrich reasoned that she could wear the same dress from town to town without anyone catching on.

The personal appearances were torture to Jean, who had never been before a live audience, school productions aside. It was common in the 1930s to accompany a movie with theatrical prologues—the last gasp of vaudeville. Theaters paid Hughes $3,500 each time Jean appeared onstage (she, needless to say, didn't see a cent of this). Jean was visibly terrified during these shows, and ad-lib writers had to be rushed to her side to keep her from making a complete fool of herself. She even became physically ill before some performances, and Marino had to carry her onstage from the dressing room.

The Harlow craze had begun to roll, and nothing could stop it, not even Jean's own misgivings. The press agent for the National Hairdressers Association offered a $10,000 prize to the person coming up with the best platinum dye; Jean's face appeared on magazines, newspapers, and billboards from coast to coast. By the time she passed through Missouri on her way back home from New York, she was billed as "Kansas City's Own Star," the proverbial overnight success.

Through all this, Jean never once saw *Hell's Angels* in its entirety. "When I was making a personal appearance," she said, "I'd always sneak in the back of the house to watch the Zeppelin airplane attack. I never failed to get a tremendous thrill out of it. I probably saw that scene hundreds of times." But she could never bear to watch her own performance. "What's more, I never intend to. If I had to look at myself . . . I'd feel there was no hope."

FOUR

WHAT PRICE HOLLYWOOD?

Portrait still from The Public Enemy *(1931)*

As 1930 drew to a close and *Hell's Angels* continued playing to enthusiastic, sell-out crowds, Howard Hughes took stock of Jean Harlow. He'd known the film would make her a star, regardless of her ability, but even he was taken aback by the public reaction: he'd created a shapely, blonde Frankenstein's monster.

Jean showed up regularly at Caddo, padding hopefully around Hughes's office waiting for her next assignment. Lincoln Quarberg worked himself and his publicity team into a tizzy cashing in on Jean's success. She was sent to every Hollywood party of the season, gave interviews to everyone from *Photoplay* and *Modern Screen* to small-town papers. Her *Hell's Angels* line, "Would you be terribly shocked if I slipped into something more comfortable?" entered popular vocabulary. Jean's fame even spread overseas. London's *Literary Digest* listed her as the seventeenth best-known woman in the world, and the British press began a long love affair with her. Jean's shocking hair, blatant sexuality, and slang-laced vocabulary went over big in England, and she was seen as the epitome of the tough-talking American broad.

Jean also acquired a new friend at about this time. Arthur Landau called one day to relate an unusual meeting with a fan. A young woman named Blanche Williams was burning up the phone wires asking for a job as Jean's personal maid. After weeks of these calls, Landau finally gave in and asked Jean to see the woman. Blanche Williams was not, fortunately, a crazed fan; she was a forceful, intelligent young woman who simply wanted a job and had the gumption to approach her favorite actress. Before Jean knew what hit her, Blanche took over her life and her home. For the next seven years, Williams served as Jean's lady's maid, secretary, companion, and friend.

An angular, no-nonsense black woman, Blanche had previously

worked for other stars and continued doing so after Jean's death. The two women became genuinely close and devoted friends, but the fact that Jean was paying Blanche's salary cannot be overlooked. In the days when most black women found their job opportunities (even in Hollywood) as servants, many sublimated their own career dreams to those of their employers. Mae West, Sophie Tucker, Tallulah Bankhead, Joan Crawford, and many other actresses were attended by such close "friends," women forced to live out their hopes and ambitions through their famous employers. That's not to say there wasn't real affection on both sides. Blanche lashed out fiercely at anyone who dared to speak ill of Jean, and continued to do so until her own death in 1984. Jean, for her part, told reporters that "I am sure I'm not a heroine to Blanche. I'm sure she never thinks of me as a 'movie star.'"

For her part, Blanche became the mother figure Jean badly needed. She put Jean on a strict budget; when Jean ordered silk stockings by the dozen, Blanche hid them away and doled them out only as needed, knowing full well Jean would give them away to friends otherwise. Jean also had a habit of dousing herself with too much perfume, so Blanche began squirreling this away as well, allowing her one ounce per month. She teamed up with Mama Jean in getting The Baby to pay more attention to her clothing. Jean loved wearing evening pajamas (a kind of silky, elegant pantsuit) to dinner parties; this horrified Blanche, who took to laying out a dinner dress and claiming that she was very sorry, but all the pajamas were at the cleaners. "I happen to own more than a dozen sets and know very well they can't all be out of the house at the same time," sighed Jean, "but I also know that I shall wear the dinner dress."

Blanche accompanied Jean to her film sets, delighting in the professional hustle and bustle, trying to pitch in and help whenever the unions let her. She wasn't supposed to assist Jean with her costumes, makeup, or hair on the set, but that rarely stopped her. She also ran errands, acted as a go-between with reporters and executives, helped with correspondence, and fed Jean her lines between takes. Jean was soon happily dependent on Blanche, and amazingly, Mama Jean never seemed to resent this intruder; she, too, needed a mother, and Blanche Williams was capable enough to keep both Jeans in line.

Jean had made a smashing debut, but Quarberg wasn't giving her a moment to rest. She was competing with an impressive crop of newcomers who had also made their mark with the public that year. Sultry Marlene Dietrich, soignée Kay Francis, pert Ginger Rogers, saucy Claudette Colbert, tough Barbara Stanwyck, and many others were yapping at her heels. Hughes and Quarberg had to keep Jean in the limelight, even if no films were ready for her. Her competition had the backing of major studios to bolster their careers, but Jean had only the eccentric Hughes, the over-worked Quarberg, and the totally useless Arthur Landau.

Caddo simply wasn't equipped to give the kind of back-up support a fledgling star needed. The major studios—MGM, Fox, Universal, Paramount, Columbia, Warner Bros.—had huge publicity staffs, makeup and wardrobe departments, voice coaches, photographers, even their own doctors and police forces. But not Caddo.

At a loss for anything else to do with her, Hughes wangled invitations for Jean to attend major parties and important nightclub openings. She went to Christmas and New Year's parties late in 1930, where guests remember her sitting in the corner like a teenaged wallflower, as Mama Jean, wrapped in ermine and satin, held forth with grace and charm. Those who hadn't seen *Hell's Angels* assumed the elder woman was the star and the shy girl her secretary or maid.

Jean became acquainted with that year's stag line and soon got her name linked in gossip columns with several eligible bachelors. MGM producer Paul Bern took an immediate liking to her, and the two became platonic friends. Bern complimented her performance in *Hell's Angels* and offered a few helpful tips. He sent out feelers to Hughes, asking if Jean might be loaned out for an MGM project.

Meanwhile, singer Harry Richman launched a sneak attack on Jean's affections. He'd recently been jilted by Clara Bow, and the publicity-hungry Richman latched onto Jean like a barnacle on a rowboat. The hard-drinking and fast-living Broadway song-and-dance man was making an attempt to succeed in films, as well as an attempt to sleep his way through every female star on the West Coast. Jean, hungry for affection since her recent separation, began a short but torrid affair with Richman, who was never shy about his conquests. His brash, loud-mouthed style soon wore thin with Jean and she, like Bow before her, broke off the affair. As a grown woman with a normal sexual appetite, Jean didn't want to hide herself in a convent, but she also didn't want her sex life splashed all over the front pages. Richman was not her style.

She was seen around town with stockbroker Ernest Torgler and several other wealthy young men, but displayed no lasting interest in any of them. Jean wanted to get back to work, and began begging Landau and Hughes to find her something to do. She was shipped out on another cross-country publicity tour while the search went on for a film. Jean, the Bellos, and Blanche found themselves racing from town to town that winter, dropped in unfamiliar, cold, and snowy streets trying to find their hotel so they could change in time for the theater appearance. In Atlantic City, Jean took advantage of a warm spell to stride around the boardwalk, unaccompanied by reporters or fans. Arriving in New York, she found a cablegram ordering her onto the next California-bound train. At long last, a film project had been found for her.

Paul Bern had convinced MGM to borrow Jean for *The Secret Six*, a tidy (but now-forgotten) gangster yarn. Produced by the studio's offshoot, Cosmopolitan, the film starred Wallace Beery as brutal stockyard worker Louis Scorpio, who is drawn into bootlegging and quickly becomes a hardened killer and crooked political boss. He is aided by major-league hood Richard Newton, played by Lewis Stone in an unsympathetic role unusual for him. Jean's part was quite small after her exposure in *Hell's Angels.*

Fourth-billed as Anne Courtland, she played a cashier hired to seduce influence from reporter Hank Rogers (John Mack Brown). Hank's reporter pal Carl was played by rising young actor Clark Gable, whose brief scenes with Jean showed a bantering chemistry; the two instantly struck sparks. Basically a good girl at heart, Anne falls for Hank and turns state's evidence when he is rubbed out. Scorpio is acquitted by a bribed jury but gets his just desserts in a smashing finale: foiled in his plan to kill Anne and Carl, he is turned in by a vengeful moll (Marjorie Rambeau) and winds up on death row. The "Secret Six" of the title is a group of crusading businessmen who make themselves unintentionally hilarious by sitting around solemnly wearing Batman masks.

Director George Hill was hardly the Simon Legree that James Whale was, but Jean still seems nervous and hesitant in this film, unsure of herself on camera. Her hair is cropped short, and MGM's makeup department went a little overboard with the eye shadow and lipstick, making her baby face look hard and coarse. While making this, her first major film at MGM, Jean met two men who would be very important in her life: one as a friend and one as an enemy. Jean had several scenes with Clark Gable, but he was as shy and retiring as she, and the two exchanged only polite familiarities during this film. Their close friendship didn't develop right away. Her relationship with costar Wallace Beery, however, was much more dynamic. The two detested each other at first sight.

Beery was a middle-aged character actor who hailed from Jean's hometown. He'd run away as a teenager to join the circus, from there going on to theater and, in 1913, films. His career slowly gathered momentum until 1930, when he exploded onto the scene with immense success playing gruff, boozy wharf rats and gangsters. Unlike Jean, Beery in private life was very much like Beery onscreen: violent, coarse, and outspoken, greatly talented but a bane to costars and employers alike. He even managed to brutalize and terrorize his first wife, the imperious Gloria Swanson—an amazing feat, rather like brutalizing and terrorizing the Statue of Liberty.

Jean was still emotionally bruised from her recent experiences, still unsure of herself and her abilities. Beery seemed to sense this, and, sharklike, went in for the kill. As Louis Scorpio, Beery had many scenes with Jean and took every opportunity to display his low opinion of her. A veteran of every form of show business, he did not take kindly to sharing the spotlight with an untested upstart, and his natural contempt for women asserted itself. Jean cowered beneath his onslaught, neither defending herself nor seeking assistance from director Hill. She simply bit her lip, lowered her eyes, and went gamely on with the scene, choking back her embarrassment. While not as much of a trial as *Hell's Angels* had been, *The Secret Six* was not a happy experience for her.

Jean worked hard on this film, getting home at seven o'clock or eight o'clock to find dinner waiting. Blanche helped wash and set her hair, laying out clothes for the next day. After a leisurely hour with the radio or a book, Jean would go to bed by ten o'clock. On days when she wasn't required on the set, she posed for publicity photos, gave interviews, or appeared at local events. On these "late days" she also socialized, with the encouragement of Hughes and MGM. The more she was seen in public and mentioned in the gossip columns, the better for her career.

The Secret Six was released in April and met with mostly favorable reviews (*Photoplay* asserted that "gangster pictures are not dead—not as long as they produce thrillers like this!"). Jean's performance, however, went largely unnoticed, though Mordaunt Hall in the *New York Times* refers oddly to her as "the ash-blonde of several other such tales." This was only Jean's second film; either Hall couldn't tell one blonde from another, or he'd seen *Hell's Angels* several times.

By the time *The Secret Six* hit the theaters, Jean was already hard at work on another project. Hughes rushed her to Universal (for a healthy loan-out fee) to work on a boxing melodrama called *Iron Man.* Universal also released two high-budget horror films that year, *Frankenstein* and *Dracula,* but *Iron Man* was just a run-of-mill programmer; hardly in the same league or worthy of the same production values. The film starred Lew Ayres (fresh from his success in *All Quiet on the Western Front*) and Robert Armstrong (still a year away from *King Kong*). The plot revolved around small-time boxer "Kid" Mason (Ayres) and his avaricious, disgruntled wife, Rose (Jean). When Mason's manager George Regan (Armstrong) molds him into a contender, the film develops into an interesting love triangle, as Regan and Rose battle for the young boxer's affections.

Regan, of course, wins; Rose's true colors are revealed when she's named co-respondent in a divorce case. The Kid loses the big fight, but emerges a wiser man, with his loyal manager by his side. Perhaps director Tod Browning didn't intentionally turn this W. R. Burnett novel into a three-way love story, but modern audiences tend to read more than a manager's loyalty into Regan's devotion to Kid Mason.

Jean stands out as the high point in *Iron Man,* otherwise a rather shabby film. Both Ayres and Armstrong turn in perfectly acceptable performances, but the character of Rose is so mean, so gaudy and outrageous that she's like a beacon in the darkness. Tod Browning certainly cannot be held responsible for the choppy editing or abominable script,

Trash personified: as Rose Mason in Iron Man *(1931)*

▼

but the painfully slow pacing is surprising from the man who would later direct the cult classic *Freaks.* What should be a short, snappy film drags out to an unbearable 113 minutes. Jean's costumes, by an uncredited designer, were the most revealing she'd ever worn (one gown in particular had a shockingly invisible bodice). The sets were probably left over from a higher-budget film; the Masons' apartment, a delightful study in art deco, appears to have been a nightclub in a former life.

Within the limitations of the script, Jean's performance was quite an improvement over earlier efforts and shows how hard she was working. She has gained authority and snaps out her lines with confidence. Flouncing in and out of scenes with more flair than she'd previously shown, she seems actually to have fun with the appalling character she was playing. Her reviews, however, were abysmal. Richard Watts, Jr., of the *New York Herald Tribune* admitted right out front that Jean "is not one of this department's favorite actresses," adding that her own trashy and artificial qualities suited the role perfectly. The *New York Times* André Sennwald liked both Ayres and Armstrong but carped that Jean's "virtues as an actress are limited to her blonde beauty." Irene Thirer in the *New York Daily News* tried to be kind—"despite all the Harlow exploitation, the young woman is practically new to talkies"—though this is hardly the sort of kindness an actress longs for.

Jean was becoming Howard Hughes's favorite yo-yo. He sent her spinning out to New York for another tour, then immediately reeled her back in for another loan-out. The year 1931 was not yet half over when Jean reported to Warner Bros. for her third film of the year. Warner's was in the throes of a gangster cycle, having begun the trend in 1930 with *Little Caesar;* they were now set to follow up with *The Public Enemy.* The following year they produced the classic *Scarface,* and RKO countered with *I Am a Fugitive from a Chain Gang.* This studio mob war continued throughout the early 1930s with countless lesser efforts, either brushed off as harmless escapism from the Depression or seen as an ominous indicator of those desperate times.

The Public Enemy was one of Jean's best films. It contains, however, her worst performance. The film chronicles the rise and fall of bootlegger Tom Powers, one of the small-time hoods who cashed in when the economic depression coincided with prohibition (1930–32). Starting small and rising to the top, Powers soon loses touch with reality and becomes both heartless and psychotic. James Cagney scored his first major success with this role; Jean was third-billed as Gwen Allen, a slumming society girl who briefly becomes Powers's mistress. Heavily made-up and unattractively coiffed, she makes three appearances on-screen.

Her final scene is particularly embarrassing. Powers has just left his current flame—the famous breakfast scene, in which Mae Clarke receives a faceful of grapefruit. Gwen is trying both to seduce Powers and to continue to keep him at arm's length; her monologue is confusingly

With Edward Woods and James Cagney in The Public Enemy *(1931)*

written, and her character badly conceived. Director William Wellman was as brilliant a craftsman as Jean would ever work with, but he was more geared toward action than romance. Struggling through the long, stilted speech, Jean is plainly uncomfortable, and the scene invariably draws rude howls from modern audiences. It ends, however, with her one effective moment. Dumped by Powers, Gwen stalks frustrated through her apartment like a caged animal; suddenly grabbing a vase, she hurls it into the fireplace. This one wordless expression of anger rings true.

Jean got along well with Cagney, but she and costar Joan Blondell didn't warm up to each other. What Blondell mistook for snootiness was probably paralyzing stagefright and dismay at her own performance. Reviews for *The Public Enemy* on its release in May were nearly all raves, but, again, Jean was singled out for critical blasts. Richard Watts, Jr., praised the film for its "Zola-esque power" and "chilling credibility," but again showed his dislike for Jean by stating (quite accurately, as it happens) that she completely ruined the seduction scene. The *New York Post*'s Thornton Delehanty included Jean in its list of performers giving "realistic characterizations," but Mordaunt Hall in the *New York Times* singled her out as the only cast member failing to live up to the overall quality of the project. A snub like that from the *Times* was particularly painful.

Jean was quite aware of her deficiencies as an actress, but had nowhere to turn for help, and the meager resources of Caddo were certainly useless to her. "I was not a born actress," she later told Carolyn Hoyt. "No one knows it any better than I. If I had any latent talent, I have had to work hard, listen carefully, do things over and over and then over again in order to bring it out." She was, essentially, learning on the job, and her dismal show in *The Public Enemy* was an unavoidable result of this hit-or-miss self training. She was still very self-conscious about her midwestern twang and attempted a cultured accent for Gwen Allen. The results were grievous: lines like "I'm going to meet my friends on the corner" came out, "Ah'm gawng to meet my frands on the coronor." Jean's voice never did acquire the silky perfection of Joan Crawford's or Claudette Colbert's. Alexander Walker once described Mae West as sounding like a kazoo blown through steel wool; he could have been talking about Jean.

Nevertheless, she was still keeping her hold on the public's attention and affection, and over one hundred cities had formed "platinum blonde clubs." Her tough-talking sarcasm and startling appearance had captured the fancy of America. Hughes recognized that the fascination wouldn't last long, but rather than grooming and training his new star, he decided to take the easy way out by continuing to loan her out.

In early summer, Jean made her only major appearance in a Fox film. The studio that had promoted sex star Theda Bara cast Jean in a

LEFT: Poster art from Goldie *(1931); RIGHT: arriving in Grand Central Station on a 1931 publicity tour (Bettmann/UPI)*

▼

remake of their 1928 silent *A Girl in Every Port,* which had starred the temperamental Louise Brooks. This new film costarred the up-and-coming Spencer Tracy and Warren Hymer, a "rube" comedian whose career faltered later in the decade.

Goldie cast Jean as a carnival performer in Calais—a high-diver who lives off the sailors coming into port. Tracy and Hymer portrayed Bill and Spike, two battling friends in the tradition of Quirt and Flagg in *What Price Glory.* The two alternate between unbearable male bonding and squabbling over the women they "possess." The plot line was offensively sexist even in 1931, and Jean was appalled by Goldie's antics. Clad in a cape and bathing suit, she (or, rather, her stunt double) dove into a barrel of water for her living, emerging wet and ready to steal her admirers' earnings.

Even more horrifying to modern sensibilities, Bill had the odd habit of "tattooing" his conquests with his signet ring, and therein lay the crux of the plot. The naive Spike falls in love with Goldie, despite Bill's warnings about her character (for the first time on-screen, a female is referred to as a tramp, a distinction Jean could have lived without). Spike refuses to listen to Bill, and Goldie proceeds heartlessly to vamp him out of his paycheck. Spike finally discovers what Goldie has been hiding under her bracelet during most of the film—Bill's tattoo—and abandons her. The male friends wind up (figuratively) in each other's arms, while Goldie is left to her life of diving and seduction.

Needless to say, the film's vogue didn't last long, and it is rarely seen today (only one print is known to exist). Cheaply made and with a silly, illogical plot, *Goldie* was a far cry from *The Public Enemy.* Jean appears embarrassed and uncomfortable, although her character's sheer silliness gave her a chance to cut loose and have a little fun. The costumes (by Dolly Tree, who later crossed paths with Jean again at MGM) were cheap and tawdry, and her male costars were as uncomfortable as she.

Irene Thirer in the *New York Daily News* took pity on Jean and suggested Hughes rechristen her "the borrowed blonde, for . . . she has been borrowed by one producing company after another." Thirer added, however, that Jean "lacks the spark needed to make her shine as a personality." Bland Johaneson in the *New York Daily Mirror* thought *Goldie* a "lively, broad, funny and a good midsummer movie," but delicately neglected to assess Jean's performance.

By mid-1931, Jean's career and spirits were beginning to sag. Since her great success in *Hell's Angels,* she'd been loaned out for four films in almost as many months, each role more god-awful than the last. She was making a name for herself, all right, as the biggest laughingstock in talking pictures.

Jean had hoped that Helen of *Hell's Angels* would be her first and last bad girl role, but she quickly learned that it was the thin edge of the wedge: casting directors had gotten it into their heads that she was the best of the bad girls. Howard Hughes wasn't interested enough in her career to try to convince them otherwise, and Arthur Landau wasn't about to derail the gravy train on which he'd hitched a free ride.

Jean, however, was getting sick and tired of it all. She'd played a tough-talking moll in *The Secret Six,* a heartless gold digger in *Iron Man,* an oversexed tease in *The Public Enemy,* and yet another gold digger in *Goldie.* And Jean wasn't the only one who thought her career was on the skids. Industry gossips already referred to the twenty-year-old actress as "last year's blonde." Her reviews were getting worse with every picture, and she was quickly becoming the butt of Hollywood jokes (Jean to Margot Asquith: "How do you do, Margott?" Lady Asquith to Jean: "No, dear, the 't' is silent—like in 'Harlow'").

She took her case to the press and whined at interviews that she was sick and tired of the ridiculous parts she was given. "I've played a series of abandoned wretches whose wickedness is never explained, never condoned. . . . How can I expect audience sympathy when I have none for the parts I've been forced to play?" Such public bellyaching was an unusual step for a young actress, but Jean was through pussyfooting with Hughes. By this point, being fired would have been almost a blessing, at least it could have restored her artistic freedom. Comedy was her forte. Jean knew this, but everyone around her seemed to have forgotten.

Finally, in the summer of 1931, fate stepped in, in the form of Columbia Studios. Frank Capra, still a youthful and fairly unknown director, requested Jean's services for the third lead in a newspaper comedy called *Gallagher.* Jean pleaded with Hughes to be loaned out for this, her first comedy since her extra days. Columbia agreed to borrow Jean for a two-picture deal, and she was delighted to get as far away from Caddo as her feet could carry her. Determined to make herself agreeable, Jean felt that maybe, just maybe, she could convince Columbia that her potential was impressive enough for them to purchase her from Hughes.

The signs were good. Columbia's leading starlet, Loretta Young, read *Gallagher*'s script and requested the title role. Talented comic actor Robert Williams was cast in the male lead, and well-known character actors Walter Catlett and Louise Closser Hale were set for supporting roles. Much to Jean's delight (and Loretta Young's chagrin), Capra changed the title of the film to *Platinum Blonde.*

Platinum Blonde was an early version of the common-man-vs.-elite-snobs comedies Capra later made his trademark. Robert Williams played Stew Smith, a wise-cracking, salt-of-the earth reporter trying to dig up some dirt on the wealthy Schuyler family. Loretta Young played his love-struck pal, and Jean the Schuyler's self-centered and pampered daughter Anne. Predictably, Smith marries Anne with disastrous results and eventually winds up in the more appropriate (working-class) arms of Gallagher.

The film isn't as substantial as Capra's later classics, but it's a friendly, folksy eighty-eight minutes, typical of the damn-the-rich films of the early Depression years. Audiences wanted to be convinced that the rich are, after all, unhappy and nasty people and that it's really ever so much nicer to be poor but honest. No one really fell for this well-meaning propaganda, but studios can hardly be blamed for trying to cheer up the masses.

Platinum Blonde was better than most such films, light on message and heavy on comedy. Williams was perfect as Smith; not terribly handsome, he was nevertheless as effective as James Stewart and Gary Cooper were in Capra's later films. His off-the-cuff bantering style would have made him one of Columbia's biggest stars had he not died later that year after an appendectomy. Today, except for *Platinum Blonde,* Williams is virtually forgotten. Loretta Young did what she could with a colorless role, but some of the minor players shine delightfully. Louise Closser Hale as the snooty Mrs. Schuyler and Halliwell Hobbes as the befuddled butler are particularly hilarious, still drawing laughs and applause in revival houses.

Jean clicked back into comedy as though she were born to it. She reacted well to Capra's direction, and he in turn was impressed with her talent and cooperative attitude. As Anne Schuyler, Jean is subdued and refined; even her voice is softer and less nasal. While her platinum hair seems inappropriate for a society girl, her makeup is considerably toned-down—except in Columbia's publicity photos for the film, in which she was given her usual tarty look. Her costumes, by an un-

With Robert Williams in Platinum Blonde *(1931)*

▼

credited designer, are soft and concealing, a refreshing change after the transparent gown of *Iron Man* and the bathing suit of *Goldie.*

Jean was also beginning to learn a few tricks of the trade, such as maintaining eye contact with her fellow performers. It's not clear whether she picked this up from Capra, Williams, or just through observation, but Jean was starting to *act,* rather than just reading her lines in a agreeable way. In *Platinum Blonde,* Jean acts *with* Williams, not just *at* him, as she'd done in *The Public Enemy.* She tugs playfully at his lapels, peering up into his face with a kittenish assurance that she's too adorable to resist. And she *is.* Jean is obviously having fun with the role and inviting us to have fun along with her. For the first time on-screen, she is thoroughly likeable.

The critics, still smarting from her former films, didn't much agree. The *New York Daily Mirror* loved *Platinum Blonde,* calling it "one of the gayest, sauciest comedies you've ever seen," but brushed off Jean as merely "effective." Her sworn enemy, Richard Watts, Jr., of the *New York Herald Tribune,* also enjoyed the film but dismissed Jean as "competent but not much more."

This hurt Jean deeply. She had enjoyed herself, diving back into comedy like a warm bath. She knew she had done well, but if the critics couldn't accept her as a comedienne, she knew her career was over.

In the meantime, she still had one more Columbia film to complete. *Three Wise Girls,* which began production in early autumn, gave Jean her first top billing, but in a project that looked pretty pathetic next to *Platinum Blonde.* She played Cassie Barnes, an ambitious but naive small-town girl who moves to New York to make her fortune. There she encounters two potential role models, Dot (Marie Prevost), a cynical typist, and Gladys (Mae Clarke), a romantic, heart-on-her-sleeve fashion model. Both Cassie and Gladys fall for married men, while Dot pins her hopes on a poor but unmarried chauffeur (played by Andy Devine, years before he became a regular in low-budget westerns). When her lover reconciles with his wife, Gladys commits suicide, prompting a sadder but wiser Cassie to leave New York. Much to everyone's amazement, her own lover divorces his wife and trails Cassie home with a wedding ring. This unlikely ending sent a mixed message to audiences: it's all right to fool around with married men, provided you're absolutely sure they'll ditch their wives for you.

While it was all very pleasant to be playing a nice girl like Cassie, Jean looked on the film with disdain. Based on a Wilson Collison story called *Blonde Baby, Three Wise Girls* was an uncomfortable mixture of wise-cracking comedy and soap opera. Screenwriter Robert Riskin was unable to create a believable character for Cassie, leaving Jean nothing to work with. Cassie appeared to be just a pliable combination of Dot's cynicism and Gladys's sensitivity, and director William Beaudine wasn't able to help Jean sort the two qualities out. She was effective in her brief comic scenes and convincingly sincere in her dramatic ones, but her appearance left much to be desired. Whereas she'd been groomed as a society debutante in *Platinum Blonde,* Jean looked more like a cheap hooker than a small-town belle in *Three Wise Girls.* Her eyes were heavily shadowed and her mouth done up in a nearly black cupid's bow, which Jean took as a bad sign. If her makeup was beginning to backslide, could her career be far behind?

She was also overshadowed by her two costars, whose roles were better suited to their talent. Silent-film comedienne Marie Prevost was terrific as Dot, providing much-needed comic relief. Prevost's career

With Marie Prevost in Three Wise Girls *(1932)*

was on the decline by 1931, and she was fighting an obvious weight problem. Despite her good showing in this and other films, she died, broke and alone, in 1937 and, like Robert Williams, is all but forgotten half a century later. Mae Clarke, who never achieved real stardom, gives a restrained and intelligent performance as Gladys, never yielding to hysterics or self-conscious melodrama.

The casting of middle-aged actors Walter Byron and Jameson Thomas as love interests for Cassie and Gladys didn't add to the film's spark. While competent performers, their glaring lack of sex appeal makes it difficult to sympathize with their girlfriends' broken hearts. Films of the early 1930s are littered with such overly made-up, aging matinee idols. Even then filmgoers looked askance at these dubious leading men, and today audiences hoot delightedly at their appearance.

Three Wise Girls depressed and unnerved Jean. After a top-rate production like *Platinum Blonde,* it was frightening to be consigned to a bomb like this, even top-billed. The costumes and sets were cheap, and even such run-of-the-mill necessities as continuity were lax: at one point, the neckline on Cassie's lingerie changes in mid-scene.

The film got a limp reception from the press, the *New York Times* dismissing it as "a nursery primer on the alleged perils of a big city," not even bothering to evaluate individual performances. *Variety* gave its honors to Mae Clarke, and though it called Jean "better than might be expected," added that she still "fails to be convincing."

Jean's one foray into comedy hadn't produced any real results, and now she found herself back at Caddo under the thumbs of Hughes and Landau. After nearly four years in films, the future was looking bleak.

Hughes announced her for several more loan-outs, including a newspaper story with the unfortunate title *Queer People.* One of the more interesting offers for Jean's services came from the newly formed RKO, which was preparing a horror-adventure film and badly needed a blonde leading lady. As Jean was the blondest in Hollywood, she was the first considered. The role wouldn't have required much acting, mostly screaming in terror. Jean was unenthusiastic and asked Hughes if a more suitable film could be found for her than *King Kong.* Jean needn't have worried. One of the biggest, most prestigious studios in Hollywood was about to rescue her from Kong, and from Hughes and Landau.

Frank Capra had been talking up Jean's talents to industry officials since she'd worked with him that summer. She had other friends in high places. MGM executive producer Paul Bern had been a casual friend since her *Hell's Angels* days, and when he saw the Capra comedy he began suggesting that MGM take a closer look at "last year's blonde." Finally, Robert Rubin and Ben Piazza of MGM's New York office arranged to meet with Jean on one of her East Coast publicity tours. They were pleasantly surprised by the shy, soft-spoken girl and impressed at the screening of *Platinum Blonde.* She told them how anxious she was to make good in films, how distressing she found her current plight, and how hard she'd work for a sympathetic studio.

Rubin and Piazza agreed with Capra and Bern, and suggested to Louis B. Mayer and Irving Thalberg that Jean just might be a valuable asset to the company

Mayer and Thalberg weren't much impressed with Jean's potential, but they were willing to give Bern the benefit of the doubt. They borrowed Jean on a probationary basis. If she made good in her first film, they would purchase her contract; if not, she would be thrown back to the sharks.

Jean couldn't believe her good fortune. Metro-Goldwyn-Mayer was the pinnacle of Hollywood glamour, a far cry from the lackadaisical Caddo or the low-budget Columbia. Formed as the result of a merger in 1924, MGM was now ruled by Mayer, one of the most intimidating characters of the film industry. Some of his employees remember him as a modern Attila the Hun, others as a paternal and well-meaning boss, but all agree that the man knew how to make movies and create stars. He left many of the artistic decisions to Thalberg, known as "the boy wonder of Hollywood," but Mayer still oversaw every phase of star-making, property acquisition, and contract negotiation.

When Jean walked through the studio gates late in 1931, MGM advertised that it contained "more stars than there are in heaven." Jean felt like the new kid in school, something of an oddball and misfit in such exalted company. "Greta Garbo and Carole Lombard and Norma Shearer seem like real movie stars to me," she told an interviewer. "I have always felt more like an outsider who got an unbelievable break in Hollywood."

It was made quite clear to Jean that she'd been hired to fill one special gap in the MGM roster, that of the sexpot. Although the studio had in its ranks four top actresses, none of them possessed the streetwise, sultry quality Jean exuded. Greta Garbo, who had been a major star since MGM signed her in 1925, was an ethereal, almost terrifying beauty, specializing in heavy-breathing roles of heartrending tragedy. She could no more crack wise or snap a garter than Jean could recite Shakespeare in Swedish. Norma Shearer and Marion Davies, both stars since the mid-1920s, had influential mentors unwilling to see them in unflattering roles. Shearer was married to Irving Thalberg, who arranged for his (admittedly talented) wife to get roles other actresses would have killed for, such as Marie Antoinette and Juliet. Davies, a wonderful comedienne, was hampered by her own sugar daddy, publisher William Randolph Hearst. Hearst simply couldn't bring himself to let Davies cut loose in the raucous comic roles at which she excelled, insisting on publicizing her as a modern-day Pollyanna. This effectively killed her career.

Joan Crawford, also an MGM alumna from the 1920s, specialized in contemporary Horatio Alger stories of strong-jawed working girls who succeed by dint of hard work and the ability to say "no" to oversexed playboys. None of these ladies was about to slip back into playing gun molls and trollops. Jean's first MGM role, her big test, would be another gun moll.

But first the studio began relentlessly grooming and publicizing her. The head of the publicity department, Howard Strickling, was a genius at divining and exploiting a star's most marketable characteristic. He knew full well that Jean had been hired as a harlot, but he was also quick to recognize her innocent girl-next-door quality and to realize that here was a new kind of sex goddess. He and Jean became allies in trying to temper her image with a little humor and innocence.

Ad on the back cover of Time *magazine in 1931—incidentally, Jean really* did *smoke Luckies.*

Jean had been appearing in advertisements since 1930: all studios had tie-ins with fan magazines and manufacturers, selling the services of stars to promote various products. This gained sales for the advertisers and exposure for the performers. Jean popped up in magazines and newspapers all over the country, plugging Lux Toilet Soap ("I learned Hollywood's secret and started using Lux Toilet Soap my first day in the studio"), Woodbury's Cold Cream ("At least twice every day I thank my dermatologist for recommending Woodbury's"), and Lucky Strike Cigarettes ("It's a real delight to find a Cellophane wrapper that opens without an ice pick"). One of her Lucky Strike ads even appeared on the back cover of *Time* magazine (October 1931).

When MGM began handling her publicity, the usual fan magazine articles were supplemented by constant fashion and beauty features. Jean's hair, eyebrows, clothing, and opinions became the subject of endless in-depth reporting. The slightest change of her hair color earned nearly as much newsprint as the rise of Fascism in Europe. Jean was overwhelmed with all this attention. Howard Hughes had set her adrift, letting loan-out studios take care of whatever publicity they cared to. Now she was the subject of MGM's well-organized star-making machinery, and it took her breath away.

It also took her eyebrows away. Various studios had been thinning and plucking Jean's brows in an attempt to lighten her broad forehead and bring her eyes out. MGM took no halfway measures: they shaved off her brows entirely, penciling new ones in. Brow-shaving had been a rather bizarre fad that had arisen and swiftly died in the fifteenth century and hadn't been heard of since. Clara Bow shaved hers in the 1920s, but the ones she drew in so closely followed the original lines that it had hardly been worth the effort. Jean's, however, were raised to alarming heights. She and Marlene Dietrich led the eyebrow brigade, which left fashionable women all over the world looking like startled drag queens. To this day, Jean's most recognizable features are her eyebrows, winging their way skyward. Many women mistakenly plucked out their roots rather than shaving the brows, leaving them uncomfortably eyebrowless when natural brows returned in the 1940s.

While Jean's first MGM vehicle was being prepared, she was marched into the portrait studio for publicity shots with Clarence Sinclair Bull, the studio's current photographer. These photos began appearing in fan magazine articles like "Jean Harlow's Beauty Secrets" and "Jean Harlow's Wardrobe" even before she'd stepped onto the movie set.

In the meantime, MGM's new starlet was getting increasingly nervous about her chances of making good. Bern tried to console her and convinced her that Mayer and Thalberg had only her best interest at heart, that he would personally oversee her career.

Jean's gratitude turned to shocked dismay when the big test film was dropped into her lap. She was to portray another gun moll. Rushing to Bern's office, she alternately accused him of leading her on and cried that she'd rather give up her career than play this role. Bern tried to explain that MGM wasn't about to gamble a big-budget comedy on an untested player, that Jean would have to earn points by playing this minor role before she could be entrusted with anything important. The humiliated executive, who really *did* have Jean's best interest at heart, began working overtime to make good his promise of a really challenging part for his protégée. But for now, Jean would have to swallow her pride and submit gracefully to her role in *The Beast of the City*.

The film was a classic brother vs. brother story, involving Jim and Ed Fitzpatrick. Jim (Walter Huston) is a police captain and Ed (Wallace Ford) a crooked cop. Jean was billed second as Daisy Stevens, a gangster's girl who entices Ed into joining a bunch of armored-car thieves. Appearing as Jim's son was eleven-year-old Mickey Rooney, in his first of three projects with Jean. This film marked the only time Jean died onscreen. In a grand nightclub gunfight, she takes a bullet in the midsection and does a wonderful tumble over a table. Indeed, the film concludes on a Hamlet-like note, with the entire cast lying dead in a heap.

The main saving grace of the project was its director, Charles Brabin. An Englishman and veteran helmsman, he was married to retired sex symbol Theda Bara and was, therefore, very sympathetic to Jean's frustration. He did his best to coax a devastating performance out of her. Bara had spent years trying to break out of the same trap in which Jean now found herself. Brabin convinced the young blonde that if she were able to prove herself a competent actress and good team player in this project, he would do his best to talk her up to studio executives for more sympathetic parts in the future. Jean was nothing if not a good sport, so she squared her shoulders and buckled down to do her best.

When *The Beast of the City* was released in February 1932, Jean held her breath. If she made good, her future was all but assured; if she flopped, she'd be condemned to playing smaller and smaller roles in

Jean's MGM "screen test"— The Beast of the City *(1932), with Wallace Ford*

cheaper and cheaper films until she sank below the surface without a ripple. Many a blonde, before and since, had made a huge splash only to wind up bitter and forgotten within a year or two (who today recalls Peggy Cummins, Joan Marsh, or the brilliant Lyda Roberti, all of whom were trumpeted as screen immortals in their time?).

Jean's hard work and Brabin's expertise paid off. Not only did critics love the film, but for the first time Jean herself was singled out for praise. The *New York Post* thought the story well written and "brilliantly directed," congratulating the cast en masse. Mordaunt Hall in the *New York Times* credited Brabin for much of the film's success, but also deemed Jean a "distinct asset." Best of all, the *New York Daily News* said that "the platinum blonde baby really acts in this one, mighty well."

These opinions hold up today. Jean's performance is quite good, and one scene in particular stands out. Daisy, attempting to seduce the gangster brother, entices him to her steamy-hot New York apartment. The segment foreshadows the film noir of the 1940s in both mood and camera work; the amoral gun moll undulating before a window overlooking the summer night sidewalks was a powerful image, one of the first memorable moments in Jean's career.

As relieved as Jean was by the film's reception, she also realized that success in another tough-broad role was a mixed blessing. This was exactly the kind of film she wanted to escape, and here she was being praised for her expertise in it. She came knocking at Paul Bern's door again, demanding that he make good his promise to change her image.

Bern had good news for her. Pleased with the response to *The Beast of the City,* MGM had decided to buy out her Caddo contract and sign her on as a full-time MGM employee (just in time for Jean's twenty-first birthday). This was the turning point of her career: no more cheesy loan-outs, no more uninterested executives brushing her off, and no more Arthur Landau. Mayer insisted she sign with the Orsatti Agency, who handled most of MGM's contract players.

Landau began phoning Jean daily, pleading to be kept on as her agent. After all, hadn't he "discovered" her? Hadn't he gotten her into *Hell's Angels?* Where would she be without him? And now that she was a success, was she going to drop him like a used tissue? Landau knew what a soft touch Jean was. She hadn't a child's good sense when it came to sniffing out phonies. Much to everyone's dismay, Jean agreed to continue paying Landau 10 percent of her earnings, although she wouldn't be using his services as an agent. Mama Jean and Marino shook their heads in disbelief, Mayer lectured her on the foolishness of charity, her friends simply sighed that Jean would wind up in the poorhouse someday. But Paul Bern was touched by this act of kindness to an old friend. He himself was notorious for similar gestures. According to actress Colleen Moore, "there used to be a saying whenever questions arose regarding money: Mickey Nielen spent it, Harold Lloyd saved it, Paul Bern gave it away."

In March of 1932 Jean began meeting with MGM lawyers to hammer out her new contract. MGM would pay Caddo Company $30,000 to release her; as Howard Hughes had long since lost interest in Jean and her career, this went without a hitch. But Louis B. Mayer hadn't counted on Jean's loudmouthed, know-it-all stepfather. Marino Bello had long fancied himself a clever businessman, and he decided that he owed it to his stepdaughter, as well as to himself, to make sure that MGM's slick lawyers didn't take advantage of her. He demanded meetings with Mayer, Thalberg, their lawyers, and their lawyer's lawyers. He even hired his own attorney, Mendel Silberberg, to hash out the legal niceties, and had the gall to pound on Mayer's door to spout outrageous demands. Jean cringed while Mama Jean beamed at her husband's great business acumen.

Mayer's lawyer wrote in frustration that "Mr. Bello has been difficult in our negotiations not intentionally so, but because he does not readily grasp the final result of the proposals." In other words, Marino

Left: Dining with Louis B. Mayer; right: celebrating the end of Prohibition, with actor Walter Huston (left) (both Bettmann/UPI)

had all the legal understanding of a five-year-old. He demanded that Jean play only starring roles, while Mayer patiently pointed out the "featured player" clause in her contract. Bello requested that MGM provide Jean with expenses for answering her fan mail, including envelopes, photos, stamps and even cardboard. He demanded that when she was sent on personal appearance tours, the studio pay not only her traveling expenses, but those of Marino, Mama Jean, and Blanche Williams. Jean would, however, agree to supply her own shoes, hosiery and underclothing for her films. To Marino's credit, he made such a pest of himself that Mayer actually wore down and granted some of the more inconsequential clauses.

Jean was to be paid a weekly salary of $1,250 for the first year; over the next six years she would receive regular raises until, by 1938, she would be earning $4,000 a week. "I'm getting twelve-fifty a week—hundreds, not dollars," she enthused to the newspapers when discussing her new contract. "And if a man with kids is getting twenty-five bucks a week, he's pretty lucky!" Privately, Jean handled her new wealth with the blasé equanimity of a girl who'd never had to worry about money.

It's true that she'd scrimped and saved during her days as an extra after her separation from McGrew and when her grandfather briefly cut her off. Supporting her mother and stepfather meant going without all the new dresses she wanted, and driving an old-model car. But unlike many of her fellow performers, Jean had never gone hungry, never had the specter of starvation or prostitution lingering over her. She was able to breeze through her days at the studios because she didn't have to rely on acting for a living. She had a father and four living grandparents back home, all of them financially secure and none about to let their Baby starve. It was very easy to reject her husband's alimony; there would always be money coming in.

As impressive as Jean's paycheck was, it paled when compared with those of other major stars in 1932. MGM's top actress, Greta Garbo, was pulling in an incredible $13,000 a week, as was John Gilbert, even though his career was in a severe decline. Paramount's new sex symbol Mae West was signed on at $10,000 a week, and Will Rogers topped the list with an amazing $15,000 a week. Marino was quick to point out this discrepancy, but was told that Jean was still an untested product. If, and only if, she made good, she would be awarded yearly bonuses. Marino kept his mouth shut for the time being, but began storing up grievances for future use.

Jean was already developing a careless attitude about her paycheck that boded ill for the future. She'd fallen into the habit of turning her salary over to Mama Jean, who gave her an allowance of $125 a week. That in itself would have been harmless enough, but what was Mama Jean's was also Marino's, and Marino could hardly be trusted.

Jean's contract went into effect on March 19, 1932. MGM owned her now. She could barely take out the garbage without Mayer's written approval. He had final say over any appearance she made in films, radio, vaudeville, or legitimate theater, for advertisements, for any books or articles she might care to write. Interestingly, the contract even had a lengthy clause regarding television appearances. TV was still in its infancy, but the studio realized that it might someday become a force to deal with.

The contract stated that MGM would "endeavor" to arrange a six-week vacation between pictures, but Colleen Moore laughingly recalled what these vacations were like. "After each picture I had a four-week break. . . . The first week they are cutting the picture and we are going back for re-takes; the second week I make publicity pictures every day, in the studio. The next week I'm interviewed, sometimes in the studio, sometimes at my house for lunch, and always the publicity man was there. . . . The last week was spent taking costume tests for the new picture. . . . So I never had a vacation while I was a star."

Jean was subject to the usual morals clause, stating that she could be summarily fired if she did or said anything that might "degrade her in society or bring her into public hatred, contempt, scorn or ridicule," an ironic proviso for someone hired to play trollops and gun molls. The studio took out extensive insurance on its new starlet, carefully explaining that MGM and only MGM would benefit from the policy. Mama Jean and the rest would have to look after themselves. One particularly heartless clause, also common in most major studio contracts, stated that should Jean's "present facial or physical appearance be materially altered or changed, or in the event that she suffer any impairment of her voice" for more than *two weeks,* she could be fired without compensation. In other words, Jean was an attractive piece of meat: if she were scarred in an auto accident, lost a breast to cancer or her figure to pregnancy, she was out. MGM also reserved the right to loan Jean out to other studios without her approval. It gave her pause, but Mayer would not yield on this point.

Now that her financial future was apparently on firm footing, Jean was able to begin a project she'd postponed some three years before—building her dream house.

Back in the summer of 1929, she and Charles McGrew had bought a parcel of land at 1353 Club View Drive in an exclusive section of Beverly Hills—atop a hill overlooking the Los Angeles Country Club, the site was conveniently located between Wilshire and Santa Monica boulevards. Not a month later, she walked out on the marriage. Jean couldn't possibly build a house on her salary, so the lot stood empty for months and then years while she shelled out property taxes on it. Now Jean decided the time was right to begin construction.

Architect William Kramer was hired to build an all-white Georgian, nine-room home. He began that spring, and MGM obligingly sent Clarence Sinclair Bull out to photograph Jean clambering happily around the construction site, chatting with workers and poring over blueprints.

The interior was designed by Russell Buntz, who continued the pastel theme inside the house, paneling rooms in pale blue or painting them ivory, with matching wall-to-wall carpeting. The master bedroom was done all in ivory and white, except for a pink dressing table holding Jean's collection of perfume bottles. The bed was imported from France and framed with a huge canopy; the master bath had onyx floors and gold-plated fixtures. One fan magazine solemnly stated that the plumbing was solid gold. Jean's own favorite addition was the huge swimming pool, tiled in green and white, complete with diving board, which the studio pleaded with her not to use.

One disadvantage of the all-white interiors was the ever-growing Harlow menagerie, which made short work of the rugs and furniture. With such a large collection of animals, claw marks, stains, and furballs soon abounded. Jean stocked up on ammonia and carpet sweepers and continued adding to the zoo; fan magazine writers found the disarray and clutter charmingly refreshing after Joan Crawford's antiseptic museum and Pickfair, the stuffy "Buckingham Palace of Hollywood" run by Mary Pickford and Douglas Fairbanks.

Jean began showing up every day at her new workplace, even before a film had been readied for her. She spent much time with Paul Bern, try-

Jean's White Palace, overlooking the Los Angeles Country Club (Bettmann/UPI)

▼

ing to sweet-talk him into finding a proper vehicle and acclimating herself to the new surroundings. Her favorite garb was a pair of loose white trousers, polo shirt, white socks, and tennis shoes. This didn't sit well with her new boss, who felt that no star should leave her home unless ready to be photographed for a fan magazine. Mayer had already impressed this credo on Joan Crawford, who obeyed with alacrity. Crawford recalled what happened when she showed up one day dressed like Jean: "I came to the studio very well dressed (I thought) in slacks with my hair back and a scarf around it. He [Mayer] took one look at me, turned absolutely red, and told me to go back home and dress the way a star should be seen in public, and to never appear looking the way 'just any woman' would. . . . I never again appeared in public, at least not consciously, looking like 'just any woman.'"

But Jean never took her star status seriously enough to buckle under as Crawford did. She and a few other renegades like Katharine Hepburn and Greta Garbo insisted on appearing comfortable to the point of sloppiness when strolling from set to set. Mayer fumed and lectured, but to no avail.

When stopped by autograph seekers, Jean tended to squeal happily and engage the fans in conversation—hardly the glamorous, standoffish aura Mayer liked his stars to project. Indeed, she began taking a fiendish delight in aggravating him. Early in her tenure at MGM, she was asked to dine at the head table during a studio visit from ex-president Coolidge. Joining her were Will Rogers, Wallace Beery, and several Barrymores. John Barrymore, a notorious practical joker, bet

Jean that she wouldn't appear at the table wearing a chiffon nightie. Much to Mayer's horror and Barrymore's delight, Jean took on the bet. Coolidge's reaction was barely noticeable, but Barrymore choked with laughter throughout the meal. He became an ardent (though platonic) admirer of Jean's, while Mayer's opinion of her dropped a notch or two.

Jean realized that her two best allies at the studio were Paul Bern and Irving Thalberg, so she began pestering them for a good film. Bern felt guilty about sticking her with *The Beast of the City* and worked hard to dig something up that might catch Jean's fancy. As it turned out, there had been a project bouncing around the studio for nearly a year that fit the bill perfectly.

Red-Headed Woman was a short story by Katherine Brush, which MGM had bought for F. Scott Fitzgerald to turn into a suitable screenplay. Fitzgerald, already in the twilight of his career, turned in a depressing, unusable script and seemed unwilling or unable to make the necessary revisions. He was fired and Anita Loos (author of the brilliant comic novel *Gentlemen Prefer Blondes*) took his place. Thalberg asked her to transform the turgid mess into a sex comedy, much to the unease of director Jack Conway, who saw nothing amusing in the story of an amoral secretary who breaks up marriages, leads men to destruction, and winds up happy and wealthy at the fade-out. His own marriage had been destroyed by a similar mantrap, and he was convinced that audiences would share his feelings on the subject. Everyone involved agreed that it would take a remarkable actress to make such a horrid tramp into a laughable heroine.

Every actress at MGM had been considered for the role and rejected. Garbo was too languid. Crawford was too intelligent. Shearer and Davies were rejected out of hand; neither of their mentors was about to assign them such an unsympathetic role. Red-headed Clara Bow was briefly considered; even aging comic Marie Dressler borrowed a red wig and jokingly demanded a test.

Paul Bern was convinced that Jean would be perfect. He knew she longed to return to comedy, to prove where her talents really lay. He recognized that Jean's childlike glee, her impish personality, would redeem the character in the eyes of audiences, and that she was the only actress capable of mixing sexual lure with wholesome innocence. He arranged for Jean to meet with Thalberg and Loos to plead her own case. She showed up for the meeting in a flaming red wig and tried to charm the two over.

"Do you think you can make audiences laugh?" asked Thalberg. "With me or at me?" "At you," Jean was told. She smiled and shrugged. "Why not? People have been laughing at me all my life." After the meeting Thalberg told Loos, "I don't think we need worry about Miss Harlow's sense of humor." Jean was officially signed on as the star of *Red-Headed Woman.*

She certainly didn't win any friends when Bern's sponsorship got her the part, but it proved to be worth the possible antagonism of her peers. The role would have been easy to botch. It required a very light touch and expert comic timing. Jean was sure she could play this part to perfection, but her employers took a wait-and-see attitude. She embarked wholeheartedly on the project, playing her vamp reputation for laughs, sending up not only the title character, Lil Andrews, but also Helen, Rose, Gwen, Daisy, and all the other humorless sluts she'd so unrewardingly played in the past. Loos and Thalberg guessed that audiences would be so touched and surprised at this about-face that any possible deficiencies in her performance would be overlooked.

Red-Headed Woman was the story of Lil Andrews, an ambitious girl from the wrong side of the tracks in Renwood, Ohio. Lil is determined to get to the top, much to the dismay of her roommate (Una Merkel) and bootlegger boyfriend. Lil barges in on her married boss, Bill Legendre (Chester Morris) and brazenly seduces him. She does not—cannot—take no for an answer. She is so single-minded, she can't even take insults or physical abuse for an answer: "Do it again—I love it!" she purrs when Legendre slaps her. She has no trouble winning the spineless boob from his wife, and she quickly marries him. Failing to charm the local elite, Lil moves on to a wealthy New Yorker, vamping both him and his amorous chauffeur. When Legendre tries to warn this latest victim, Lil shoots him (one of the few false notes in the film). Escaping prosecution, Lil flees to Paris and is last seen hobnobbing with the upper crust, her oversexed chauffeur still in tow.

Lil was an entirely new and refreshing kind of trollop. She didn't glower or breathe heavily behind cigarette holders. She was humorous, good-natured, and full of glee. This was an upwardly mobile young lady with whom depression-era girls could identify. She wanted to claw her way out of poverty and a dead-end career the only way she knew how, and went about it with a childlike cheer that made her more a role model than a figure of scorn.

The *Red-Headed Woman* set was a happy one, which helped calm Jean's nerves. She was unsure about the red wig, but cameraman Harold Rosson eased the tension by making small talk and comparing golfing tips (both were avid golfers, and Rosson had occasionally teed off with Marino). Jean soon got used to the wig and even grew to like it, although she assured fan magazines that "as soon as the picture is finished this red hair is going to be given a nice place among my souvenirs." She also made a point of burning as many bridges behind her as she could, stressing that she'd been "trying for a long time to get away from the type of character started by *Hell's Angels.* Perhaps if I can prove that I can do more than one thing I will be given a chance to play a variety of roles in the future."

FIVE

STRANGE INTERLUDE

Portrait still, ca. 1934

At least one MGM executive had faith that Jean's time had come. When *Grand Hotel* opened at Grauman's Chinese Theatre on April 16, the most visible couple attending were Jean Harlow and Paul Bern. This was the first public notice that the two were more than good friends.

Bern's acquaintances weren't surprised at the pairing. During his years in Hollywood, the slight, balding forty-three-year-old producer had managed to get his name linked with some of the industry's top sex symbols, including Joan Crawford, Mabel Normand, and the ill-fated beauty Barbara LaMarr. LaMarr was one of First National's stars in the 1920s, and Bern had allegedly attempted suicide after her fifth marriage. LaMarr died in 1926, under circumstances which have never been fully explained.

When Bern squired Jean to the *Grand Hotel* opening, Hollywood gossips winked at each other and whispered that it was another case of a grateful young starlet making herself "agreeable" to an influential executive. *Red-Headed Woman* was still shooting, so most people didn't know that Jean was on her way up and no longer needed that kind of "protection." Daily rushes indicated that her latest performance might make her a major star, on a par with Crawford and Davies.

No one was willing to believe that she might care for Bern for his own sake. Writer Carey Wilson and producer Al Lewin spotted them at the premiere and recognized Bern's bent for molding impressionable young actresses. "He's got that goddam Pygmalion complex," said Lewin. "He's hellbent on finding someone to make over and fall in love with."

After this, their first date, the two returned to Bern's newly built home in Beverly Hills. It was a strange, isolated house at 9820 Easton

With Paul Bern at the 1932 premiere of Grand Hotel; *note Jean's wig, from* Red-Headed Woman *(Bettmann/UPI)*

Drive, near Benedict Canyon. Set back some three miles from the main road, it looked like the abode of a Hans Christian Andersen gnome: all gables and turrets, surrounded by pine trees and footpaths, with bizarre rainspouts carved as portraits of Bern's silent-screen-star friends. There was a large swimming pool and a bevy of servants: John and Winifred Carmichael were his butler and cook; Harold Garrison his chauffeur, and Clifton Davis his gardener.

When Jean returned to her Club View Drive house late that night, she told Mama Jean that Paul was the first man who hadn't chased her toward the bedroom on their first date. Jean was a divorcée, not a schoolgirl, and not averse to a sexual relationship. But she was also old-fashioned and more interested in romance than sex—tired of outrunning wolves. Paul Bern seemed more interested in her mind than her body; this was an unusual experience for Jean and it intrigued her.

Paul Bern believed in her. He recommended books he liked, helped coach her speaking voice, encouraged her writing talents, introduced her to European manners and morals. For a homespun girl from the Midwest, this was a revelation: a man who kissed your hand, saw you to your door without trying to break it in, and took "no" for an answer. Before long, Jean had fallen hard. She was able to overlook Bern's lack of good looks and sexual drive. After several dates, she actually felt a sense of relief that here at last was a man who took his time. She wasn't going to let this one get away.

In the meantime, she returned to work on *Red-Headed Woman* with renewed vigor and with Bern's constant support and supervision. Jean was now the official protégée of one of MGM's top producers, and the cavalier treatment she was used to became a thing of the past. The better she was treated, the better her performance got; the better her performance, the more respect she received on the set. It was obvious to director Conway that Jean was stealing the film from her more experienced costars, and that it had nothing to do with Bern's sponsorship. An actress may *get* a good part due to higher influence, but it's up to her to prove herself. Jean was just plain good.

As the film wrapped in late May, Jean wrote to friend and fan Stanley Brown, "Can you imagine ME singing—or, rather, TALKING to music! Ye Gods, I get in one morning and Mr. Conway says, 'Jean, it won't take you long to learn this song, will it?' I guess I nodded a few times and proceeded. My Lord, what procedure!"

The film was an exciting one for her, but also exhausting: "I got beaten, fired a gun, and delivered a long speech in FRENCH. Other than that I did nothing but work." Her social schedule during filming was curtailed. She and Bern saw each other largely during the day, when one or the other could escape for a quick lunch or brief dinner date after viewing the day's rushes. But both the hard-working actress and the driven executive were home in their respective beds by ten at the latest. Both worked six-day weeks, so their courtship had to be taken in fits and starts. It's no wonder that film people found it so difficult to marry outside the profession; outsiders couldn't cope with the hours.

Free evenings were spent in Bern's home, reading. Jean had confessed her literary ambitions, terrified that he would laugh at her impertinence. Instead, Bern suggested that she begin thinking of writing a novel—nothing overly ambitious, but a story the studio might buy for a film project. He recommended books, and the Victrola in her dressing room became silent as she spent free moments perusing works of European and American literature and philosophy. She never brought these books to the set, as she knew the kind of ribbing she'd get from cast and crew. It was bad enough that the press had caught on to the "bombshell and the egghead" story. A similar situation arose some twenty-five years later, when Marilyn Monroe began dating playwright Arthur Miller; both couples found it difficult to withstand the obvious jokes and public spotlight on their private romance.

The story of Jean's showing on the *Red-Headed Woman* set was being kept under careful wraps. Nothing prejudices reviewers so much as telling them how terrific a performance is going to be. This all changed in mid-June when the film opened to glowing reviews. Irene Thirer in the *New York Daily News* called it "Red-hot cinema . . . lurid and laugh-enticing." Bland Johaneson of the *New York Daily Mirror* found it "filled with laughs and loaded with dynamite," and Lucius Beebe of the *New York Herald Tribune* called it a "fast and at times hilarious satirical comedy" (although he also thought it translated the "viciousness" and "gratuitous snideness" of the Brush story to the screen *too* well).

But more importantly, Jean herself garnered the first unreserved raves of her career. She'd been given at best grudging admiration for her dramatic roles, mostly suffering the slings and arrows of the worst scorn. Now she was suddenly proclaimed the triumphant centerpiece of a successful film. The *New York Daily News* made a special point of noting that "the ex-platinum Jean Harlow now sparkles as a titian siren, her emoting improved immeasurably along with the change of her tresses. Harlow gives a splendid performance, making the picture more of a character study of a woman who trades on her physical charms than a narrative romance." The *Mirror* called her performance "amazing . . . out-Bowing the famed Bow." Only the *Tribune* wondered if the audience was applauding "Miss Harlow's satirical characterization . . . or from the belief that she is the hottest number since Helen of Troy."

The acclaim was well deserved; *Red-Headed Woman* is a thoroughly delightful film and still holds up after more than fifty years. Jean is surrounded by a fine cast, including Una Merkel, who appeared in three more films with her. Merkel's personality shouldn't have meshed well with Jean's, as they were both tart, wise-cracking blondes; but somehow they avoided canceling each other out and made a fine pair. Chester Morris was appropriately stuffy as Legendre, and character actors Lewis Stone and Henry Stephenson were excellent in minor roles.

The small but crucial part of Lil's oversexed chauffeur was played by MGM contract actor Charles Boyer, who had been a big hit in his native France but was dying in America. Boyer was so disgusted at being cast in this bit part that he insisted his brief but important footage be deleted in France, which must have confusingly altered the plot line for French audiences. Boyer didn't make it big in the U.S. until 1938's *Algiers* (in which, by the way, he *never* said, "Come wiz me to ze Casbah").

MGM's star costume designer, Adrian, arrayed Lil in a wonderful series of revealing, gaudy outfits. For a formal party to which her guests wear socially correct silks and chiffons, she bursts onto the scene in an outrageous creation of shimmering threads, looking like a Ziegfeld girl gone berserk. To make up for the "subtle" red hair (the film was, of course, black and white), Jean was given a great deal more makeup than usual; huge eyes and a bee-stung mouth helped emphasize Lil's trashy personality.

With bit player Charles Boyer in Red-Headed Woman *(1932)*

Jean was also given her first full-blown temper tantrum in *Red-Headed Woman.* These comic fits would become a trademark for her, used frequently in her later films. Waving her little fists about, shrieking wildly, eyes popping, and shoulders thrust forward, Jean spat out her lines at breakneck speed, somehow making these tantrums endearingly comic rather than grating. Her smile, like that of a mischievous five-year-old, also went far to mitigate Lil's appalling actions.

Loos thought it wise to let the audience know immediately that this was a comedy, so she inserted three vignettes right after the opening credits: Lil gazing into a mirror and purring, "so gentlemen prefer blondes, do they?"; Lil buying a dress after the saleswoman assures her that it is indeed transparent; and Lil snapping her boss's photo into her garter, where it would "do some good." After that, even the slowest audience would realize they were permitted to laugh at this woman.

Religious groups, however, weren't laughing when *Red-Headed Woman* was awarded the Hays Office seal of approval. Write-in campaigns were directed to MGM and to exhibiting theaters, but the studio surprisingly held firm and refused to withdraw or reshoot the picture. Jean herself was the target of adverse criticism, as moralizers seemed unable to separate the actress from her role. This would plague her throughout her career and would be one of her greatest heartaches.

Lil Andrews, against all rules of censorship, went happily unpunished for her sins at the end of the film. Bad women had been portrayed on-screen before, but the loosely enforced Hays Office censorship code stated that they must either repent or be punished. Lil does neither. The same year that *Red-Headed Woman* was released, several characters even more morally bankrupt than Lil Andrews appeared on-screen: in *Baby Face,* Barbara Stanwyck played a gold-digging tramp who made Lil look like a Girl Scout; Stanwyck's character, however, repented when the right man came along. The sadistic half-caste played by Clara Bow in *Call Her Savage* went through the tortures of the damned before earning her happy ending, and Greta Garbo's *Mata Hari* went to the firing squad not so much for her spying as for her seduction of innocent Ramon Novarro.

Red-Headed Woman was banned entirely in Germany and England, which put a substantial dent in MGM's profits. Interestingly, England's royal family kept a print to show guests at Buckingham Palace, despite their government's official condemnation of the film.

On June 20, Jean and Paul Bern took even their closest friends by surprise when they announced their engagement. "We waited until after *Red-Headed Woman* was released to be married because I insisted on it," said Jean. "I don't want people to say I had married him to further my career." People, of course, said it anyway. Among those violently opposed to the marriage was Jean's old classmate Irene Mayer Selznick. A good friend of Bern's, she felt the match would be a disaster and snubbed Jean whenever the two met.

Jean and Bern took out a marriage certificate, accompanied by a battery of reporters and cameramen. Jean smiled delightedly throughout the ordeal, and even the camera-shy Bern managed an uncomfortable little grin. Marino was well in evidence, leaning over Jean protectively to make sure he figured in all the photographs.

The wedding was planned for the Fourth of July weekend at Bern's home. As his pine-enclosed lawn was hardly suitable for a reception, Mama Jean happily suggested that they hold a garden party at the Club View Drive house the following morning. She and Marino began phoning caterers, sending out invitations to guests and press alike. If their Baby was going to marry a prominent man, they were going to make sure the entire Western World knew about it.

During their brief engagement, Paul sat Jean down and had a long serious talk about his past and their future. He was well acquainted with his bride's history, but Jean knew very little about her husband or the impact his past might have on their lives.

Paul Bern Levy was born in Wandersbach, Germany, in 1889, into a large Jewish family. One source gives him seventeen siblings, but this seems excessive even for the nineteenth century. The Levys moved to New York City when Paul was nine; after graduating from public school, he entered the New York Academy of Dramatic Arts. This is not to imply a colorful, man-about-town demeanor—quite the opposite. Even as a youth, Paul was introspective and thoughtful, more inclined to Strindberg and Chekov than the Ziegfeld Follies.

ABOVE: Jean Harlow and Paul Bern announce their engagement, June 20, 1932; RIGHT: Dorothy Millette, date unknown (both Bettmann/UPI)

▼

In 1911 he began working as an actor, without much success. Lacking the looks and personality to succeed onstage, Bern began taking jobs as stage manager and writer for various stock companies up and down the East Coast and around the Midwest. Around this time, he met an attractive young redhead named Dorothy Roddy Millette, a leading lady with the Ben Greet Players. Paul and Dorothy were kindred souls from the start, and the actress was delighted to find a serious, intelligent young man who shared her interests and ambitions. The relationship quickly deepened.

In 1914 Bern entered the film industry while Dorothy continued working in stock companies. They moved in together, living in New Jersey rooming houses (even then, many middle-class people working in New York found it cheaper and more convenient to commute). Paul's career began rising: he joined Paramount Studios on Long Island, soon switching to a job as film cutter at Goldwyn. Before long, he'd worked his way up to assistant director and screenwriter.

Paul and Dorothy were finally able to afford Manhattan and moved into the Algonquin Hotel in the midst of the theater district. The famous literary "round table" had not yet formed, but the hotel was already a well-known gathering place for intellectuals and theater folk.

By this time, Paul and Dorothy had come to a decision that would affect the rest of their brief lives. Although registered as Mr. and Mrs. Paul Bern, the couple did not marry. Today, few people think twice about living out of wedlock, but things were very different in 1918. It couldn't have been a professional choice, as neither of their careers would have suffered from a marriage. Paul's family and Dorothy's (still living in her native Indianapolis) might have objected to a mixed-religion union, but that would surely have been more palatable than *this* arrangement. Paul was paying the bills, so there was no reason for Dorothy to register at all, much less as "Mrs. Paul Bern."

The relationship may well have been a platonic one, but there was obviously some strong emotional tie between Paul and Dorothy, which kept them together in this sham marriage through the rigors of two high-stress careers. As Paul's fortunes continued to skyrocket, Dorothy's languished. They began to consider California, where more and more films were being produced. With Paul's influence, Dorothy felt she could at least get a foothold in the film industry. Being a New York stage actress carried some weight then, and with the help of her "husband," she could surely bluff her way into stardom.

Then, in 1921, she fell seriously ill.

Descriptions of this illness are frustratingly vague and mysterious, and her hospital records were destroyed decades ago, so there is no way of knowing the exact nature of her problem. Newspaper clippings and interviews refer to "dementia praecox," a catch-all phrase used to describe anything from mild depression to schizophrenia. Conflicting sources hint at amnesia, "paralysis of the mind," and even long-term coma. No mention is ever made of drug abuse or a suicide attempt, and Dorothy's emotional state earlier in life is merely a matter of conjecture. In short, the exact nature of Dorothy's sudden and devastating collapse remains maddeningly unclear.

In any case, Paul could no longer care for her at the Algonquin. She was moved to the Blythewood Sanitorium in Greenwich, Connecticut. Much to his surprise, Paul discovered that their years together in New York State had given them the status of commonlaw spouses, and that he was legally responsible for her care. He opened a bank account for "Mrs. Paul Bern" and supplied Dorothy with $175 a month to cover her insurance and hospital bills. Then he packed his bags and moved to California.

By the time Dorothy had sufficiently recovered to move back to their Algonquin suite, all traces of her husband were gone, except for the monthly check. She was given to understand that their marriage was over. If she wanted Paul to continue supporting her, she was to stay in New York and be a good girl. Dorothy was to get on with her life and let Paul get on with his. But she couldn't find it within herself to let go. She became a recluse who lived for Paul's letters and for his brief, infrequent visits. She was sure that someday, when she was well again, he would come back to her.

Paul Bern had no intention of coming back. He saw his future beckoning on the West Coast, and that future didn't include a half-cracked wife. To be fair, Paul never cut off Dorothy's hush money, but he did cut off her emotional lifeline, abandoning her to semiwidowhood.

The 1920s were good years for Paul, who joined Metro in 1925, moved to Pathé in 1928, and returned triumphantly to MGM later that year as assistant to Irving Thalberg. Several times a year he went to New York in search of writers and performers, paying a hurried and upsetting visit to Dorothy at the same time.

His quiet intelligence and sympathetic attitude were prized in an industry not known for introspection or philosophy. Struggling young actresses flocked to Paul for advice and reassurance and were refreshed by his gentlemanly behavior. Paul listened as well as talked, and this, too, was unusual in the Hollywood male. Journalist Adela Rogers St. Johns, in her usual semihysterical prose, began referring to him as "The Father Confessor of Hollywood" and, more embarrassingly, "The Motion Picture Christ."

Paul moved into a Spanish hacienda just off Sunset Boulevard with his two best friends, Carey Wilson and John Gilbert, and the three began disporting themselves in a very unchristlike manner. Wilson had recently separated from his wife, and Gilbert was enjoying an on-again, off-again relationship with his ex-wife, actress Leatrice Joy. "The house and its occupants became a legend in the film colony," remembered Joy. "Charlie Chaplin lived only a block away and spent many evenings with them reading plays aloud, experimenting with homemade gin, and sometimes trying to commune with other kinds of spirits via Ouija boards and automatic writing." Colleen Moore recalled that "it was a miserable run-down place, and those three *nuts* lived there. The parties were incredible. They almost blew up the house once experimenting with analine dyes. There always seemed to be a near-fatal accident in that place but things always turned out all right."

Carey Wilson was the closest to a normal, well-adjusted person of the three. Bern's permanent depression seemed lifted by Gilbert's natural high spirits, and Gilbert's self-destructive antics were somewhat tamed by Bern's calming influence. Sheer momentum eventually broke the group up, and Bern began building his own home. This was his situation when he and Jean first met.

Paul told Jean of his involvement with Dorothy Millette, but he delicately left out some important facts. Jean knew there was a woman in his past, someone down on her luck who Bern was helping to support, but she *didn't* know he was legally bound to her by the laws of New York State. Paul was pretty cloudy on some points himself: Would he have to obtain a "commonlaw divorce" before marrying? He didn't want to lose or unduly frighten Jean, so it was simpler not to tell her the whole truth. Jean, who was still forking over 10 percent of her salary to Arthur Landau, didn't find it hard to believe that Paul would support an ex-girlfriend in need.

As part of his wedding gift, Paul gave Jean the deed to his new house. It was mortgaged to the roof, but it was the thought that

The Bern–Harlow wedding party: guests include Great Aunt Jetta (left), Mama Jean (second from left), cousin Donald Roberson (second from right), and Marino Bello (right).

▼

counted, and besides, neither he nor Jean was the sort to worry about finances. Both were well-paid by MGM, their careers on the upswing, and money was the last thing on their minds. Jean was even beginning to enjoy her personal appearances. Unlike the *Hell's Angels* tours, these were well-received and relaxed affairs. Wearing her red wig, she would appear onstage after the film ended, say a few words and answer a few questions. The acclaim and applause were a welcome change after the derision and catcalls of only a year ago.

On Saturday evening, July 2, Jean Harlow and Paul Bern were married at Bern's home by Judge Leon Yankwitch. John Gilbert served as best man, and Marino Bello gave the bride away. About a dozen guests were present, including Irving and Norma Thalberg, Virginia Bruce (the future Mrs. Gilbert), David and Irene Selznick, Jean's friend and stand-in Barbara Brown, Mama Jean, and several close relatives of the bride and groom. Jean's father and stepmother did not attend, nor did Louis B. Mayer.

The bride wore a white silk gown with a deep fringe, low-heeled shoes (so as not to tower over her husband), and no makeup, appearing all of sixteen years old. The men wore business suits, except for Marino Bello who, with his usual flair for just the wrong gesture, wore a tuxedo.

The guests left soon after the ceremony, and the newlyweds retired to the master bedroom. That wedding night has become a source of contention for Hollywood scholars due to a 1964 biography claiming that Bern beat Jean severely with a cane, sending her screaming into the night, effectively ending the marriage. Author Irving Shulman depicted Bern as an impotent, disturbed sadist, and claims Jean fled to ex-agent Arthur Landau's home that night. "The little bastard's a maniac! A dirty, rotten Goddamned sex fiend!" Shulman has her crying, covered from head to toe with bruises and insisting that Bern, infuriated with his inability to have sex with Jean, had savagely bitten, beaten, and all but killed her. ("You're just a rotten awful fag with a dangle half the size of my pinkie!" quotes Shulman in his inimitable style.) Not only the beating was denied by Jean's friends, but the language in which it was couched—"If Jean had used the kind of language that is in Shulman's book . . . my husband would have washed her mouth out with soap," snorted one of her champions.

What Shulman had forgotten was the presence that night of Blanche Williams, who slept in the next room and would have happily killed anyone who harmed Jean. She found the newlyweds in bed the next morning, unbruised and drinking orange juice. She accompanied Jean to the reception at the Bellos' home, where Bern joined them later.

Colleen Moore and Marion Nixon had arrived early and chatted gaily with Jean as she changed into her garden party frock. The party was the social event of the season, and even the weather cooperated as a flock of stars and executives descended on the Club View Drive home for an afternoon of socializing and getting their names well placed in newspaper accounts.

Again, this party was depicted by Shulman as a day-long horror, the terribly injured Jean hobbling about red-eyed and sobbing. Moore scoffed at Shulman's account: "If he had said that athletic, tennis-player, good swimmer Jean had beaten up Paul, the story might have had some credence," she laughed. "Jean would have floored him. . . . But my rebuttal is based on more. . . . I was at the reception.

"Now, if she'd been covered with black and blue marks or had marks covered with make-up, we would have known it. You can't fool an actress about covering make-up. Jean had no marks, no make-up. If she was anything other than her usual self, she was happier." According to Moore and others at that party, the Berns were obviously in love. Hollywood, if not Shulman, recognized this as a happy match.

The next day the newlyweds returned to work; neither had time for a honeymoon.

After the success of *Red-Headed Woman,* it was essential for Jean to follow up with another blockbuster. Hollywood had always been full of one-film wonders, and Jean was not so secure on her throne that she could rest easily. She'd found her niche as a comedienne, at last, and MGM admitted that her next film should capitalize on this talent. With her new fame and new husband, Jean felt on top of the world. At twenty-one she had her life just where she wanted it.

Screenwriter John Lee Mahin recalled that Jean's next film, *Red Dust,* started as an unlikely choice. Based on a Wilson Collison play purchased by MGM in 1930, "it came in as a 15-page treatment . . . and was a very purple melodrama about a poor little slaving whore." Joan Crawford and Norma Shearer were considered for the role but turned it down. The project bounced around until 1932, when Mahin thought of turning it into a comedy. After a few quick conferences with Bern, it was announced on July 14 that Jean would costar with John Gilbert in *Red Dust.*

She was genuinely thrilled. "It gives me the opportunity to play in a real, down-to-earth [film]," she told reporters. "*Red-Headed Woman* was a step toward my goal, but *Red Dust* is just about a realization of my hopes." Jacques Feyder was assigned to direct, and Hunt Stromberg put in charge of production. John Gilbert's career was badly in need of a hit, and casting him opposite Jean might give it the necessary shot in the arm. Costume and makeup tests began in late July while Mahin continued revising the script.

Then he caught an advance screening of a Clark Gable film and ran into Stromberg's office raving about the up-and-coming actor: "There's this guy, my God, he's got the eyes of a woman and the build of a bull. He and Harlow will be a natural." Production was halted, and Gable replaced a brokenhearted John Gilbert, whose career continued to slide. He died four years later. Victor Fleming, who had a reputation as a rough-and-ready director, replaced Feyder, who returned to his native France indignant. With supporting players Mary Astor and Gene Raymond (whose hair was nearly as platinum as Jean's) in place, production resumed on August 19.

Red Dust was one of the "tramps in the tropics" stories so popular in the 1920s and '30s. The fad was begun by *Rain,* the 1922 play based on a Somerset Maugham story. Jeanne Eagels had scored a huge Broadway success in the role of the good-hearted, wisecracking whore Sadie Thompson, and Gloria Swanson's 1928 film version earned her an Oscar nomination. While Jean was making *Red Dust,* Joan Crawford was filming her own version of *Rain.* It was perhaps her finest performance, and one of the most effective dramatic films of its era. Critics, however, hated it, and Crawford always regretted the film. Today it's regarded as a classic.

Back on the *Red Dust* set, Clark Gable wasn't happy with the story or script; production ground to a halt while more changes were made. Jean bounded about with the double happiness of a honeymooner and a newly successful star. She found close companions in both Gable and Mahin, and began bringing her Victrola out of the dressing room and onto the set. This had already become the trademark of any Jean Harlow soundstage: jazz records blaring merrily between takes, Jean grabbing any passing partner and whirling him off in a foxtrot.

No reporter or executive had trouble finding Jean's dressing room; they just followed the strains of Bing Crosby or Cab Calloway right to her door. Jean's room was situated directly over Greta Garbo's, which caused some concern at the front office. An assistant director knocked on the Great One's door and asked if Miss Harlow's records were disturbing. "Noooo," sighed Garbo in her weary-of-it-all moan, "I used to play happy music, too . . ."

Clarence Sinclair Bull was the photographer in charge of production stills for this film, and he later recalled the sense of fun Jean brought to the sittings. He was terribly frustrated by her hair, which was nearly impossible to light correctly. By the time the lights were arranged to highlight her deep-set eyes and bring out her receding chin, her platinum hair registered on film as a white smear. One night after shooting some publicity stills for *Red Dust,* Bull noticed a hospital set at the far end of the soundstage. What caught his eye was an adjustable surgeon's lamp. He and Jean raced over just as a stagehand was dismantling it and asked if they could borrow the lamp for an hour or two.

Bull was excited by the results: he could finally set up lighting to flatter Jean's difficult bone structure, then adjust the "boom" lamp above and behind her to set off her hair to its best advantage. After the session, the obliging stagehand turned his back while Jean threw her coat over the lamp and she and Bull smuggled it back to his studio. He christened it "Harlow's Halo" and reserved it solely for her use, keeping it well hidden in case the prop department came looking for their missing light.

Red Dust *poster art (1932)*

With good friend Clark Gable in Red Dust, *summer 1932*

Like many stars, Gable had an intense dislike for these photo sessions. They took place during their "free" time, so it was like staying after school to do extra homework (Garbo and Norma Shearer had to be dragged kicking and screaming into the studio). Jean, however, had a grand time posing for the camera, managing to coerce Gable into the studio sometimes after filming wrapped. She'd crank up the Victrola and alert Bull that he'd better rush over if he wanted a few shots: "They'd kid around and wrestle until I'd say, 'let's heat up the negative.' And they burned it clear through. I've never seen two actors make love so convincingly without being in love. How they enjoyed those embraces. And the jokes and laughter."

Jean's lifelong friendship with Gable began during this film. The thirty-one-year-old actor had much in common with Jean: both were only children from the Midwest, both had married young and throughout their lives showed a preference for older "parent figures" when choosing spouses (in 1932, Gable was married to middle-aged society woman Ria Langham). Both Jean and Gable were marketed as sex objects, and both felt supremely embarrassed by it. Neither was secure about their acting ability, but they found they could kid around and bolster each other's confidence.

Their friendship was strictly platonic, and it was particularly refreshing that no fan magazine or gossip columnist raised an eyebrow at these two sex symbols gamboling like a couple of bear cubs. Gable was romantically linked with nearly all of his female costars, but no one ever suggested that his interest in Jean was anything but brotherly. To do so was to court a sock on the nose, as Gable was very protective of his "kid sister."

In the hands of Mahin and Fleming, *Red Dust* was turning into an interesting mix of sex comedy and adventure. Although the film took place in Indochina, all the sets were built on the MGM back lot. Hundreds of thousands of dollars were invested in the film and in building up the Harlow-Gable team. The set took up an entire soundstage, and was composed of eight separate rooms built around a central compound, complete with a working river. Live moths were released before each take to ensure authenticity (the moths either immediately froze to death or electrocuted themselves in the lighting equipment). MGM bought up all the straw matting on the West Coast to furnish the set, and all of this trouble and expense was relayed daily to a panting publicity department.

As finally scripted, the film took place on a rubber plantation run by Dennis Carson (Gable). When a fledgling assistant and his prissy wife, Gary and Barbara Willis (Gene Raymond and Mary Astor) arrive, they are accompanied by Vantine (Jean), a prostitute on the lam from the law. Vantine cheerily settles herself in for a long stay and cattily observes the affair heating up between Carson and Barbara Willis. When Carson finally rejects Barbara out of loyalty to her unsuspecting husband, the neurotically repressed woman shoots him. The Willises, obviously unfit for life in the tropics, hightail it back to the States, leaving Vantine to nurse an appreciative Carson back to health.

The film was certainly the steamiest of the year—the men were unshaven, the women rumpled, and everyone bathed in sweat (actually, the set was rather chilly and the makeup crew had to chase the cast around with atomizers of "perspiration" between takes). The script was rife with sexual innuendo, and the plot had everyone (except poor Gene Raymond) merrily hopping from bed to bed.

Jean's character was considerably softer and more sympathetic than Lil Andrews in *Red-Headed Woman*. Although there was no doubt about Vantine's profession, her wisecracking was offset by a sentimental vulnerability. In one scene, upset by a rejection from Carson, she scrapes out the parrot's cage and snaps at the bird, "Whadda *you* been eatin', cement?" "It'll be unpleasant if she says it angrily to the parrot," reasoned Mahin, "but if she's crying at the same time, if she's broken hearted, then it's funny and it's sweet."

Mahin and Jean conspired to put as many of these redeeming touches into her character as they could. While Jean was happy with the film as a whole, she was also uneasy about playing a prostitute; the relentless cheapness of her characters was still a source of distress. She found both a playmate and an ally in Mahin, an attractive young man who looked a bit like Tyrone Power. If their friendship ever went beyond the platonic stage, they were very discreet about it. Their names were never romantically linked.

On her nights off, Jean settled into her new husband's home and accustomed herself to being a wife again. Mama Jean and Marino continued living at the Club View Drive house at Jean's expense; evenings not spent with Paul were spent at this second home. In fact, Jean seemed unable to break away from her mother and frequently stayed overnight, a habit which had annoyed her first husband. The Berns were seen at the required openings and parties, but most free evenings were whiled away in front of the fireplace, reading. Jean's friends looked askance at her enthusiastic accounts of this school-room marriage, and wondered how long the high-spirited girl could be happy in such an atmosphere. "All I want out of life," Jean told Colleen Moore, "is to be able to sit at Paul's feet and have him read to me and educate me."

Moore recalled a party the Berns attended, obviously in love and gazing at each other like the newlyweds they still were. Paul had instructed Jean to refer to her fellow guest Prince Ferdinand Liechtenstein as "Your Serene Highness." This threw her into such a state that the prince laughingly told her to drop the formalities, and she happily called him "toots" for the rest of the evening.

As Moore helped Bern on with his coat at the end of the party, she noticed something weighing down his pocket. "It was so heavy, I said to him, 'what's in your pocket—all my silver?'" Bern produced a .32 caliber pistol and told her, "We live up in a lonely canyon, and someone might try to hurt my darling."

Paul's fascination with guns was one of the few things that bothered Jean about her husband. Another was his dark, fatalistic humor. Jean was an open, uncomplicated girl, the very image of the corn-fed farmer's daughter. Her easy good humor was in stark contrast to Bern's morbid preoccupation with death and the occult. His friends Gilbert and Wilson recalled that Bern made almost a study of suicide, discussing it at such length that even those two eccentrics got the willies. Jean had never been introspective, and this sudden exposure to a dark, probing mentality unnerved her.

Her own philosophy of life was astonishingly complacent and well-balanced. "I'm fortunate in that respect," she later told interviewer James Reid. "I was born with a fairly happy disposition. Nothing bothers me." In what must have been an oblique reference to Bern, she sighed, "Some people *like* to suffer. Mental sadists, I call them. And I don't want to be one of them. If I have one problem so baffling that it can't be solved, I tuck it away. Some day I may find the answer." This carefree attitude must have been quite foreign to Bern.

Friends noticed that the Berns got on each others' nerves occasionally; that Jean could be thoughtlessly cruel to her husband. Douglas Fairbanks, Jr., recalls attending a social function with them, during which Jean repeatedly groped his leg under the table. Fairbanks, an intelligent and humorous but exceedingly stuffy young man, was horrified. Of course, Fairbanks was one of the more attractive men in Hollywood, but Jean certainly wouldn't have made a *serious* pass with her husband sitting nearby (and probably packing a pistol, at that). It's more likely that she was trying to shock the rather formal actor, and succeeded admirably. Puncturing stuffiness was one of Jean's favorite pastimes, although in this case her prank was badly timed and inconsiderate. Fairbanks, a friend of Paul's, never quite recovered from his pawing and avoided Jean thereafter.

Anita Loos recalled another incident, in which she accompanied the Berns to a football game. After Paul had made sure the two ladies were comfortable and supplied with all the hot dogs and soda they wanted, he asked if there was anything else he could get for them. "Yes, daddy, I'll take one of those," Jean giggled, pointing to the starting lineup. Jean and Loos had a good laugh over that one, but Loos later realized how hurtful such a remark must have been to the middle-aged bridegroom.

Jean did, however, get along well with most of Paul's friends, especially Carey Wilson and his fiancée, actress Carmelita Geraughty. Jean had always sought authors rather than actors for company, and the Wilsons became her closest friends. She also socialized with top MGM executives Thalberg and Selznick, due to their friendship with her husband. Indeed, while Norma Shearer was considered by many jealous actresses to be the First Lady of MGM, Jean's marriage had certainly made her the Second.

As the summer wore on, Jean noticed that Paul was acting more distracted than usual. She was busier than she'd been in ages, working six- and seven-day weeks on *Red Dust.* She threw herself wholly into the role of Vantine, the first that satisfied her ambition of playing "a good girl with a streak of badness or a bad girl with a streak of goodness."

What Paul knew, but Jean didn't, was that Dorothy Millette had fled her New York exile and come in search of her errant husband. In April, when news of the Bern–Harlow romance had hit the national press, Dorothy flew west and moved into San Francisco's Ambassador Hotel. She sensed she was up against something bigger than a mere flirtation, that she was going to lose Paul once and for all if she didn't act. Dorothy began writing and calling Paul, who continued sending her checks but put off any personal contact. By the time he and Jean married, he was fully aware that his other wife was closing in like an avenging angel, demanding an explanation of this gross betrayal. A reckoning was coming as the summer ended and Labor Day weekend approached.

On Saturday, September 3, the Berns worked at the studio on their pictures. They were expected that night at a party thrown by Frederic March and Florence Eldridge. When chauffeur Harold Garrison drove Bern home, he was told that Jean would be working late and staying with the Bellos and that Bern didn't want to attend the party alone.

Paul told Jean he might stop by for a late-night dinner, but called up pleading a bad headache. He worked on a script in his study until early the next morning, when the servants saw him finally turn out his light and go to bed.

Jean spent Sunday with the Bellos and at the studio. Marino was packing for a fishing trip he planned to take on Labor Day with Clark Gable, and Jean decided to spend the night with her mother again. She phoned Paul and invited him to dinner, and he said he'd try to make it.

There were strange goings-on at the Bern house that Sunday, while Jean visited with her mother. Neighbors claimed to see a veiled woman in a pink dress drive up in a chauffeured limousine; shortly afterward, they heard the sound of someone swimming in Bern's pool and a woman (not Jean and presumably not Mrs. Carmichael, the cook) arguing with Bern. The same veiled woman was spotted leaving after midnight. Neighbor Slavka Vorkapich, who saw her, noted that the car "leaped down the hill at such speed it skidded 100 feet when it reached the bottom." For someone who had chosen a secluded house on a dead-end street, Paul Bern had managed to select the nosiest neighbors in California.

Jean stopped by for a brief visit at seven P.M. When she left an hour later she took the Carmichaels with her to help Mama Jean prepare for dinner. Jean told Paul goodnight, in case he decided not to follow. Paul kissed her and said casually, "Well, I'll be seeing you." Shortly thereafter, he called her at the Bellos' and told her his headache was worse, that she'd have to spend the night without him again. Jean, concerned, called several times that evening to see if he was all right, but no one answered.

On Monday morning, the servants began arriving at the Berns' home to prepare for the day. While tidying up the grounds, Clifton Davis found two brandy glasses—one broken—by the poolside. Mrs. Carmichael noticed that a piece of cake she'd left in Jean's dressing room against her possible return the night before was missing. She thought that odd, as Jean *hadn't* returned, and Paul didn't eat cake (it obviously never occurred to her that he was perfectly capable of throwing away stale cake).

John Carmichael went to the master bedroom to see if Bern was awake yet. There was no answer to his knock, so he entered with a breakfast tray. Paul Bern was lying in a pool of blood, half in and half out of the dressing room, with part of his head missing. Carmichael let out a yelp and fainted.

The other servants came running. Bern was naked, lying face down with his head turned toward the bedroom door. Blood covered the wall where a bullet had lodged, and his pistol lay by his side. The Carmichaels did what Paul and Jean had always instructed them to do in case of emergency: they called MGM.

Within the hour, Louis B. Mayer, Irving Thalberg, and David O. Selznick arrived, bringing with them MGM security chief Whitey Hendry. Word spread quickly, and various publicists, writers, and studio hangers-on gathered, although many who later claimed to have been at the death scene must have been bragging. If everyone were telling the truth, the room would have been packed to the ceiling. Mayer noticed a suicide note on the mantel: he read it and quickly stuffed it into his pocket before calling the police at nine o'clock.

Officers Condaffer and Ryan didn't arrive until eleven o'clock, which must have been a very uncomfortable two hours for that sizable crowd in the death room. After apologizing for the delay, the policemen began taking statements. For every simple question asked, they got seven different answers. For an apparent suicide, there was an awful lot of hemming and hawing.

Mrs. Carmichael, sniffing around the house for clues, had come up with a woman's yellow bathing suit hanging in a closet. It was damp, and it wasn't Jean's. Harold Garrison claimed he'd driven Bern to the Ambassador Hotel in San Francisco the day before for a two-hour visit. Clifton Davis told of the two brandy glasses, claimed he'd heard the Berns arguing of late, and hotly insisted that his employer had been murdered. Glaring at Mayer, he also insisted that he'd seen two suicide notes, and that Mayer had at least one in his possession (the second note, if it ever existed, was never found).

Howard Strickling, who'd arrived with the rest of the crowd, convinced a reluctant Mayer to hand the note over to the police. "Dearest Dear," it ran, "unfortunately this is the only way to make good the frightful wrong I have done you and to wipe out my abject humiliation. I love you. Paul. You understand that last night was only a comedy." It was perhaps the most unfortunately worded note in the history of suicide and was to haunt Jean for the rest of her life. Had Mayer fully realized the consequences, he would have been well advised to keep it in his pocket.

The police continued their interviews while Bern's body was photographed and packed off to the coroner's office. Thalberg asked if he could be excused, so he could fulfill the unpleasant task of informing Bern's bride that she was now a widow. Norma Shearer picked him up and drove him to the white mansion on Club View Drive. "I waited in the car across the street while Irving went inside. Then he appeared on an upper-floor balcony. It had a railing around it that hid most of him but I could see his shoes and the cuffs of his trousers. . . . He paced back

Reporters gather outside the Easton Drive house following Paul Bern's suicide, September 5, 1932.

and forth until Jean came out. I could see her slippers and the hem of her negligée. They stood facing each other for a minute, then she seemed to wilt. Irving took her back into the house, then he came out and sat beside me in the car, white-faced."

For the first time in her life, Jean confronted real tragedy. Her mother was of no help whatsoever. True to form, Mama Jean collapsed into hysterical tears. Blanche Williams, made of sterner stuff, called Jean's doctor, Robert Kinnicott, who rushed to the house and put both Jeans under sedation while Blanche frantically summoned Marino back from his fishing trip. He raced home, diplomatically dropping Gable off first, so as not to involve him in the mess. Inspector David Davison and Chief of Detectives Joseph Taylor arrived to interview Jean, but Marino (referred to in the papers as "Count" Bello, which must have pleased him no end) refused, saying she was in no shape to answer questions. As the death was obviously a suicide, the officers didn't want to intrude, but stated that they "would not close the case until [they] had secured a statement from the widow."

Coroner Frank Nance announced that he would call an inquest to iron out "certain discrepancies." Although the powder traces on Bern's head and the trajectory of the bullet clearly indicated suicide, Nance was annoyed by the contradictory stories he was hearing from the seemingly hundreds of people who knew "why" Bern had died. Every servant, neighbor, and friend felt compelled to tell his or her story to the police and newspapers, and Nance wanted either to get the stories straight or stop them once and for all. Jean's attorney, Mendel Silberberg, tried to talk the coroner out of an inquest; after all, a handwriting expert had proclaimed the suicide note genuine, if vaguely worded. What else did he want? But Nance held firm and planned to summon the widow to a grand jury investigation.

Paul's brother Henry flew in from New Rochelle, New York, that evening. During a layover between flights he told reporters that he knew of no motives, that Paul and Jean seemed perfectly happy. John Gilbert and Carey Wilson, saddened but not surprised by their friend's death, testified to police that he had often spoken of suicide—in an academic way—had attempted it at least once before, and was prone to sudden and deep depressions. Meanwhile, several sources had leaked the existence of Dorothy Millette, and the hunt was on for this new mystery woman.

MGM's chief physician, Edward Jones, wired to Mayer from his Honolulu vacation, "Understand motive. Will leave at once to testify for you and Miss Harlow, if necessary." This brought one more disturbing element into the case: Who had notified Jones? What was this "motive" he understood? It was only Monday night, and already Bern's death was becoming clouded by rumor.

The Monday evening papers carried front-page headlines about Bern's suicide. Dorothy Millette, back in her San Francisco hotel room, read Paul's published suicide note. She knew that she had irrevocably lost him, and that she herself had probably pushed him over the edge. She couldn't live with that loss, and she couldn't live with that guilt. That night, Dorothy boarded the *Delta Queen,* a commuter ferry bound for Sacramento. She found the most secluded deck and stood in the late summer darkness until the boat was in mid-voyage. Then she jumped into the cool waters of the Sacramento River.

Jean awoke Tuesday morning with the cold realization that she was alone again, with no husband, no strong shoulder to lean on. The sounds of Mama Jean's muffled sobs and Marino's ineffectual consolations told her that she was again the only adult in the vicinity. Jean knew her career was in grave danger, and that Paul had put it there. Just as he had brought her to the heights, his death threatened to drag her back down. Jean didn't have time to mourn right now; she had to fight for her professional life.

She put on a simple dress and agreed to meet with the police that morning. Still shaking and tearful, she told them that "there was nothing wrong with our marriage. It was a wonderful marriage. I loved him dearly." When the suicide note was brandished before her, Jean said quietly, "I have no idea what it means. The 'frightful wrong' he apparently believed he had done me is all a mystery. I can't imagine what it means." Then Jean clammed up. She never again made a public statement about her husband, leaving amateur detectives to come to their own conclusions.

Chief among these was, of course, the ex-novelist Irving Shulman. His unintentionally hilarious version of the "comedy" involved Bern donning a huge dildo and "strutting around the room . . . piling conceit upon conceit, dancing, strutting, Paul burlesqued a worship of the phallus . . . and they clung to each other like children surrounded by an evil enchantment." Just why this episode might have occasioned Paul's suicide is never explained; indeed, Shulman was never able to cite any sources for this unlikely version of the "comedy." As he also misquotes Bern's suicide note in his book, one is advised to take this story with vast caution.

Paul Bern's final note has been a source of confusion and speculation for many years, and Jean always maintained it was, indeed, a mystery to her. One fact has always been overlooked when analyzing it, however. There was no envelope, no superscription. Very likely, the note was not meant for Jean at all, but for Dorothy Millette.

Paul *had* done Dorothy a frightful wrong by marrying another woman while legally bound to her. He'd abandoned Dorothy in New York and run off to California, rarely visiting her and even denying her existence. As for the statement, "last night was only a comedy," it's probable Paul referred to Sunday night, as he knew the note would be found Monday morning. There is evidence that Dorothy was in the house that night and may have been there when Jean dropped by at seven o'clock. If it's true that neighbors saw Dorothy leave hurriedly around midnight, she may very well have been present when Paul shot himself. She'd just have time to return to San Francisco by boat or train, read Paul's message in Monday's papers, and take her own life in despair.

It's significant that a man involved so closely with two women would address his note to "Dearest dear," not to "Jean" or "Dorothy"—although had Mayer found an envelope embarrassingly addressed, he would certainly have destroyed it. Paul Bern's final message has never been fully explained. Jean, as usual, refused to comment.

The "helpful" Dr. Jones arrived from Honolulu to issue two contradictory statements: Bern had killed himself because of severe and ongoing depression; Bern had killed himself because he was physically unable to consummate his marriage. Dr. Jones, in short, did nothing but cloud the issue further. The impotence theory was more sordid and, naturally, caught on. What else could the "abject humiliation" have meant? Just think: the world's leading sex symbol married to a eunuch! Simple depression, even bigamy, couldn't compete with that.

Jean refused to comment.

Many people have subscribed to the impotence theory. In America, sex was—and is—thought to be at the root of everything. Irene Selznick regretted cold-shouldering Jean at the time and subsequently felt that she was "heroic" in defending her "impotent" husband's name. "You can hold your head up—you have nothing to be ashamed of," she told Jean when they next met.

Henry Bern hotly denied the impotence rumors and offered to supply a list of women who could deny it from experience. Fan dancer Sally Rand laughingly said that Bern may have had a lot of problems, but impotence was certainly not among them. Yet the rumor would not die, and most people still believe that Paul Bern killed himself out of sexual frustration. All of Jean's biographers have clutched the theory as though it were a life raft. Shulman based his book upon it. On close examination, though, the theory falls apart.

There are too many conflicting stories for anyone to divine the truth at this late date, so Paul Bern's sexual prowess will have to remain an unanswered question. But it's difficult to believe that his suicide had anything to do with sex. Bern would have been dealing with any such problem for years, and doing so admirably (remember his close relationships with LaMarr, Crawford, Normand, and even Millette). Why should his marriage to the sympathetic Jean suddenly prompt him to kill himself? Even those who insist that Bern was impotent believe that Jean knew of it beforehand and simply didn't care. She was not sexually fixated, and she loved Paul enough to make up for any physical disability. It is much more likely that Dorothy's showing up pushed the already neurotic man over the edge.

Jean didn't answer District Attorney Buron Fitts's subpoena dated September 7. Dr. Kinnicott explained that she was too ill. Jean wanted to be loyal to Paul but also to save her own neck. She might do both by keeping her mouth shut. Mayer tried to stir up sympathy for the grieving widow by circulating a story that has become Hollywood legend: the sobbing Jean crying, "I just can't go on living without Paul, with all those fingers pointed at me," and making a break for the balcony; and Mayer, in best melodramatic fashion, snatching her back from certain death. He was intent on publicizing the image of a suicidally grieving widow protecting the name of the sadly impotent Paul Bern. It was far preferable to that of a third party in an illegal marriage.

On September 8, Jean finally appeared before the grand jury. Sequestered in a room in Los Angeles's Ambassador Hotel with a stenographer recording statements in shorthand, she answered the questions of Coroner Nance and jury foreman William Widenham. Her testimony was never made public, and all records were conveniently "lost," but Widenham stated that Jean had "answered all of our questions and seemed more than anxious to present the facts and clear up the case."

When the accumulated evidence was put before District Attorney Fitts, he proclaimed himself perfectly satisfied that Bern's death was a clear-cut suicide. Mayer had been a good friend of the late Los Angeles

District Attorney Thomas Woolwine, and used this to get the current DA to go easy and not exploit it for headlines. The investigation was formally closed on September 12. Jean refused to comment.

Paul Bern's safe deposit box was opened at the Culver City Bank of America by the Deputy State Inheritance Tax Collector, Theodore Pettit. With Jean anxiously looking on, Pettit unearthed three of Bern's wills: two dated 1925 and 1927, which left a $2,500 annuity to Dorothy Millette (*not* Dorothy Bern) and bequests to his family; and one dated July 29, 1932, leaving his entire estate to Jean.

On Sunday, September 11, Paul's ashes were interred in Inglewood, California. Just one week before, Jean had bid a casual goodbye to her husband, expecting him at dinner that night. Now she was heavily veiled, assisted into the service by Marino and an MGM staff writer while fans crowded the barricades for autographs and photographers snapped photos for the evening editions. Jean appeared close to collapse, but, in fact, she was summoning up an amazing reserve of strength, strength that even those closest hadn't suspected. The next day, Jean returned to work.

She did this for several reasons: out of consideration for her coworkers, for her own peace of mind, and out of fear for her job. Jean was well aware of the morals clause in her contract, and despite Mayer's assurances, she wasn't about to take any chances. She had to court public opinion right now, convince her fans that she was a grieving but brave widow worthy of sympathy and not a mantrap who deserved to be hounded off the screen. Rumors were flying that Mayer had already offered Jean's part in *Red Dust* to Tallulah Bankhead and Joan Crawford, so she knew how far she could trust her "understanding" boss. Popular stars such as William Haines, Fatty Arbuckle, and Pola Negri found themselves out of luck when fans turned against them. Jean was hedging her bets.

Marino led Jean and a private nurse through a secluded side entrance to the studio, after carefully alerting the press—no sense wasting a good photo opportunity. Victor Fleming had scheduled a broad comic scene for the day, figuring that would be easiest on Jean and her costars. For the next three days, she cavorted seminude in a wooden rain barrel while Gable teased and dunked her. No usable film was obtained that week, but Fleming was right: the ice was broken; Jean's youth and inner resources were slowly bringing her back.

Not only did Jean's appearance on the set help her own emotional state, it accomplished a minor miracle of public relations. Opinion was definitely turning in her favor. Clark Gable told the press that Jean had carried on even after collapsing on the set, and had "more guts than most men." Lionel Barrymore marveled at such fortitude in one so young, and Marie Dressler offered solace and support to the young widow.

Marino Bello and MGM employee Willis Goldbach assist Jean following Paul Bern's funeral (Bettmann/UPI).

▼

Newspaper and fan-magazine coverage became more sympathetic, even as Jean stonewalled reporters and refused point-blank to discuss her husband's death. This in itself gained her a new respect. Just as gangsters have their code of silence, the film industry appreciated Jean's refusal to rat on one of their own. She was gaining the reputation of being a good team player. If her performance in *Red-Headed Woman* cemented Jean's professional standing as an actress, her performance after Bern's death cemented her acceptance by the film community.

On the day that Jean returned to work, two Japanese fishermen discovered Dorothy Millette's body entangled in the reeds of the Sacramento River. The hotel room key in her pocket led to her identification. No note was found, but the desk blotter in her room showed that the word "justification" had been written with some force by the occupant. After an autopsy and inquest found her death to be a suicide, poor betrayed Dorothy Millette was buried in the East Lawn Cemetery, Sacramento. Jean paid for the funeral.

Not long after, another will was brought forth by Dorothy's survivors, one that left Paul's entire estate to "Mrs. Dorothy Bern." This is just what Jean's attorney had feared, and the legal battle would rage for four more years, when Dorothy's sister and a brother-in-law were awarded a grand total of $2,000. By that time, both Paul and Dorothy had been long forgotten by all but Jean.

SIX

BLONDE BOMBSHELL

Portrait still, ca. 1934

Mama Jean and Marino earned their keep that autumn of 1932, providing a nest in which Jean could recover from the events of the summer. However ineffectual Mama Jean had proven in the past, she more than made up for it now. As soon as The Baby came home from work on *Red Dust,* Mama Jean was ready with a healthy dinner to force down her throat, a full complement of rattle-brained stories, boxes of new frocks to examine, occasionally a new puppy or kitten to play with. Jean, exhausted after a day's work and the strain of her coworkers' sympathy, sank happily back into childhood each night and slowly regained her strength.

Paul Bern's home was immediately put up for sale. Blanche, Mama Jean, and Marino had hastily emptied it of Jean's belongings, omitting anything that may have reminded her of those few brief months with Paul. The house was quickly snapped up by a real estate broker anxious to capitalize on the recent tragedy; there are always people ready and willing to live in such places. (Its 1969 owner, Jay Sebring, was murdered at Sharon Tate's nearby home.)

Red Dust completed filming around the first of October, and Jean ventured back into the photo studio. No cheesecake shots were taken (this would have been considered tasteless even by Hollywood standards); instead, a few somber character studies got her back into the swing of things. She'd not yet consented to any interviews, but finally agreed to let Adela Rogers St. Johns speak to her for *Liberty* magazine.

St. Johns, who was noted for being a mother hen to many stars (and quite a Hollywood team player herself), put out a favorable article restating the impotence theory in no uncertain terms. She even claimed that the late Barbara LaMarr had tipped her off some five years earlier. Jean had resigned herself to the fact that the public wanted to believe

Paul had killed himself in shame over his failure to perform his "duties," and that Jean was standing by her man in true-blue fashion. Although she never went on record with such statements about Bern, she ceased denying popular rumors and theories, letting her fans think what they would.

Jean had many supportive friends helping her through this period, and this was more than just luck. Since her arrival in the film capital, Jean had been acquiring and keeping new pals at a great rate—not just hangers-on anxious to associate with stars, but loyal friends who stuck by her in times of need. Some were stars themselves: Dolores Del Rio and her husband, MGM art director Cedric Gibbons, became close friends, as well as bandleader Johnny Hamp and his wife, Ruth. In the aftermath of Paul's death, a protective group crowded around Jean, sheltering her from outsiders. Harold Barnard, one of the doctors who treated her during this time, also became a good friend. He and his wife lived nearby, and Jean began visiting on Sunday mornings. The maid would let her in at the crack of dawn, and Jean sneaked quietly around the kitchen preparing breakfast. One morning that fall, Dr. Barnard awoke to the sound of voices nearby—very nearby. He opened his eyes to see Jean sitting next to him on the bed, cross-legged, chatting away with Mrs. Barnard as the two chowed down on breakfast. Jean was on the mend.

Her love of animals was also a solace to her. In addition to Oscar the Pomeranian, she found herself surrounded by two alley cats ("good cat" and "bad cat"), a goldfish named 'Erbert (presented to her by a fan), six ducks, a Norwegian huskie named Tiger, one of Rin-Tin-Tin's litter (a platinum blonde named Duncie), and a Persian cat named His Royal Highness, who had a habit of teasing the neighbor's police dog beyond endurance ("the next dog that comes in our yard is going to know just what a .38 feels like," Jean wrote to a friend).

Jean never really "got over" Paul's death. The suicide of a spouse is not something a person sheds like last year's fashions. After her initial shock and grief, she experienced other understandable emotions: guilt, anger, confusion. Could she have somehow prevented his death? Perhaps if he'd been able to discuss Dorothy with her, she would have understood. Or would she? *Did* their sex life have something to do with it? Jean read so incessantly of this motive that it was beginning to haunt her. On the other hand, she was furious with Paul. How could he do this to her, and to himself? What if *she* had been the one to discover his body that morning? How could he shoot himself in their bedroom? What hostility that betrayed! And Paul was an MGM executive. He knew full well that his death might have ended Jean's career.

Although she eventually put her feelings about Paul in some perspective, she never forgot him. Jean was lucky to have her work, her family, and her friends all conspiring to get her back into life. She was

With a member of the Harlow menagerie (Bettmann/UPI)

▼

young and exceptionally healthy. Her powers of recuperation were tested for the first time and showed her to be strong and self-reliant. After *Red Dust* opened, Jean began coming out of her seclusion, paying off Paul's considerable debts, and continuing to socialize with his friends. Carey Wilson and Irving Thalberg visited frequently, Thalberg assuring her that *Red Dust* looked to be an enormous success and reassuring her about her career.

Thalberg was right. *Red Dust* attracted huge crowds and became a major money maker for MGM. The Gable–Harlow team became the first successful pairing of talking pictures. Not since Greta Garbo and John Gilbert had a couple thrown off such sexual sparks. The widely known fact that Jean and Clark were just good friends didn't seem to put a damper on audience enthusiasm for them. *Time* magazine compared Jean favorably with Jeanne Eagels's performance in *Rain,* an enormous compliment. The same magazine cattily noted that "audiences . . . watched her face for traces of tragedy, found none." Indeed, some of the film's success might have been due to morbid curiosity about the Widow Bern. But if they had come to gawk, they stayed to cheer.

The *New York Times,* while not overly impressed with the script, gave honors to the Gable–Harlow team and noted a sudden increase of platinum blonde moviegoers, another indication of Jean's growing popularity and influence. But perhaps Jean's crowning glory was the winning of Richard Watts, Jr. The *New York Herald Tribune* critic had been an outspoken enemy of Jean's since the beginning of her career, unfailingly pounding her into the ground with each review. Nothing she did impressed Watts, and his reviews always gave Jean a shudder of nauseous fear. "The flagrantly blonde Miss Harlow," he wrote when *Red Dust* opened, "who hitherto has attracted but intermittent enthusiasm from this captious department [quite an understatement], immediately becomes one of its favorites by her performance in *Red Dust.* . . . She proves herself a really deft comedienne. . . . In addition, however, to being amusing, she manages to create a credible character and to make the girl she plays a most engaging and sympathetic person."

The reviews were almost all like that. (The only sour note came from syndicated columnist Robert R. Ring, who felt Vantine would have been played better by Joan Blondell; to give Ring his due, Blondell *would* have been quite good.) Jean was even given the dubious distinction of making her debut in Nazi Germany, when *Red Dust* finally passed Hitler's censors in late 1933, after being banned twice. The Third Reich's opinion of Jean has not been handed down to posterity, although her German ancestry and ultra-Aryan appearance must have gratified them.

Jean reached the peak of her powers in *Red Dust.* At the age of twenty-one, she was in full control of her talents. While her performance in *Red-Headed Woman* might have been brushed off as beginner's luck, Vantine proved that Jean's career was assured for some time to come. Thoroughly comfortable on-screen, emanating both assurance and joy, Jean was a delight. Tossing off lines from the side of her mouth, knowing just which ones to emphasize and which to downplay, she'd become that rarest of Hollywood creations, the beautiful clown. While other actresses dabbled successfully in comic roles, it was mostly the gawky or unattractive who made lifelong careers of comedy.

Before Jean's rise, the teaming of sex and laughter was all but unheard of, as though being funny automatically unsexed a woman. Only Mabel Normand had managed to combine the two, and she died just as Jean achieved her first success. Many beautiful women had timidly ventured into comic roles: Clara Bow, Marion Davies, Constance Talmadge, Colleen Moore, and Florence Lawrence had developed these skills to an extent. But most funny women—to this day—divest themselves of sexual overtones.

In the early years, the unattractive Louise Fazenda and Marie Dressler epitomized the comic woman; by the time Jean entered films, her contemporaries were Fanny Brice, Beatrice Lillie, Gracie Allen, the middle-aged Billie Burke, and Zasu Pitts. In Jean's wake, however, women were given the chance to excel as comics without sacrificing their feminine allure. By the late 1930s, Carole Lombard, Claudette Colbert, and even Garbo had followed her lead. (Mae West was a rule unto herself, almost a female female impersonator.)

In the years following Jean's death, the comic field became more open to beautiful clowns, though they remained rare: Marilyn Monroe, Judy Holliday, Lucille Ball, Kay Kendall. Most of the women we consider comic geniuses are still the oddballs—not unattractive, but quirky enough to disqualify them from the tag of sex symbol: Carol Burnett, Gilda Radner, Bette Midler, Lily Tomlin. Jean had blazed the trail for all of them, proving to the world (and, more importantly, to the studio executives) that a sex symbol could make audiences laugh.

By the time Jean voted for Franklin Roosevelt that November, she was well on her way back into society. For the time being her escorts were either Mama Jean or Marino, or "safe" studio employees like Howard Strickling and Vic Orsatti. Jean didn't attend premieres or large parties, but stuck to quiet dinners or dull, studio-sponsored events. No one had the nerve to ask her out on a date, and, indeed, romance was the last thing on her mind. She became friendly with her cameraman, Harold Rosson, who had quietly offered his condolences and had done everything he could to assure that those "traces of tragedy" *Time* had looked for didn't appear. Just as he'd provided assurance on the *Red-Headed Woman* set, Rosson again proved a friend in need.

After the great success of *Red Dust,* Jean was given some time off while MGM considered its next move. She'd earned the respect of

Mayer and Thalberg, and they felt she was entitled to a vacation before her next project—besides, the film had to be carefully chosen so that it would not retard the impetus of Jean's success. She was a full-fledged star now, but no star was too secure to be careless in choosing her vehicles. Even Garbo might be laid low by one or two bad films, as happened later in the decade.

Jean spent that Christmas reading bedtime stories to children at a Los Angeles toy shop, as part of a charity drive sponsored by the Assistance League, a popular Hollywood organization. She signed autographs, gave out toys, and accepted donations while hordes of children piled onto her lap. She thoroughly enjoyed it, and it provided priceless public relations for her at the same time.

She and the Bellos bade farewell to 1932 with a New Year's trip to Agua Caliente, a popular South-of-the-Border resort. Jean developed a gambler's streak and spent a good deal of time at the casino, becoming a demon with the dice (as the crews on her sets soon learned). She found her skill at the roulette table impressed locals and visiting celebrities alike. Her biggest success at Agua Caliente was impressive enough to be mentioned in *Vanity Fair,* not noted for detailing the gambling excesses of film stars: during her twenty-fourth birthday celebration, Jean put down a $2 bet and let it ride for eight straight passes, setting an unofficial casino record when she walked off with $10,240. Not all of her visits were as successful. But Jean learned from the sad lesson of Clara Bow, who had piled up serious gambling debts. Jean kept her losses to a manageable level, however, and thus her gaming was treated as "cute" by the press.

She was also seen keeping company on the dance floor with one Servando Osornio, a Mexican physician described as "a friend of the family." Even the Hollywood press was sympathetic enough not to censure this romance, her first since Bern's death. The mysterious Dr. Osornio vanished from the gossip columns and Jean's life after she returned to Los Angeles.

Most of Jean's vacation time was spent on the golf course, polishing up her game. She was enthusiastic but lazy, getting bored after five or six holes and letting someone else finish for her. For exercise she much preferred swimming, tennis, or plain old walking. Her home contained a private gym, complete with a "rolling machine," a bizarre contraption of pulleys and hard rubber rolling pins believed to squeeze the fat off desired body parts. The room also contained a steam cabinet (which Jean referred to as the closet in which she kept her skeleton). But her usual way of keeping weight down between pictures was her old childhood starvation method, preferred by many stars. She'd simply give up anything remotely fattening or tasty when working.

In January, Jean was back in Hollywood awaiting her next assignment and still breathless from the events of the past year. Jean had become a star, a bride, and a widow within the space of nine months. The new year found her finally beginning to enjoy the fruits of her labors: steady work, adulation, and a decent income.

Gratefully throwing off the image of the Widow Bern, she returned to being Jean Harlow. The tradition of wearing black for a year following a spouse's death had already ceased by 1932 (World War I had made that convention too appalling), but it was still considered proper for widows to wear dark, unadorned clothing and stay out of the limelight for several months. Jean fulfilled this obligation, and now put her old-maidish clothes back into the closet. With the new year she started her new life, dating, dancing, and enjoying herself.

Anita Loos, who had so successfully created *Red-Headed Woman,* was asked to go through her files and find a suitable story for Jean and Clark. The pair was dynamite at the box office, and MGM wanted a quick follow-up to build on the chemistry. Loos dusted off one of her old short stories and teamed with writer Howard Emmett Rogers to create another costarring vehicle, *Hold Your Man.* Sam Wood directed Jean for the first time; Hal Rosson was again in charge of photography.

Hold Your Man, which began filming in early spring, was a classic text-book case of split personality. In a misguided effort to soften the public image of the stars, MGM convinced Loos and Rogers to turn the hard-boiled tale of two swindlers into a parable of reformation through Love. The results were predictably schizoid.

The film starts out as a bright, sexy comedy of no manners, as con artist Eddie Hall (Gable) and Ruby Adams (Jean) meet when the police chase him into her Brooklyn apartment. The two are soon passionately involved, to the dismay of their current sweethearts, the sympathetic Al Simpson (Stuart Erwin) and the not-so-sympathetic Gypsy (Dorothy Burgess).

Things go swimmingly until Eddie convinces Ruby to lure a married man to his apartment. Once they're in a clinch, Eddie will burst in as her outraged brother and shake down the unsuspecting victim. But Eddie accidentally kills the man in a fit of jealous rage, blows town, and leaves Ruby to take the rap. She's sentenced to a women's reformatory (in which she's forced to wear an unattractive uniform and a dreadful center-parted hairdo). When Ruby discovers she's carrying Eddie's baby, the film goes weak at the knees and turns into a half-baked melodrama. Eddie resurfaces, completely reformed, and the two conspire a jailhouse wedding to give their baby a name. The film closes on the happy family en route to Cincinnati, where Ruby's ex beau Al has arranged a job for Eddie. (Al has to rank as the sap of the century: earlier he'd offered to marry Ruby and raise Eddie's child.)

A film divided against itself cannot stand, and *Hold Your Man* simply folds up halfway through. Both stars give intelligent comic performances with suitable material, and the opening scenes are electric with sexual tension and roughneck humor. But neither Jean nor Clark was adept at teary-eyed drama, and their attempts at it were fairly pathetic. The sight of Gable sobbing, begging a priest to marry him to Ruby, was not a high point in his career.

The reformatory scenes were, however, fascinating. They show a cross-section of characters unusual in 1930s films: black, white, Jewish, Oriental. The good-natured camaraderie of the women, their intrigues and rivalries, would have made an entertaining movie. Indeed, the only saving grace of that heavy-handed last-minute wedding is the inmates' conspiracy to bring it off.

Jean was called upon to sing the film's title song, which posed unexpected problems. It was discovered that her vocal range encompassed exactly three notes, and songwriters Arthur Freed and Nacio Herb Brown had somehow to write a song around them. The result was one of the most forgettable tunes of the decade. Jean found she wasn't even able to do justice to those three notes; instead of dubbing, the authors gave up and suggested she hum some of the words. Jean talked her way through the introduction, then hummed through the chorus:

> *Give him love that will hmmm-mmm-mmm,*
> *With a kiss that will hmmm-mmm-mmm*

and so on. Incredibly, MGM used the song again later that year for Winnie Lightner in *Dancing Lady.* It once again failed to ignite enthusiasm and has not been heard since.

Other than that unhappy musical interlude, Loos recalled *Hold Your Man* fondly: "Every day is a gala day on the set of a Harlow–Gable picture . . . work is play to both of them." Jean's Victrola was hauled

Jean and Clark Gable gather 'round the jigsaw puzzle between takes of Hold Your Man *(1933).*

With Paul Hurst, Clark Gable, and Garry Owen in Hold Your Man

▼

out, to the aggravation of the sound technicians listening to playbacks. Jean also purchased a huge jigsaw puzzle, which she set up in an out-of-the-way corner; she and Gable attacked it between takes, and other crew members either helped or, occasionally, hid pieces. Loos spent much time on the set, delighting in the good-natured razzing the stars gave each other. "Underneath their sharp jibes lies deep friendship and respect," she later wrote, "but one would never guess it from their incessant exchange of hot shots."

Jean called Clark "you big Ohio hillbilly," and he in turn christened her "the chromium blonde." Gable did, however, praise Jean's abilities, telling Loos that "she sets a pace for me that keeps me on my toes every minute. . . . She anticipates every move and meets you more than halfway. When it comes to weighing dramatic values, Jean's scales need no adjusting. . . . Sam [Wood] says that she is a mindreader and kidnaps his thoughts before he can express them."

The pair loved childish pranks, like staging a mock feud for one innocent reporter. Expecting the usual raves, the poor woman was amazed when Gable deadpanned, "the trouble with Harlow is that she's mean. . . . I don't call her down because she is a woman, but someday I'll forget myself. Have you noticed her sitting around with her shoes off? Well, she does that because she can't think without twiddling her toes. Her brains are in her feet." Jean sneaked up behind Gable, feigning fury, as he continued his tirade: "And what about a dame that can't live without a gramophone going? She doesn't seem to realize that if I don't give a good performance in this picture there won't be anything for the audience to see." At this point, Jean jumped in on cue, yelling insults and throwing shoes while the alarmed reporter beat a hasty retreat. "He razzes me every minute," Jean later explained, "in hopes of getting my goat—and sometimes he does. In a big hot love scene the other day he whispered, 'Jean, you've got your eyebrows on upside down.'"

Somehow, *Hold Your Man* got finished in this playroom atmosphere, and Jean took a three-week vacation while her next few projects were lined up. When the film opened in June, the two stars were widely applauded, but the movie itself was panned mercilessly for the botched-up job it was. The *New York Times* was hard put to explain the audience's favorable reaction, attributing it to "the popularity of Mr. Gable and Miss Harlow. Certainly there was little else about the film to merit such a response." The *Times*'s reviewer enjoyed the film's first half, but understandably felt that "the sudden transition from hard-boiled wisecracking romance to sentimental penitance provides a jolt." Most critics agreed: the Gable–Harlow popularity continued unabated, but would need better material to thrive.

Jean's name began showing up in gossip columns again. When she began going regularly to Santa Monica's Miramar Café, a romance with orchestra leader Jay Widden was inferred. She and Howard Strickling were seen meeting for lunch on Sundays, and it was implied that Jean was planning to cop yet another MGM bigwig. She was spotted with a well-known polo player from San Francisco and on dates with Canadian Frederick Booth. Both were turned into torrid affairs. But Jean was notoriously close-mouthed about her sex life. If any of the above-named gentlemen shared her bed, they all had the decency to keep quiet about it, and Jean herself never kissed and told.

She got in trouble over a man only once, and was horrified at the resulting publicity. The man in question wasn't an executive or well-bred polo player, but boxer Max Baer, in town to film *The Prize Fighter and the Lady*. Baer (the father of Max Baer, Jr., Jethro of "The Beverly Hillbillies") was a golfing buddy of Marino's, as well as a possible victim of his notorious financial scams. Jean invited Baer to a party that spring, where he endeared himself to no one by tossing several fully dressed female guests into the pool. Jean was not amused and kept her distance thereafter.

Mrs. Baer was in the process of filing divorce papers; gossip columnists put two and two together and came up with the obvious conclusions: Jean had broken up the happy marriage. Everyone involved (except Baer, who needed all the free publicity he could get) denied that

Jean was involved in the break-up. Mrs. Baer admitted that Max would probably relish an affair with the Blonde Bombshell, but insisted that "I know Jean has no feeling romantically for him." Jean was furious, huffing, "I've been over on the set of *The Prizefighter and the Lady* several times, watching the big fight scenes between Max and Primo Carnera—but so has every other star on the lot. . . . I bet I haven't seen him five times in my life—and never once alone!"

Angry and embarrassed, Jean curtailed her socializing and kept her private life private. She restricted her dates to the men in her professional life, directors, writers (like Mahin), and a cameraman, Hal Rosson. Not even the nosiest columnist could call her on that.

MGM, pleased with the success of their all-star *Grand Hotel* in 1932, decided to purchase the Broadway play *Dinner at Eight* as a follow-up. Contrary to all rules of finance and one-star pictures, the studio had crammed *Grand Hotel* with Greta Garbo, John and Lionel Barrymore, Joan Crawford, and Wallace Beery. When box-office receipts showed this to be a good moneymaking strategy, they freed up as many stars as possible for the spring of 1933 and *Dinner at Eight.* The stage show had been quite a hit and was currently touring the country. A biting comedy by George S. Kaufman and Edna Ferber, it revolved around snobbish New York society coping with the Depression as well as personal traumas.

Billie Burke and Lionel Barrymore were signed on to play Millicent and Oliver Jordan, hosts of the title dinner party. Among the guests (each with his or her problem) were aging actress Carlotta Vance (Marie Dressler), corporate raider Dan Packard (Wallace Beery) and his adulterous, social-climbing wife, Kitty (Jean), and alcoholic matinee idol Larry Renault (John Barrymore) and his agent, Max Kane (Lee Tracy).

Clark Gable and Joan Crawford were lined up to play Dr. Wayne Talbot (Kitty's current lover) and the Jordans' daughter Paula (Renault's current lover). Sadly, both stars opted out and the roles were filled by the serviceable but unexciting Edmund Lowe and Madge Evans. To be fair, Lowe and Evans were talented performers, but certainly no Gable and Crawford.

Jean decided not to attend the Los Angeles theatrical production of *Dinner at Eight,* as she "wanted to be free to play the part as it seemed most natural to me and without the unconscious thought that I was trying to do better than another actress, probably more gifted than I." The thought of being cast opposite so many big names gave her a major case of the jitters. "I got the part," she nervously told a friend, "but I'm simply panicky. I'll be completely snowed under and become The Face on the Cutting Room Floor." It's true that the role of Kitty wasn't a large one; this was more of a stock company, with each performer building on the others' scenes.

Marie DRESSLER
John BARRYMORE
Wallace BEERY
Jean HARLOW
Lionel BARRYMORE
Lee TRACY
Edmund LOWE
Billie BURKE
IN
DINNER AT 8
A Metro-Goldwyn-Mayer PICTURE

Above: the cast of Dinner at Eight *(1933) gathers for an impromptu Coca-Cola promo.* *opposite, top:* Dinner at Eight *poster art; opposite, left: Portrait still from* Dinner at Eight; *opposite, right: with Wallace Beery in* Dinner at Eight *(Academy of Motion Picture Arts and Sciences)*

▼

Director George Cukor, known for handling difficult stars, was called in to play ringmaster. This was especially welcome with characters like Wallace Beery; while Jean was thrilled to be working with Dressler and the Barrymores, the thought of playing Beery's wife gave her indigestion. Luckily, Dan and Kitty Packard were supposed to detest each other. She and Beery wouldn't have to dig too deeply to make *that* believable.

Dinner at Eight was filmed in only thirty-two days, wrapping up in mid-April. "We made the picture pretty close to chronological order," Jean recalled, "so we could all feel the dramatic power of the climactic scenes." The speed of this film haunted Cukor for years; whenever one of his projects went over schedule, producers would remind him testily of *Dinner at Eight*'s one-month shoot. Cukor had been worried about Jean's ability, but by the time they were finished he had nothing but praise for her, in later years comparing her favorably to Marilyn Monroe and Judy Holliday.

Marie Dressler was also proud of Jean, claiming her as a protégée. Dressler was infuriated by the Hollywood truism that "any young and conspicuously good-looking actress owes her box office appeal to her beauty. . . . In *Dinner at Eight* [Jean] had to throw a bomb in the works by proving that she is a first-rate actress! The plain truth is, she all but ran off with the show!" This, from Dressler's posthumous autobiography, meant more to Jean than all her good newspaper reviews. She stood in awe of the older actress.

Of course, Wallace Beery wasn't as appreciative. As his on-screen wife, Jean had to spend more time with him than any other cast member, which she took as a personal curse from the gods. She could have been whiling away the time with Dressler or Barrymore, but instead bore the brunt of her old foe's bad temper. The *Dinner at Eight* set was a far cry from the rowdy playground of *Hold Your Man.* Cukor kept everyone on a tight rein, and when they weren't filming, the cast was posing for publicity photos or going over lines. Cukor brooked no nonsense, and Jean kept her Victrola in the dressing room for this film. She was anxious to appear grown-up and professional in the presence of her costars, who between them boasted a total of some two-hundred-fifty years onstage.

Luckily, Jean and Beery were professionals first and enemies second. Their on-screen shouting matches and insults are the high point of the film, although Beery's manhandling of Jean looks painfully realistic. *Dinner at Eight* showcased its cast brilliantly and is one of the most fondly remembered films of the 1930s, with good reason—it's a rare treat from beginning to end, one of the magical instances wherein script, cast, and director meshed perfectly.

Screenwriters Frances Marion and Herman J. Mankiewicz had to soften the acidic Broadway play considerably for film viewers; characters were made more sympathetic, and the ending was brightened up a bit. But the film version is still enjoyably biting.

Jean, Billie Burke, and Marie Dressler stand out among the cast, but there's not a bad or uneven performance in the lot. Kitty Packard, as played onstage by Judith Wood, was a "slightly faded wild-rose"; Jean turned her into a Kewpie doll with social ambition—stupid when it suited her purposes, but with the gears always turning. Shifting suddenly from vapid baby talk to sneering threats, she makes Kitty a totally believable character, grasping, spoiled, and foolish, but at the same time so totally honest that one can't help but like her.

Burke was both touching and hilarious as the scatter-brained, self-centered Millicent Jordan, and Dressler gave a broad but effective portrayal of over-the-hill sex symbol Carlotta Vance, barging into her scenes like a well-dressed grave. Lionel Barrymore managed to tone down his crotchetyness, and brother John's hammy touches were perfect for his role. He was essentially playing himself, and it must have been a brave casting director who approached him for the part.

Even the minor roles were expertly cast and played. Though no Joan Crawford, Madge Evans (who as a child posed for the Fairy Soap ads that have become camp classics for their unfortunate slogan, "Have you a Little Fairy in Your Home?") was suitably intelligent in her performance. Two minor actors in the film point out frighteningly the ups

With Hilda Vaughn between takes of Dinner at Eight *(1933)*

and downs of a Hollywood career. Edward Woods, who had costarred with Jean in *The Public Enemy,* was relegated to a walk-on as a bellhop; and the breathtakingly handsome Phillips Holmes (a rising star of 1930–32) played the tiny part of Ernest DeGraff.

The old saying about there being no small parts, only small actors, is borne out by Hilda Vaughn, who played the small but riveting role of Tina, Kitty Packard's lazy, nasty maid. Vaughn had some success on Broadway but never really made it in films. As Tina, she stole one climactic scene from Jean: suddenly shifting from brainless, shiftless maid to icy blackmailer, Vaughn creates a sense of genuine menace and revenge. Jean wisely underplayed the scene, realizing that giving Vaughn free rein made it all the more effective.

Kitty Packard was set like a jewel in an all-white bedroom by art directors Hobe Erwin and Fred Hope, and Adrian gave her what was to become Jean's most famous costume, the silver silk satin gown she wears to the climactic dinner. It fit Jean like a coat of paint, giving rise to rumors that the dress was either sewn or glued to her each day (rumors fueled by photos of Jean propped against a slant board between takes). But bias-cut silk satin drapes so smoothly that it always gives that appearance. Jean's dress slipped on over her head; it fit so slickly that she couldn't wear underclothes with it. To this day, white satin dresses are called "Jean Harlow gowns," and when the 1930s are evoked in period films, costume designers try to recreate the *Dinner at Eight* dress.

Dinner at Eight spent a lot of time in the editing room; one last-minute emergency developed when the Italian government objected to Carlotta's dog being named Mussolini. "Tarzan" was deftly dubbed in, though Dressler's lips are obviously still saying "Mussolini." The film wasn't released until mid-August in major cities, and didn't arrive in smaller towns until autumn. Not a discouraging word was heard from the press, who all but did nip-ups praising the film and its cast.

"It lives up to every expectation," said the *New York Times.* "It is one of those rare pictures which keeps you in your seat until the final fade-out, for nobody wants to miss one of the scintillating lines." Indeed, the final scene was a classic moment in comedy: as Kitty Packard chirps about having read a book the other day, Carlotta Vance grinds to a halt and exclaims, "Reading a book?" "Yes, it was all about civilization or something, a nutty kind of a book," Kitty explains. "Do you know the guy said that machinery is going to take the place of every profession?" "Oh, my dear," purrs Carlotta, "that's something you need never worry about."

Laughter, curtain, applause.

Bland Johaneson of the *New York Daily Mirror* called *Dinner at Eight* "a great picture—you can't afford to miss it," and made a point of stating that "among all these great performers it is little Jean Harlow who stands out. . . . Harlow is magnificent." By this time, Richard Watts, Jr., of the *New York Herald Tribune* was wholly won over to Jean's charms, also singling her out for praise: "It seems to me that Miss Harlow, an increasingly delightful actress with each picture, plays . . . with such high spirits, comic gaeity and shrewd knowledge—or perhaps instinct—that . . . she is quite the hit of the evening."

Jean was out-performing Barrymores and, more importantly, Beery. She was on top of her profession and climbing higher with each film. The Bern scandal was safely in the past, and she'd emerged from it brighter than ever. As a reward, MGM let her take off to the Chicago World's Fair while they fashioned a high-budget showcase film around her.

In Chicago, Jean finally met her number-one fan, a middle-aged copywriter named Stanley Brown. Brown had begun writing fan letters after *Hell's Angels,* when Jean still had time to answer each one personally, and the two developed a correspondence. He called her "little fellow" and she called him "my safety valve," detailing in depth the aggravations and tribulations of her work. Brown wasn't the only fan she took to her heart. Jean loved writing letters and sat in her dressing room typing notes to everyone from a Chicago chorus girl to a New York doorman.

She and Brown hit it off, and Jean asked him to be her escort to the fair. She dragged him onto every ride and all the exhibits, happily stuffing herself with hot dogs, as Brown fretted over her dress, holding nap-

Immortalized in pastel: fan magazines from (left to right) 1934, 1931, and 1935

▼

kins to catch the mustard. After disembarking from the Ferris wheel, the pair were chased by fans into a freak show, where Jean stood enraptured for several minutes by a three-headed sheep. Back in the glaring sunlight, they fought off crowds, though Jean tried valiantly to sign autographs and wondered aloud, "How do you suppose they get that way, Stan?" "These fans?" he asked, prepared with a deep psychological statement on mass hysteria. "No," Jean replied dreamily, "those three-headed sheep."

Before returning to California, Jean visited her maternal grandparents and her father. She also kept in close contact with her great aunt, Jetta Roberson Chadsey, and favorite cousin, Donald Roberson, a handsome young man who soon followed Jean to Los Angeles. Despite the Carpenters' divorce, Jean had something most sex symbols lacked—a large, close family always ready to protect and nurture her. Her immediate sex-bomb predecessor, Clara Bow, had been badly damaged by her upbringing, which included a psychotic mother and an abusive father; the stage mother of Judy Garland and the horrors of poor Marilyn Monroe's childhood have likewise become the stuff of legend. But Jean always had Kansas City to return to. As over-protective as Mama Jean may have been, she would happily have killed for her daughter, and what Jean lacked in siblings was more than compensated for by her vast assortment of friends and relations.

When Jean returned to work that summer, she found a pleasant surprise waiting for her. MGM had redecorated her dressing room in white French provincial. The collection of star dressing rooms, fondly called The Bordello, were completely revamped in 1935. The building was a coed affair with shared balconies, like a cheap motor court. Each dressing room consisted of an outer foyer (in which reporters might cool their heels) and an inner sanctum used for dressing, learning lines, and resting. Male stars had downstairs rooms, and the women dressed upstairs—an odd arrangement, considering how difficult it must have been to climb stairs in long gowns.

Another surprise greeted Jean when she found herself sued for $1,009.50 by actress Jetta Goudal and her set designer husband, Harold Grieve. They had been commissioned to redecorate Paul Bern's home when the newlyweds had moved in, and were not willing to let the matter slide. Jean was in quite a fix; she'd paid off Paul's debts and had sunk the rest of her cash into the Club View Drive house. She was essentially penniless.

Negotiations were made for MGM laywers to pay off the Grieves, and Jean would repay the studio in one large chunk at a future date. The matter was carefully hidden from the press and public. It would have proven embarrassing for Jean to admit her financial situation (especially in Depression-ridden America, when her salary seemed astronomical). The Grieves were willing to keep the matter hushed up as well, realizing that the lawsuit wouldn't reflect well on them. Hounding widows into bankruptcy was not considered good PR, and Goudal's career didn't need another downward shove.

On August 31, Jean's grandfather Abraham Carpenter died in Kansas at the age of ninety-one. As she'd just returned from a vacation, Jean decided not to attend the funeral; she barely remembered the Carpenters, and even her father rarely saw them. MGM obligingly covered up with a press release stating that the star was too busy with current projects to travel. Her grandmother, Dianna Beale Carpenter, died in her sleep of a stroke just four months later; Jean again begged off and avoided the trip home.

The press release had a lot of truth in it, as Jean *was* quite busy by the end of August with her latest film. After her recent successes, Mayer and Thalberg decided she was a valuable enough property to merit special attention. Her next film must not only keep Jean in the public eye, but must cement her reputation as a brilliant comedienne. While Jean had been riding Ferris wheels in Chicago, MGM had mounted a frantic search for a suitable film.

The studio purchased two stories, *Lulu Belle* and *The Ritz Bar,* looked them over carefully, and shelved them. MGM confidently announced that Jean and Gable would be costarring in *Nora,* then just as confidently said, no, they'd changed their minds; Jean would appear in *The Hollywood Revue of 1933.* Or, perhaps, *Night Life.* Or maybe not. None of these films ever saw the light of day, and MGM was still without a decent vehicle for their newest star.

As he had with *Red Dust,* John Lee Mahin rode to the rescue for Jean's next film. "That came in, again, as a very purple movie," he recalled, "a treatment about this poor girl who worked all her life and in the end committed suicide." The girl in question was a film star, and the unproduced play Mahin read was a Hollywood tragedy by Caroline Francke and Mack Crane, later titled *Bombshell.* Mahin's sense of humor asserted itself after a first reading; he saw the play as an unintentionally funny statement about Hollywood and its stars. Well versed in Jean's own sense of the ridiculous, Mahin knew she would delight in biting the hand that fed her.

Mahin and director Victor Fleming got in touch with Irving Thalberg and convinced him that *Bombshell* and Jean were made for each other and MGM gratefully tabled their latest brilliant idea for her—*Red-Headed Woman in Paris.* Although most people today assume that *Bombshell* was based on Jean's own life, it was an open secret in 1933 that Clara Bow had provided the inspiration. Fleming had been one of Bow's many fiancés and gleefully wrote the It Girl's tribulations into the life of heroine Lola Burns. Mahin also knew Bow and attested to the fact that she "lived in a virtual madhouse of leeches, drunks and hangers-on. . . . As fast as the exasperated star threw one group out the front door, another came in through the back." One of the more obvious tip-offs was the heroine's private secretary blackmailing her and embezzling funds; Bow's own secretary had been tried on just such charges in 1931. MGM, in fact, should have been very grateful that Bow did not sue for defamation of character, as she had due cause.

Bombshell began filming on August 11, starring Jean as Lola Burns, character actor Lee Tracy as her manic press agent Space Hanlon, and Frank Morgan as her overbearing father. Swedish actor Nils Asther was cast as phony society playboy Gifford Middleton, but he felt the role was too small for an actor of his stature. MGM obligingly dropped Asther's option and cast Franchot Tone. This was Jean's first of four films with Tone, who specialized (much to his disgust) in playing spineless society wimps. His marriage to superstar Joan Crawford didn't help his inferiority complex. Tone was far from happy with this role but, seeing Asther's professional demise, was smart enough to grin and bear it.

As finally scripted by Mahin and Jules Furthman, *Bombshell* was essentially plotless; just a month in the life of Lola Burns, reigning sex symbol at Monarch Studios. Lola (like Jean) lives in a white mansion overrun with animals, and is growing weary of her image as a home-wrecking vamp. Her nerves are further plucked by her deranged press agent, her blowhard father and brother, a love-struck director (played by Pat O'Brien; the character was based on Fleming's experiences with Bow), and various lovers and crazed fans.

Jean greatly enjoyed poking fun at herself and allowed Mahin and Furthman to include many self-mocking inside jokes. A brief introductory montage shows audiences salivating over scenes from *Hold Your Man,* and Lola sparring with Primo Carnera (an oblique reference to Jean's recent troubles with Max Baer). Lola is called to reshoot "some *Red Dust* scenes with Gable," and the famous rain barrel from that film

Frank Morgan holds forth to an unbilled actress while Lola Burns (Jean) fumes in Bombshell *(1933).*

was revived for an on-the-set scene. "Thank goodness it was not necessary for me to get in the rain barrel in *Bombshell,*" Jean later laughed. "I had to pick too many splinters out of myself the last time." Jean's dressing room was used for several shots, and some fascinating scenes of The Bordello can be glimpsed as Lola rushes to and fro on the back lot.

Bombshell is perhaps the best source of information on what it was actually like to be a star in the golden era of movies. Lola Burns stood for every overpaid but overworked, harried but glamorous Hollywood actress. The cluttered confusion of the film sets, the camaraderie of the makeup crew, the frenzied dealings with studio brass, reporters, and fans both good-natured and malevolent; it was all put on film with wit and honesty. Lola emerges as an exaggerated combination of Jean and Clara—temperamental but humorous, cynical but sentimental, and hopelessly naive.

Lee Tracy was an unlikely costar, an actor reminiscent of the late Robert Williams from *Platinum Blonde.* A veteran of vaudeville, stock, and Broadway, Tracy specialized in fast-talking, wisecracking reporters and con men (he'd been in *Dinner at Eight,* but he and Jean had no scenes together). At thirty-five he looked twenty years older, and his appeal was not sexual. Yet he provided the perfect foil for Jean, matching her shout for shout, sneer for sneer. After seeing her in action, he observed, "Jean has a natural sense of comedy and timing that one only expects from veterans of the stage or vaudeville."

Franchot Tone and Pat O'Brien threw off fewer sparks; the role of neither was as smartly written, and neither actor was an adequate match for Jean. Tone was particularly unhappy as Gifford Middleton, written as a satire of his own screen image. This inside joke is lost on modern audiences, who are unaware that the overblown lines were written to parody the genre. "Your hair is like a field of silver daisies," pants Middleton. "I'd like to run barefoot through your hair!" Lola sighs, "Not even Norma Shearer or Helen Hayes in their nicest pictures were ever spoken to like that." Such dialogue was *not* meant seriously. Even Space Hanlon sneers, "He looks like an athlete. I wouldn't want him puttin' his foot in *my* scalp!"

Jean tore into the role like a puppy with a rag in its mouth. Since her dressing room was filmed in several shots, she kept Lola Burns's three sheep dogs boarded there (to the distress of MGM's sanitation crew; the newly remodeled room was swiftly ankle deep in fur). Filming went smoothly except for a technician's strike, which held up location shots on Wilshire Boulevard. Every time the scene was set up and ready to shoot, a contingent of strikers would give forth with obscenities and Bronx cheers, bringing the day's work to a halt.

Jean was also enjoying the company of cameraman Harold Rosson. The two began golfing together on weekends, both with and without Marino as chaperone. Rosson, a thirty-eight-year-old New Yorker, had been working in films since 1915. His was an impressive family in the industry. Brothers Arthur and Richard were successful directors, and sister Gladys was Cecil B. DeMille's right-hand assistant. Hal himself was the top cinematographer at MGM, having been purchased from Paramount, where he'd been Gloria Swanson's favorite cameraman. At his new studio, he was entrusted with many top projects, including all of Jean Harlow's films.

A short, balding gentleman with a quietly cynical manner, Rosson reminded many of Paul Bern. It's true, Rosson was nearly twice Jean's age and hardly the Clark Gable type fans expected, but there were also many differences. He was sturdier than Bern, both physically and emotionally. A quiet and soft-spoken intellectual, he was also a realist—much more likely to curl up with a book about modern cinematography than Schopenhauer's *Studies in Pessimism.* He was kind, fatherly, and somewhat dull. Jean had once again found her dream man.

SEVEN

IT'S LOVE I'M AFTER

Portrait still, 1935

In mid-September the *Bombshell* company took off to Tucson for location filming. Both Jean and Franchot Tone were expert riders, so their horseback scenes were played without doubles or laughable rear-projection. The film was nearly wrapped; Tucson was cool and romantic at night—it was quite a vacation for cast and crew. Jean and Hal Rosson took long walks in the desert after sunset and dined together every night. Their long friendship took a romantic turn.

They'd met when Jean first arrived at MGM in 1931 and immediately became friends. Rosson supported her acting ambitions and propelled her career with his superb artistry behind the camera. "Every morning as soon as I walked on the set, Hal seemed instinctively to know my frame of mind," she said. "If I were feeling low or depressed or worried about something, he invariably found an opportunity to whisper, 'brace up, honey, you'll live through it.'" The pair began golfing and swimming together. Whether he knew it or not, the way to Jean's heart was to provide the paternal figure she longed for.

The romantic atmosphere of Tucson went to their heads, and Jean found herself reliving another September night six years earlier: She and Hal Rosson eloped. On the evening of September 18, they met pilot Allen Russell, who made a living whisking couples off to impromptu weddings. Jean had the presence of mind to don something old (her suit), something new (her hat), something borrowed (a pair of gloves), and something blue (a turquoise clasp). The rickety plane arrived at the Yuma airport around four A.M., where they were met by airport manager John Redondo and his truck. Redondo relayed the fugitive couple to E. A. Freeman—Yuma's "marrying justice of the peace"—a license was quickly issued, and the marriage hastily conducted, with Russell and Redondo as witnesses.

"Miss Harlow had little to say," recalled the justice. "They seemed to be in a hurry, but neither Miss Harlow nor Mr. Rosson was nervous. The bride and bridegroom seemed to be very happy and were smiling when I finished marrying them . . . but I was too excited to notice much." After the ceremony, the newlyweds and their witnesses breakfasted in a tiny, empty desert café before flying back to Los Angeles.

The marriage took Hollywood completely by surprise; no one had taken the Harlow–Rosson relationship seriously. Mama Jean was more surprised than anyone. For once, The Baby hadn't confided in her. At Hal's apartment, Jean telephoned the Bellos with the good news. Mama Jean was hurt and shaken, not a good beginning for her daughter's third marriage. But she quickly pulled herself together and agreed to host a wedding breakfast the next morning at the Club View Drive house. She and Marino called MGM and started pulling arrangements together. Reporters, caterers, and friends were awakened at dawn and told to clear their calendars.

The next morning, Jean and her new husband sat beaming for the photographers and spoke to a contingent of reporters. Rosson wore a business suit and Jean a tennis dress. Everyone brimmed over with happiness, except Mama Jean, who was visibly haggard and upset. This was the first time since the McGrew elopement that The Baby hadn't consulted her on a major decision. As for Marino, once he had been assured that his place in the white palace was safe, he took Rosson to his heart and set about trying to win over the taciturn cameraman.

"I know this is one Hollywood marriage that will last," Jean told the press. "I am as confident of him as a husband as I am that he is the best cameraman in the world. . . . He is just old enough to enable him to be my mentor." Rosson, for his part, looked slightly dazed.

Jean's friends were divided in their opinions. Some thought Hal Rosson bore an unhealthy resemblance to Bern, that Jean was trying to recapture those brief happy moments she'd had with him. The more Freudian-minded wondered why Jean kept marrying Mont Clair Carpenter facsimiles. How deeply had her parents' divorce affected her? Had Jean been plunged into a never-ending search for her daddy?

She could have bedded down with any good-looking actor she chose, but Jean's libido was more complex than that. She felt safe and comfortable with men like Rosson, Bern, W. S. Van Dyke, Cedric Gibbons, Carey Wilson. Not all these relationships were sexual, but all followed the same pattern. The men were successful in their fields and not threatened by Jean's fame or public image. They were intellectually superior to her, appealing to her great appetite for self-improvement—as well as feeding her feelings of inferiority. They were all quiet, subdued men—very much like Mont Clair Carpenter.

The marriage to Rosson was also an attempt to escape the Bellos. Jean loved her mother dearly and was dutiful to the point of being a

Newlyweds Jean and Harold Rosson hold a press conference, assisted by an exhausted Mama Jean and a delighted Marino Bello, September 19, 1933 (Bettmann/UPI).

doormat, but Marino was beginning to get on her nerves. For years fan magazines had made much of the great mother-daughter love, and the fact that the grown-up sex star still lived with her Mama. One suspiciously gushing article has Jean enthusing, "I am happier, more contented and have more freedom of action under my parents' roof than I would if I moved away. . . . I can have more fun with them than with any other two people in the world." The fact that Marino was not Jean's father and the roof in question was built and paid for by the daughter went conveniently unmentioned.

Jean was beginning to worry about Marino's influence on her mother and on her own welfare. Carmelita Geraughty recalled one visit when "Jean took me into his bedroom and showed me what was in his clothes closet—custom-made suits, hand-made English shoes, Hombergs . . . Jean said, 'Look at this! And I have to pay for it all!'"

Although Jean's role in *Bombshell* was based on Clara Bow, many noticed a resemblance between Lola Burns's father and Marino Bello. "Pop" Burns pushes his way onto his daughter's sets and publicity, extorts money from her associates for shady investments, spouts off about

the influence he'd had on her career, and finally becomes such a nuisance he's banned from the studio. By late 1933, life was imitating art: Marino Bello and Pop Burns had become one.

Jean's friends wished the star had taken a tip from Lola, who finally explodes at her family and hangers-on: "You're nothing but a pack of leeches! Where does my money *go.* I never see any of it! I'm getting pretty tired of being the golden goose around here—a glamorous bombshell, eh? A glorified chump, that's what I've been!" Hollywood has seen few more striking examples of a star who should have learned from her role.

Jean and Hal Rosson moved into a $250-a-month suite at the Chateau Marmont, an exclusive and well-known establishment catering to the film crowd. (The Sunset Boulevard apartments have seen many stars and scandals, including the 1982 death of John Belushi.) Mama Jean and Marino continued living with their phalanx of servants on Club View Drive; Blanche Williams, of course, accompanied Jean. The Rossons planned a Hawaiian honeymoon and began furnishing their new home.

On September 29, Jean was awarded one of the more unusual glories of stardom: fixing her hand- and footprints in cement at Grauman's Chinese Theatre (now called Mann's Theatre). The tradition began in 1927, and publicists contend that there is enough room to accommodate stars well into the twenty-first century. Jean's ceremony was so swamped with ticket requests that a change had to be made in tradition. After a showing of *Dinner at Eight,* she appeared onstage with theater owner Sid Grauman and did the honors before a *paying* audience. She stepped lightly into the mixture of cement, plaster of Paris, and ground silver, then placed her hands and three lucky pennies into it, signing, "To Sid, in sincere appreciation" with large, flowing calligraphy. The next day, the semidried block was placed in the theater's forecourt, and Jean was photographed signing autographs and recreating the footprint ceremony. The block was cemented in place, as was Jean's standing when *Bombshell* opened two weeks later.

Bombshell is perhaps Jean's best film and contains her most brilliant performance. Those who thought it impossible for her to top *Dinner at Eight* were proven wrong. The *New York Times* called it "wild fun . . . a merry, fast-paced diversion" and found Jean "thoroughly in her element." Richard Watts, Jr., could now be counted on for raves and didn't disappoint: "*Bombshell* . . . provides the first full-length portrait of this amazing young woman's increasingly impressive acting talent. . . . Miss Harlow reveals again that gift for an amalgamation of sophisticated sex comedy with curiously honest innocence which is the secret of her individuality. There can be no doubt that she is a distinguished performer."

Post-signing ceremony at Grauman's Chinese Theatre, 1933

▼

Bombshell (on November 6, MGM changed the title to *Blonde Bombshell* in response to disgruntled, literal-minded fans who'd expected a war film) remains Hollywood's funniest and most honest look at itself, although viewers should be warned not to sit too close to the screen. The film is a high-decibel one, with every other line shouted at breakneck speed. There isn't a false note in the production. Jean plays the brief dramatic moments with effective simplicity, distinguishing them from the "fake dramatic" scenes in which Lola takes herself a bit too seriously. When overcome by "the right of all womanhood" and suddenly intent on adopting a baby, Jean makes us laugh at the empty-headed sincerity of the mother-to-be. But when she's denied the adoption, she brings an honestly heartbreaking and tragic note to the scene. There's a fine line between intentional and unintentional comedy, and Jean was accomplished enough to delineate the two.

Louis B. Mayer proved surprisingly difficult about Jean's marriage to Hal Rosson. As a honeymoon gift, he ordered Rosson to leave his bride and journey to Mexico for filming of *Viva Villa!* starring—of all people—Wallace Beery. Rosson refused, Jean fumed, and nasty memos circulated. Jean had never left the continental United States and had been looking forward to their planned Hawaiian honeymoon. The Rossons held firm, and Mayer finally gave in, assigning another cameraman to the Mexican project. But the harm had been done, and Jean was becoming suspicious of her bosses' good wishes and intentions. She was already chafing at her salary. She was making $1,500 a week and was set for a $500 increase in 1934, but felt she should be earning as much as Crawford and Shearer. Hal Rosson was pulling in $15,000 a year, considerably less than his wife, but he let her know that *he* was a professional, a high-ranking cinematographer, while she was merely an actress. Indeed, the cracks in the marriage had already begun to show. At one large party Jean gave, Hal appeared from time to time in the doorway to his study, eyeing everyone cynically and fuming. When one man tried singing to brighten up the party, Rosson made so many sarcastic remarks that Jean rushed to her bedroom in tears of fury and embarrassment.

She hoped the Hawaiian honeymoon would rekindle the friendship that had led to the hasty wedding. By mid-October, most of the hard feelings between the Rossons and MGM had been smoothed over, and the couple were planning their itinerary. The studio even had a treat for Jean. On her return, she would costar with her friend Marie Dressler in *Living in a Big Way* (Jean would play Dressler's adopted daughter). Mama Jean had shyly submitted herself for the Dressler role, a suggestion that provoked much hilarity in the front office. Just to keep Jean happy, though, a publicity story was fabricated to the effect that perhaps Mama Jean might soon appear in one of her daughter's films. In the meantime, Jean and Dressler were scheduled for costume tests.

Jean had been feeling under the weather for a few days, but ascribed it to nervous excitement about the honeymoon or nervous aggravation about Mayer's recent behavior. Then, during the evening of

In 1934, with husband Harold Rosson (Bettmann/UPI)

October 15, she was struck with terrible abdominal pains, chills, and nausea. Rosson immediately suspected appendicitis, but Jean insisted her mother be summoned before they started for the hospital. Arriving at Good Samaritan Hospital at four A.M., Jean was rushed to emergency surgery. Rosson was right. Her appendix had nearly burst.

Dr. Sidney Burnap performed the operation and told reporters that Jean "was resting easily and would recover barring complications." In those pre-antibiotic days, any surgery was fraught with danger, but Jean was otherwise in perfect health and was up and chatting within twenty-four hours. About a week later, she arranged for a special screening of *Bombshell* for ambulatory patients and staff. Rolling grandly into the visiting room in her wheelchair, she played hostess for the event, signing autographs and trying to cheer up less fortunate patients. Her own recovery took about two weeks, and Jean sneaked quietly home on Halloween. By that time, any thoughts of a honeymoon were ended. Hal Rosson had his studio duties, and MGM was expecting Jean on the *Living in a Big Way* set for costume fittings. She was heartbroken, angered at having missed out on the romantic vacation she'd hoped would bolster her marriage. Moreover, Mayer brushed off her salary request without so much as a civil reply.

The honeymoon was over, and not just for the Rossons. Jean had been pressuring Irving Thalberg for more mature roles. With her recent successes, she felt she had the leverage for more input into her scripts. Nearly all her studio shots were cheesecake, and Jean felt that one more reference to her hair color would send her over the edge. She told contract player Pat Ellis that she was tired of being identified as "the platinum blonde" first and an actress second. Jean half-heartedly fantasized about someday buying a wig and acting in local summer stock productions, just to see if there was more to her talent than a shining head of hair.

Staying at home and recuperating from surgery agreed with Jean; with Rosson's salary and her own vacation pay, she puttered around the house or visited the Bellos while her husband went to work. It was almost like the movies, playing housewife and having dinner on the table when Hal got home. She also moped about her recent differences with MGM and made the mistake of spouting off within earshot of Marino. Never one to let bad enough alone, Marino put a flea in Jean's ear about striking for better pay and more control over her roles.

For an actress to go out on strike was almost unheard of in 1933. Garbo, of course, was a law unto herself. When unhappy, all she had to do was sigh, "I t'ank I go home now" and take off for Sweden. This sent MGM into such a tizzy that they welcomed her back on any terms. But such methods were not for just anyone. Nils Asther was canned after objecting to *Bombshell,* and John Gilbert found his career in ruins after antagonizing Mayer. Even Norma Shearer thought twice before turning down films, and actually to stay at home demanding more money and artistic freedom was the height of folly. It wasn't until 1936 that Bette Davis made news by walking out on Warner Bros. That studio had similar headaches with James Cagney and Humphrey Bogart, but it was Davis who finally called their bluff. "An actor in genuine distress had no other recourse but refusal to work," she recalled in her 1962 autobiography. "I could be forced into putting on a grass skirt and doing a hula if it so pleased my masters." It wasn't only bad films that irked Davis, but also Warner Bros.' refusal to renegotiate her contract. When she (and Jean) had been signed as starlets, they were paid standard salaries. But when they went out on strike, both actresses still labored under those starlet contracts, although they were among the most profitable workers in their studios. Another trap was the infamous suspension clause. If a performer went on strike, the studio simply sat back and suspended her salary. The performer was legally barred from working in any other medium during this time—no films (if another studio would have had the temerity to hire her), no radio, no theater. If a suspended player hummed a few bars of *Sweet Georgia Brown* during a dinner party, she could be hauled into court and sued. Moreover, the suspension time was tacked onto the *end* of the current contract. If Jean had decided to sit out the remaining five years of her MGM contract she would resurface in 1938 to find that the clock had stopped and those five years remained an obligation. It wasn't until Olivia De Havilland sued Warner's in 1943 that this standard clause was toppled.

Jean wanted in 1933 what Davis later sued for: a salary commensurate with her box-office draw, a renegotiated contract, and more artistic freedom. When she was sent the script for *Living in a Big Way,* Jean returned it with a curt note saying that Marino Bello would be in touch with MGM's lawyers, Hendrickson and Greenwood. Bello called the next day and demanded a salary increase to $5,000 a week, saying he would come by to renegotiate for "his" client.

Mayer exploded. Jean was not Marino's client; she was signed with the Orsatti brothers. MGM would be happy to welcome Jean back, but refused to work through the cantankerous Mr. Bello. Mayer's secretary tried to reach Jean on the phone, but she hid under the covers and let Marino handle the matter for her. Jean's requests were quite reasonable—admirable, even—but her studio, her friends, and her husband thought she was crazy to let her stepfather negotiate. Only Mama Jean was glowing with the thought that her Baby was finally giving Marino his proper due as a businessman.

MGM dangled tantalizing projects before Jean to tempt her back to work. *The Age of Larceny,* costarring Clark Gable; the Booth Tarkington story *Presenting Lily Mars* (eventually given to Judy Garland in 1943); and even a South Seas story called *Paradise,* with Johnny Weissmuller, perhaps an attempt to make up for the canceled Hawaiian trip. Jean stood firm, with predictable results: in mid-November, MGM put her on suspension and cut off her salary.

With the redecoration of the Chateau Marmont apartment and the continuing expense of the Club View Drive house, Jean all but panicked. Hal was no help at all, telling her that she was being foolish and childish. Rosson had detested Bello at first sight and refused even to discuss anything concerning him. Jean began spending her days with the Bellos and letting Marino reinforce her self-righteous fury against MGM.

The press had a field day. Mayer released his version of the quarrel, conveniently omitting Jean's request for artistic freedom and her anger at the suspension clause. In his story, Jean was simply a greedy little girl who wasn't satisfied with $1,250 a week; she was "unappreciative of what they have done for her in her personal troubles and elevating her into stardom class."

In an attempt to woo public opinion, Jean went to the fan magazines. After all, it was pretty hard to drum up sympathy for a woman earning that kind of money during the Depression, when most women—and many men, for that matter—had no income at all. Ruth Rankin of *Photoplay* nevertheless conceded that "Jean's salary is less than that of several stars who do not line up the customers at the box office half so successfully" and granted her a forum for her complaints.

"You can't fight with your friends," Jean was quoted, "and Louis B. Mayer is the best friend any girl in the world could have. . . . I would trust him implicitly to do the best thing for me, always." Jean was no fool and felt it best to get that bit of diplomacy out of the way before complaining of her financial woes. She listed the monthly expenses she accrued, including, "ten thousand photographs and letters a month . . . two secretaries . . . a personal maid and a hairdresser. . . . Also essentials such as insurance have much higher rates for picture people."

Oddly, no mention is made of Jean's artistic complaints or her public image. Friends and studio files confirm that one of her chief concerns was the cheap tramp roles she was playing; the platinum halo was beginning to strangle her and she wanted more serious roles that would stretch her talents. None of this appears in the *Photoplay* article. Either Jean never brought it up, Rankin was seriously edited by MGM, or the entire article was a studio ploy to discredit Jean further.

Jean managed to cut her suspension time by filing for vacation, which she was due. The studio couldn't suspend a vacationing performer, so her salary resumed while Marino and Mayer fought in the confines of MGM's conference rooms. This went on into the first weeks of 1934.

While Jean couldn't act during these negotiations, there was nothing in her contract to keep her from writing. Ever since childhood, she had a burning ambition to write—poetry, fiction, anything. She always kept a notebook with her, in which she jotted phrases and wisecracks for future use. Surviving scribbles such as "Shoot if you must this curly head—but make it a close-up, sir, she said" and "Nowadays a woman is ashamed to put on enough clothes to keep warm—except in the seclusion of her own home" were found in a desk drawer after her death. Jean decided to make good use of her lay-off and called Carey Wilson to sound him out. Wilson was one of MGM's top writers and was very well acquainted with Jean's literary bent. She was always dashing up to him with story ideas for his films, and even got—posthumous—billing as cowriter for one of his Dr. Kildare films.

With Rosson sneering at her acting accomplishments, Jean was propelled into taking up the pen again—or, rather, the typewriter. She was a slow but determined hunt'n'peck typist, often pounding away at her fan mail in between takes on the set. Ever since Paul Bern had suggested she write a screenplay, she'd been keeping notes and mulling over plots. Jean thought in the terms of film: what would be a fun, interesting plot for a movie? What kind of role might she like to play?

Jean spent most of 1934 writing her novel, a romantic drama, with the help of Wilson. With Hal working late at the studio, she spent evenings with Wilson and Geraughty at their home; Geraughty would pad around with coffee and snacks while Jean paced back and forth, running her fingers through her hair and talking nonstop. Wilson took notes and tried to bang out a manageable plot. As a screenwriter, he was used to working under these conditions.

Both Jean and Carey Wilson had been working in movies for so long that their idea of "plot" was rather jaded. A simple story of a man and a woman, based on character and mood, never occurred to them. Jean's book began developing into a fun-house of romantic improbabilities, bizarre twists, and overly cute characters. Considering some of the plot lines MGM had handed her, this wasn't surprising, but Wilson didn't lay as heavy a hand on her meanderings as a good editor would have.

As Jean busied herself with her book, Louis B. Mayer finally convinced Marino Bello and his phalanx of lawyers to come to an agreement. Jean's banishment was over, and on January 26, 1934, she received her new contract. Her demand for $5,000 had been fended off, but her salary *was* increased to a more impressive $3,000 at forty weeks per year. This was a seven-year contract, with regular pay increases ending at a weekly salary of $5,314.75 by the time it expired in 1941.

Mayer told Jean that they were anxious to have her back; that if she were willing to let some matters slide, he'd agree to renegotiate some of the "minor" artistic points when her first option came up in 1935. Jean was itching to get back to the set and decided to be a good sport. Despite the work on her book, she missed the studio. Days spent with the Bellos and evenings with Wilson served only to remind her that her marriage was deteriorating.

MGM decided to capitalize on Jean's writing project and had her photographed sitting chirpily before typewriters, billed as "Sex Symbol Turned Author." She sold the rights to the book, titled *Today Is Tonight,* to Cosmopolitan (an MGM offshoot run by William Randolph Hearst). The Orsatti brothers handled the negotiations, and Jean told interviewer W. H. Mooring that "at the moment I am merely haggling with the publishers as to whether I get a dollar or a dollar seventy five."

She tried to make light of the book, knowing that it hadn't come up to her expectations. "I had some spare time," she laughed to Mooring, "and a stray idea or two, so I started to put them down on paper. Then someone looked over my shoulder and suggested I ought to keep right on til I'd enough to fill a book."

Today Is Tonight was not published in Jean's lifetime. The manuscript went back into her desk drawer, though periodically she would haul it out and begin rewriting. Occasionally, she'd show up at Carey Wilson's door with a sheaf of papers, and the two would try to pound them into shape, but Jean was too much of a realist to believe that she was another Edith Wharton or even an Elinor Glyn. After a year or two, she lost hope that *Today Is Tonight* would ever go to press or be filmed.

Via a circuitous route, the novel eventually reached the public. Mama Jean inherited it from her daughter, and she in turn left it to Ruth Hamp, who sold it to the unconventional Grove Press in 1965. *Today Is*

At a 1934 premiere with Marlene Dietrich and (left to right) directors Rouben Mamoulien and Josef von Sternberg (Bettmann/UPI)

▼

Tonight, out of print for years, has become a rare collector's item. It holds up well, despite universally condescending and sarcastic reviews. The *New York Times,* significantly, hired a humorist (Richard Lingeman) to review the book. "Harlow writes!!?" was the ominous lead-in to his column. He savagely rips into *Today Is Tonight,* dismissing both the book and its author as "real camp . . . an authentic object of Pop Americana." When Lingeman finally forces himself to consider the substance of the book rather than its datedness or its author's reputation, he describes it as "untrammeled romantic fantasy, lit sputteringly by flippant, good-hearted glimmers of wit and permeated with gush."

The book's main flaw wasn't style, but content: a plot that started lazily enough, then took on more unlikely twists and turns than it could handle. *Today Is Tonight* is the story of Judy and Peter Landsdowne, wealthy Westchester socialites still madly in love after three years of marriage. Things begin to go wrong by chapter nine: Peter is blinded in a riding accident, and he and his business partner, Bill Reynolds, lose their brokerage firm. Judy tries to stave off financial collapse by, unbeknownst to Peter, working as a high-paid showgirl; she disguises her working hours by convincing him that day is night and night is day—hence the book's title. Peter discovers her subterfuge and eventually recovers his self-esteem by writing a newspaper column called—tastelessly enough—*Broadway by a Blind Man.* After a brief flurry of uncertainty when Judy falls in love with Reynolds, all ends happily with the Landsdownes facing the future reunited and optimistic.

Only Charles Dickens could have written his way out of a plot like this. Had the book been a simple, less ambitious character study of the Landsdownes' coping with poverty and blindness, it might have been quite effective. There are many good moments, and the story does hold the reader's interest. There is some wonderful dialogue, and the genuine affection between Peter and Judy is well depicted, as when she recalls her previous naive hopes: "We both agreed exactly what day and what year we were going to die together, quite simply, quite peacefully and quite happily. We would both suddenly realize that this was the day, and we'd talk over just how flawless it had all been, and then we'd both go to sleep and will ourselves away."

One line of dialogue must have given Hal Rosson a turn. Judy taunts her husband by snapping nastily, "I had an affair with a prizefighter!" It's an indication of her sagging marriage that Jean would rag Rosson like that about Max Baer, and it's not likely that he'd have taken the joke gracefully. Carmelita Wilson later affirmed that Jean was responsible for all of the book's dialogue, and the bantering does sound like her surviving letters: friendly, funny, and bright, but sometimes falling into coy, self-consciously cute humor. Certainly, Peter's blindness is handled realistically. Rather than becoming noble and self-sacrificing, he turns maudlin, morose, and depressed. All in all, *Today Is Tonight* was no worse than many successful romantic novels.

By the time Jean returned to work early in 1934, the Rossons had realized what a mistake their elopement had been. They'd been two pals somehow propelled by romance or loneliness into a hasty decision. They soon began driving each other crazy. Hal was a night person, Jean a day person. Jean loved socializing, Hal hated it. Jean took her career lightly, as she took most things in life; Hal was a clear-eyed, driven professional—a workaholic. None of this would have mattered if they'd been genuinely in love, but their differences only emphasized how foolish the marriage had been.

Hal's main complaint (and a reasonable one at that) was the amount of time Jean spent with the Bellos. It was pretty clear by now that the apron strings tying Mama Jean and The Baby were unseverable. Hollywood was touched but Rosson disgusted when Jean turned twenty-three on March 3 and, to celebrate, bought her mother a new car.

Marino was another unwelcome prize package, constantly trying to impress Rosson with his latest business venture or dropping well-meaning but irritating suggestions concerning his son-in-law's career. Even Jean was getting fed up with Marino, who frightened her by engineering her recent strike. She *had* wound up with an increased salary, but she still had little artistic freedom and, worse, had lost the friendship of Louis B. Mayer. Bello was beginning to unnerve her.

It was lucky that Jean returned to work when she did. On March 4, the day after her birthday present to Mama Jean, she was sued for $2,654 in back taxes. Marino was supposed to be handling Jean's personal finances, and she was shocked that, even with her new salary, she was in deep financial trouble. But Jean *was* working, and her mother managed to jolly her out of any misgivings.

Sadly, Jean never appeared with her friend Marie Dressler in *Living in a Big Way*. The film was shelved early in 1934 as Dressler's health failed. She'd been fighting cancer since 1931, and after finishing her last film retreated to her Beverly Hills home to complete her autobiography. By the time Jean returned to work, Dressler's condition had worsened. She died on July 28 at the age of sixty-four.

MGM stuck Jean instead in an unexceptional gold-digger comedy called *The Girl from Missouri*. She spent February and March in story conferences and costume fittings, as well as starving off the weight she'd gained during her layoff. Jean had an extremely healthy appetite, and despite her love of swimming and tennis, had put on a few pounds. She wore a charm bracelet to remind her to diet. Among the figurines dangling from it were a dancing girl (how she *should* look), a movie camera (*why* she had to look that way), and a pig (how she *might* look if she weren't careful). She also had to get her vacation-tanned face back to its porcelain paleness and followed an MGM-suggested routine that also became a life-long habit of Joan Crawford's—and was later immortalized in the opening moments of the film *Mommie Dearest*. MGM actresses were instructed to wash with cold cream in the morning, then immediately splash ice water on their faces, breasts, and arms. This was believed to work both as an astringent and to firm up muscle tone.

When Bette Davis returned from her strike in 1937, Warner Bros. showed good faith by casting her in *Marked Woman,* a thoroughly enjoyable film. MGM was either less forgiving or less farsighted. *The Girl from Missouri* was Jean's weakest project yet, not even as witty or pleasant as *Hold Your Man*. Jean's shooting schedule on *The Girl from Missouri* was typical for a nonmusical picture. Before production even started, she met with Adrian for costume consultations. They discussed various ideas with director Jack Conway, then met several times to go over the sketches and for preliminary fittings. Publicity photos were taken, and lights had to be set up. Lighting had to be matched exactly to Jean's complexion and bone structure, so she had to appear for all initial sittings, before her stand-in Barbara Brown could take her place on the set.

When actual shooting began, Jean and her husband (who was once again assigned to photograph her) had to be on the set and ready to go by 9:00 A.M. Jean generally awoke first and was in her dressing room by half past seven. While the hair and make-up crew worked her over, she'd have a bite of breakfast and review the morning's script changes with Blanche. If the previous day's rushes hadn't looked quite right, notes from Conway would indicate what had to be reshot.

Work started at nine o'clock on the dot, and was the first time she and her husband saw each other that day.

There was generally a lunch break around noon, unless some critical shot couldn't be put off. Union regulations stipulated that afternoon break, and only an emergency could provoke a director into defying the union. During lunch, Jean conducted interviews while having her hair and make-up freshened. She worked until about a quarter of six in the afternoon and generally sent out for coffee and snacks for the crew before wrapping up. She spent twenty minutes removing her make-up and putting on street clothes, then went to view the day's rushes until half past six or seven o'clock. Arriving home by eight o'clock, she ate a quick dinner, washed her hair, and went to bed. She and Hal rarely socialized; few film folk did on "school nights."

Jean's friend Anita Loos collaborated with her husband, John Emerson, on *The Girl from Missouri.* The film borrowed many elements from Loos's novel *Gentlemen Prefer Blondes,* which had concerned itself with the gold-digging adventures of two wisecracking but naive showgirls. *Gentlemen Prefer Blondes* had already been adapted for stage and screen, but Loos, apparently having run dry on ideas, juggled the plot and characters a bit more to come up with a watered-down script. The novel had been one of the brightest, most stinging books of the 1920s. This film was bland and uninspired. Jean was cast as Eadie Chapman, the fiercely virtuous daughter of a woman who runs a notorious nightclub. Eadie and her friend Kitty (played by tough-talking comedienne Patsy Kelly) flee to New York to make their fortune.

The film began production on March 29, and was Jean's first project to come under the jurisdiction of the newly adopted "Production Code." This Code was to have a major impact on Jean's career—even this film's title became a headache under the industry's newly born concern for censorship. The working title had been *Eadie Was a Lady* (taken from a popular show tune); MGM was advised to change it to something less "suggestive." *Born to be Kissed* and *100% Pure* were submitted but, not surprisingly, rejected, before the innocuous *The Girl from Missouri* was finally approved.

The Production Code rocked the film industry. Pre-Code films have a certain naughtiness, a gritty realism that later became taboo. Look at early Mae West and W. C. Fields films like *She Done Him Wrong* and *Million Dollar Legs* and compare them with the 1940 disaster *My Little Chickadee,* in which the stars were so hobbled by industry standards that all color and spice was squeezed out of the finished product.

Censorship had not been an issue in the first two decades of the industry. Turn-of-the-century films were aimed at the huddled masses, so naughtiness was part and parcel of their appeal. *The Athletic Girl and the Burglar* and *How Bridget Served the Salad Undressed* weren't nearly as risqué as the titles implied, but they also weren't meant for upper- or middle-class families. By 1910 enough complaints had been lodged by religious and reform organizations to nudge filmmakers into a relaxed self-censorship. Still, Fox Studios had little difficulty releasing their Theda Bara films. Complaints were made, but censorship was strictly local. If one theater rejected a film, a nearby one might still snap it up. Miss Bara was able to disport herself in costumes that even today would cause problems on television. Seminudity, risqué situations, sexual innuendo were all exploited in films—but they were, on the whole, employed with a wise restraint. Filmmakers realized that overtly shocking scenes would alienate a large part of their audience.

This was the situation until the early 1920s, when an unprecedented series of scandals threatened the industry with government-dictated censorship. The decade got off to an ominous start with the mysterious death of Olive Thomas. Thomas, a promising young star, died in Paris of mercury bichloride poisoning. She claimed on her deathbed that she'd mistaken the pills for sleeping tablets, but the press played it up as a drug-related suicide, a symptom of the immoral Hollywood life-style.

Worse was to come. In September 1921, popular comedian Roscoe "Fatty" Arbuckle was falsely implicated in the death of a starlet during a party in Arbuckle's hotel suite. Arbuckle was eventually acquitted, but the publicity ruined his career. He was boycotted by the public and many of his coworkers, and reduced to directing under a pseudonym, William B. Goodrich ("Will B. Good").

While the Arbuckle trial was still under way, another crisis arose with the (still-unsolved) murder of director William Desmond Taylor. Actresses Mabel Normand and Mary Miles Minter found their careers shattered when their connection to Taylor became public. Although neither was implicated in the murder, their mere association with Taylor was sufficient to damn them.

That March, matinee idol Wallace Reid entered a drug rehabilitation center. Reid, thirty, had been the epitome of the all-American man during his eight-year career. Handsome, athletic, a family man, and musician, he represented all that was clean and wholesome about the industry. He'd apparently become addicted to morphine after a work-related injury, and studio doctors kept him supplied so as not to disrupt his filming schedule. With the support of his wife, actress Dorothy Davenport, he attempted to kick his habit, but died in the effort early in 1923.

Rather than cover up the cause of her husband's death, Mrs. Reid became an avid antidrug crusader. She directed and starred in such films as *Human Wreckage,* and the public was told in graphic detail the facts concerning Wallace's death. This did not, of course, reflect well on the morals of the film community, which had been highly suspect anyway.

It was obvious that something had to be done. The public, religious groups, and even governmental bodies were calling for strict control of films and filmmakers. The major studios decided that some form of self-censorship would have to be enacted in order to keep outside forces from taking over the industry. Postmaster General Will Hays was called in to head the newly created Motion Picture Producers and Distributors of America, Inc. Film historians generally regard Hays as a villain or buffoon, but he was simply a well-meaning official trying to fill a difficult position. He'd been known in Washington for crusading against various forms of pornography, and his highly moral reputation made him a natural choice for this job.

During this period, a morality clause was inserted in all actors' contracts. If an employee embarrassed the studio through homosexuality, adultery, undue political activities, and so on he or she could be fired without appeal. Several performers were forced into the closet to protect their careers, and the studios, not eager to fire popular players, began to cover up both legal and romantic affairs. This strategy often backfired; if any hint of a cover-up was suspected, outlandish rumors arose that were usually more harmful than the simple truth.

The Hays Office was fairly lax in enforcement during the 1920s. Most theaters were operated by major studios, which submitted their films to the Hays Office for approval. If a renegade or independent producer tried to sneak a film by, he would have a hard time finding a theater to exhibit it. By 1927 it was decided that a more uniform code was needed, so a first draft of regulations was adopted industry-wide. This consisted of twenty-five rules covering sex, profanity, religion, international relations, and depiction of crime and violence. The Code declared that specified subjects or situations "shall not appear in pictures produced by members of this Association, irrespective of the manner in which they are treated."

Even so, some leeway was permitted. Jean's lingerie scene in *Double Whoopee* should have been deleted (the Code proscribed "licentious or suggestive nudity . . . and any lecherous or licentious notice thereof by other characters in the picture"), but was allowed to slip by. Ernst Lubitsch's *The Love Parade,* in which Jean was an extra, included a lot of double entendre and suggestive situations, which should have been cut under those regulations. In 1930 the Code was, in fact, tightened up by religious leaders Martin Quigley and Father Daniel Lord. Twelve applications, each with numerous subheadings, outlined industry standards. Nevertheless, the Code was still regarded in the same light as Prohibition—an annoying, difficult-to-enforce law that could be gotten around with a little adroitness.

Censors of the time recognized that the industry had cleaned up its act considerably, and studios were occasionally able to fudge the rules. Thus, a chorus girl in *Flying Down to Rio* was able to crack, "Whadda these South Americans got below the equator that we haven't?" and Clara Bow could visit an openly gay nightclub in *Call Her Savage.* Prostitutes were sympathetically portrayed in *Red Dust, Grand Hotel,* and *Rain,* and were even allowed happy endings.

These films of the early thirties exude a refreshing joy and freedom. Industry standards were such that impropriety could be implied, as long as it wasn't brazenly displayed. This creatively challenged screenwriters to try and "put one over" on the censors. Shaking hands with a departing male, Mae West purrs, "I see ya still got that hand trouble"; Jean, warned about inhospitable tropic nights in *Red Dust,* shrugs, "Guess I'm not used to *sleeping* nights, anyway"; and in *The Scarlet Empress,* Marlene Dietrich's husky guard hands her a bullwhip and begs her to "punish" him for his insolence.

Columnist Paul Harrison noted that Jean's films were "more closely checked by censors than those of any other actress, including Mae West. Likewise, the Hays Office was particularly critical of her still pictures taken for publicity." West and Jean came in for heavy fire, as both women combined sex with humor, and sex was no laughing matter to the Hays Office. The Code stated that "the sanctity of the institution of marriage and the home shall be upheld," and that seduction is "never the proper subject for comedy."

The Hays Office had passed *Red-Headed Woman,* but religious leaders were thrown into a mild state of hysteria when they realized that gold-digging, bed-hopping Lil Andrews was seen at the fade-out to be happy, healthy, and unrepentant. MGM was informed in no uncertain terms that this was not to happen again.

Mae West, who wrote her own dialogue, became especially frustrated and eventually returned to the stage. Fleischer Studios was even ordered to lengthen Betty Boop's cartoon skirts and eliminate suggestions of drug use, bestiality, and promiscuity. Jean was discreet enough to pay lip service to censorship in the press, no matter how put-upon she felt in private. "Censorship was the greatest thing that ever happened to the industry," she was quoted as saying. "The movies had grown lazy; they were buying laughs and thrills with smut. Now, at least, there is good writing." These public statements didn't seem to placate the censors when it came to her films.

The viewing public—the highly moral segment, anyway—felt the forces of evil were winning the battle against the Hays Office. Early in 1934, the Legion of Decency was formed by the Roman Catholic Church. Other morally outraged groups had been nagging the film industry as well, but the Legion had a powerful weapon in reserve: excommunication. Catholics were ordered not to attend any films the Legion had banned. Philadelphia's Cardinal Dougherty went one step further and ordered his parishioners not to attend *any* films. The flames were being turned up under the Hays Office, which many felt had been entirely too lenient. With religious groups yapping at its heels, the film industry realized that a stronger and more strictly enforced code was needed.

Joseph Breen was called in to head the Censorship Board, and a new, lengthy code was written, one that left no room for quibbling. Any film that didn't meet the standards was denied the Hays Office seal of approval—a death sentence.

Scripts had to be approved by the Hays Office before filming could commence. The reviewing process continued during the actual filming, frequently resulting in costly rewrites and retakes. When the film was finally edited, it had to go through one final check before release. A rejection at this point would be extremely difficult to correct, as the cast and crew would already be committed to other projects, sometimes at other studios. "Putting one over" on the Hays Office became a costly risk to take.

The new Production Code went into effect in June 1934 and consisted of dozens of "principles" and "applications," which were explicitly spelled out. "No picture shall be produced which will lower the moral standards of those who see it," the Code states, and goes on to burble about "correct standards of life" and "correct entertainment." Moral films were compared to uplifting sports such as baseball, while immoral films were likened to "cockfighting, bullfighting and bear baiting." All this seems pretty broad, but the Code goes on to spell out page after page of what can and cannot be depicted, mentioned, or implied. Some rules covered situations no studio in its right mind would have filmed in the first place: children dealing or taking drugs, full frontal nudity, explicitly shown rape, abortion, or execution, and the use of currently popular derogatory terms. But other rules posed problems. Indecent dances, vulgarity (such words as "chippie" and "nuts" are singled out; the "tramp" in *Goldie* would never have gotten by), ridicule of religion, the law, or the family, and even the mention of homosexuality or adultery were forbidden. Crime was not to be condoned, explicitly portrayed, or glamorized. Costumes were not to permit "indecent or undue exposure." Liquor was to be presented with discretion and "good taste." Lustful embraces and suggestive posture were not to be shown. And, oh yes, animals were not to be *tripped.*

This is the Code that remained in force from 1934 until 1968, when the current ratings system was implemented.

The Girl from Missouri plainly shows evidence of the newly enforced censorship. While the characters Jean had previously played reveled in their raffishness, Eadie was frankly ashamed of herself. Even Kitty Packard in *Dinner at Eight* had clawed her way up the social ladder with infectious glee, but Eadie Chapman honestly felt unworthy of the millionaires she tried to capture.

Defense of her virginity is her raison d'être, but her moral standards seem confused. While Eadie will not sleep with a man she genuinely loves, she's willing to sell herself for the price of a wedding ring to the highest bidder. She instantly proposes marriage to every unattached, wealthy man she meets; no matter what his faults may be, as long as he's rich and willing, she will marry him. This is her idea of "virtue," and it's no wonder her friend Kitty eyes her askance.

Eadie's inferiority complex is not among her more attractive qualities. She sees herself as stupid, brassy, and common, and offers to take etiquette, English, and French courses in order to measure up. While Tom Paige (Franchot Tone) and, eventually, his father (Lionel Barrymore), admire her fighting spirit, that is exactly the quality of which Eadie wishes to "cure" herself.

Adrian's costumes were uncharacteristically designed to make Jean look cheap and vulgar. More significantly, nasty remarks were directed at Eadie's platinum-blonde hair. Whereas Jean's hair had previously been her characters' crowning glory, Eadie is taunted for it. Throughout the film, she is referred to as a "platinum chisler" and a "cheap blonde." These lines cannot have pleased Jean, who was increasingly disenchanted with being upstaged by her own hair. She was already toying with the idea of darkening it. No doubt Eadie, after entering the social elite, would do the same. Platinum blonde hair would never go completely out of style, but by the time of *The Girl from Missouri,* it was becoming associated with cheapness.

The film finally finished at the beginning of May. Jean was looking forward to a solo vacation in the Midwest. MGM allowed her this family visit as a tie-in to the film. As long as she made enough public appearances and gave enough interviews, the studio was more than willing to grant her time off. But just as Jean was ready to leave, she was called back for emergency retakes.

"My last few letters have been full of complaints, but I think I'm justified in this one," she wrote to Stanley Brown. "Stan, I was to leave Monday. . . . So I packed and did all those last-minute things and then, this morning, I get a call from the studio. So I go out, and guess what! The studio heads had decided I should have a stepfather in the picture for the protection of my honor! The picture has been previewed and I can't figure out for the life of me where there's a spot they can get a stepfather in and then get him out again. So that means no trip for me to Chicago or at least my stay will be cut down something fearful. So, I ask you, what's the use?"

A brief scene was inserted into the film's opening, in which Eadie's new-found stepfather orders her into her mother's disreputable nightclub. Far from protecting her honor, this adds a disturbing element; how *has* he been grooming his stepdaughter for her "career," and why is she so desperate to escape his influence?

When filming resumed, more than the script had been changed. Ray June had replaced Hal Rosson as cameraman. Jean couldn't laugh this off, as she had earlier rumors of marital discord, but no one on the set had the nerve to confront her on so delicate a matter. Her coworkers walked on eggshells waiting for the press to discover this change of personnel. They didn't have long to wait.

On Sunday, May 6, Carey Wilson and Carmelita Geraughty were married at the home of Phil Berg and Leila Hyams. Jean served as matron of honor, and seemed her usual cheerful self despite the unexplained absence of Hal Rosson. Rumbles were heard from the attending reporters, and soon one asked Jean officially to deny rumors that her husband had moved out of their apartment.

"But it is true," she told the startled reporter. "Hal moved out Saturday and is living at the Hollywood Athletic Club."

May 6, 1934: Jean (second from right) at the wedding of friends Carmelita and Carey Wilson (center), where she announced her own impending divorce

The Wilson-Geraughty nuptials were promptly forgotten, as reporters crowded around the matron of honor. Far from being annoyed, the newlyweds found Jean's timing propitious, at once taking the public gaze from their own private moment and convening an instant press conference for their friend. Jean told the assembly that "it's the only way out for both of us. I feel it's wrong for us to live together when we obviously are uncongenial. Hal will probably find some other woman who will make him happier than I could have done."

Jean no sooner arrived home when Louella Parsons was on the phone. Jean read a statement prepared by MGM's publicity department and impatiently denied that she and Rosson would "be better friends than ever and will probably see more of each other." Brushing off this chumminess as unlikely, she said, "our marriage is finished. There will be no reconciliation. . . . We simply were not meant for each other. There is no other man or woman. . . . Believe me, it's just that our marriage isn't right. Hal isn't to blame—I am not to blame—we haven't quarreled, but we are temperamentally unsuited to each other." *Screen Book* actually published the statement as an apology from Jean to her fans, as though she were obliged to ask forgiveness for her own misfortune.

On Monday morning Jean and Blanche packed up the accessories of yet another marriage, ready to move back to the Bellos. Her chauffeur Clifford Davis (not to be confused with Paul Bern's troublesome gardener Clifton Davis) drove the Wilsons to their honeymoon travel connection. On the way home, Davis sideswiped motorcycle officer Arthur Bain. Davis pulled over and got out, suddenly grabbing Bain's gun and ordering him into Jean's car. He then threatened another nearby officer, Elihu Goldsen, and struck a female bystander with the gun. Ordering two more passersby into the car, he drove away, pursued madly by a contingent of Beverly Hills police. They managed to corner him and force him out of the car. Miraculously, none of the hostages was harmed. Davis was wrestled to the ground (no doubt with a great deal of enthusiasm), and Jean's car and chauffeur were impounded. Davis's sudden outburst was never fully explained, and Jean remained silent on the subject.

When *The Girl from Missouri* was released in August, the *New York Times* review was surprisingly favorable. Perhaps the overly publicized censorship and production problems had lowered his expectations, but André Sennwald thought the film was "studded with explosive comedy twists" and that Jean "provides the film with much of its effectiveness." He also stated that she "simply must be accepted as a fine comedienne in her particular sphere," denying the condescending theory that "not all of her humor is intentional."

Photoplay, which didn't turn up its nose at its advertisers' offerings, advised readers that *The Girl from Missouri* was "noisily defiant, ripsnorting and raucous . . . fast and furious adult fare." Richard Watts, Jr., of course, found something nice to say about Jean: "this increasingly astonishing young actress plays her role with . . . engaging freshness."

In late May, Jean appeared before Judge Elliott Craig to file for divorce. She was accompanied by Mama Jean and a horde of journalists, but not by Hal Rosson. He had become quite ill shortly after the separation with what the more romantically inclined called a broken heart. Actually, he had contracted polio. The nature of his disease kept Jean from his bedside, but she phoned him constantly at the Orthopedic Hospital. Polio often results in permanent disability or partial paralysis, but Rosson was lucky and swiftly recovered. He recuperated at his sister's home during midsummer.

At her divorce hearing, Jean gave eight minutes of testimony, assisted by lawyer Oscar Trippet. Charging mental cruelty and incompatibility, she outlined the times Rosson had embarrassed her before guests, stating that "he was so rude and insulted them so that I finally refused to ask them to come to the house." She claimed he belittled her profession and talent, so upsetting her that her work was affected.

All this was very routine, and the attending press was stifling yawns. Then Jean innocently added a charge they pounced upon with howls of glee. She was tired at the studio every morning because Hal read in bed. If Trippet advised her to add that tidbit, he certainly wasn't familiar with the press. The "reading in bed" charge became a Hollywood joke within hours. The rest of the testimony was dropped into wastebaskets as papers regaled their readers with fantasies of the owlish Rosson curled up contentedly with *The Wall Street Journal* as his sex bomb wife fumed in satins and lace nearby. To this day, film historians smugly state that Harlow divorced her third husband on this one and only charge, which would hardly have stood up in court.

The actual reasons for the break-up were many and varied. In some ways, neither party was to blame, and in other ways both were. For her part, Jean seemed incapable of a mature, full-time relationship, at least with Hal Rosson. She simply couldn't, or wouldn't, accept the fact that being a full-time wife precluded being a full-time daughter as well. Given the choice between Mama Jean and a husband, she invariably fled to Mama's side.

Rosson, for his part, seemed quite baffled by his young wife. If he'd wanted a chipper but meek housewife or a serene and adoring fan, he married the wrong girl. When he realized Jean was just a high-spirited Mama's girl, he couldn't make the effort to coax or charm her back to his side. Instead, he withdrew into his cave and snarled. The two pals of 1933 had become adversaries by mid-1934.

Jean was granted an interlocutory decree, which would make her a free woman by March 12, 1935. Leaving the courthouse, she told reporters that she intended to stay single, cynically citing her three "marriages of inconvenience." Happily, absence makes *some* hearts grow fonder. She and Rosson eventually became friends again.

Harold Rosson moved to London to complete his convalescence, and soon married Yvonne Crellin. His career continued to flourish. He shared a dual Academy Award in 1936 for his work on *The Garden of Allah* and went on to film *The Wizard of Oz*, the young Marilyn Monroe in *The Asphalt Jungle* (1950), and Gene Kelly's *Singin' in the Rain* (1952). After his retirement in 1967, he moved to Palm Beach, dying in 1988 at the age of ninety-three. He was very touchy on the subject of Jean Harlow and declined all interviews that veered in that direction.

Late in the spring of 1934 Jean met the last love of her life. William Horatio Powell was born in Pittsburgh in 1892 and moved with his family to Kansas City, Missouri, in 1907. After a brief stay at the University of Kansas, Powell entered the theatrical profession in 1912, leaving Kansas City the year after Harlean Carpenter's birth.

After a lackluster but steady career on the stage, Powell entered films in 1922. His menacing, dark good looks typed him as a villain, a role he played in such films as *Romola, Beau Geste,* and *The Last Command.* When talkies came in, his excellent speaking voice propelled him to greater success; he starred in four Philo Vance detective films and began developing a gift for light comedy. By 1934, Powell was working at MGM and had recently completed the immensely popular comedy detective film *The Thin Man*, with Myrna Loy. This established both stars as leading comic actors on the MGM lot.

With *The Girl from Missouri* finished, Jean began seeing more of Powell during her free time. Her divorce was no sooner out of the headlines than Powell–Harlow stories began surfacing. One piece was headlined JEAN HARLOW SINGLE AGAIN and subheaded YES, SHE LIKES BILL POWELL.

Their first date was hardly promising. One Sunday afternoon Powell invited Jean on a springtime drive to Santa Barbara for dinner. She'd been working late the night before and slept soundly the whole way up and the whole way back again, awakening only long enough to pack away dinner. Powell didn't know whether to be amused or insulted, but after Jean laughingly repeated the story to friends, he decided to take it in fun. The episode was even written into their film *Reckless.* Jean's ability to poke fun at herself was refreshing to Powell, who spent most of his time with an older, stuffier crowd: Warner Baxter, Richard Barthlemess, Ronald Colman, and their wives.

William Powell possessed qualities that had always attracted Jean. Like Bern and Rosson, he was significantly older than she—nineteen years—successful, and highly intelligent. His professional image carried the class that Jean's lacked, and Mama Jean approved of him. Actress Maureen O'Sullivan said that Jean "was very much in love with

Dining at the Trocadero with last love William Powell: the look on Jean's face says it all (Bettmann/UPI).

Bill, and talked about him constantly. She respected him because of his intelligence. She was always anxious to increase her knowledge, and she felt she could learn a lot from Powell." Friends had made almost identical remarks about Jean's two previous husbands.

Powell, in turn, found Jean's presence flattering. At forty-two, the attention of an attractive twenty-three-year-old was quite welcome. In addition, Jean reminded him of his second wife, Carole Lombard. They both had the same irreverent sense of humor and a healthy perspective on their careers. But neither Jean nor Powell was ready to jump into a commitment. Jean was a three-time loser, and wasn't blind to the fact that in Powell she'd found yet another father figure. Powell had also been divorced twice, and his conservative nature asserted itself when confronted with romance. In a surprisingly revealing interview, Powell snapped, "Don't talk to me about love. I know nothing about it, having failed at it twice." Remarks like that, accurately quoted or not, would not have been lost on Jean.

Powell had a son from his first marriage, and didn't particularly want more children, whereas Jean was anxious to start a family while she was still young. Unlike most working women in the 1930s, film stars were financially able to balance career and children. Jean wasn't as highly paid as many other stars, but she would easily have been able to afford motherhood. While her schedule wouldn't have permitted her much time with her children (a problem about which many Hollywood offspring later complained), she had a built-in babysitter in Mama Jean.

Jean and Powell seemed determined to present themselves to the public as "just pals" at the beginning of their affair. Jean was sick and tired of being hounded by the press as a red-hot mama, bedding down with all of her male friends. Powell, on the other hand, was never a romantic idol. Indeed, his marriage to Carole Lombard had been as surprising to Hollywood as was Jean's to Paul Bern. Lombard was depicted as a climber and gold-digger, Powell as a susceptible older man. Although the marriage lasted only two years, the couple remained good friends and frequently socialized. Jean also became close to Lombard, who was involved with Clark Gable by the mid-1930s.

Soon Jean and Powell were on everyone's guest list. Both were popular in the film community, and their friends viewed the romance with concerned good will. Powell's intimates were worried that he would be hurt by another blonde sex symbol, but at the same time hoped Jean might bring the rather morose actor out of his shell. Jean's friends weren't sure her bruised ego could stand another marital failure, but kept their fingers crossed that, maybe, she'd found Mr. Right at last.

Gossip columnists were quick on the uptake, and the couple was cornered at various nightclubs, the wrestling matches at Wrigley Field, and once at a department store buying kitchen utensils "for a friend." Every outing was fuel for the fan magazines. When Powell joined Jean and the Bellos on a two-day trip to Del Monte in August, the four were hounded by photographers and reporters. As if to prove Powell's presence was mere coincidence, Jean and her parents left on a tour of Yosemite while Powell went on to Huntington Lake.

One night, Jean and Powell attempted a quiet dinner at a popular Hollywood restaurant, only to find that a legion of fans had collected at the front door, waiting to pounce as soon as the couple stepped outside. Powell had the maitre d' send his car around to the back, but when he and Jean exited through the kitchen into a back alley, they found themselves outmaneuvered and surrounded by autograph seekers. Left to himself, Powell might have ducked and run, but Jean found the situation flattering and amusing. She began talking with fans and signing autographs until she and Powell were flattened against the wall by the excited crowd. Still laughing and chatting, the pair hoisted themselves onto some trash cans and perched there, posing for photographs until Powell's chauffeur rescued them.

In late 1934 an unwelcome ghost arose from Jean's past. Paul Bern's suicide had been briefly in the news the previous year, when District Attorney Fitts vaguely mentioned reopening the case. Jean resignedly offered her services, but the flurry died down. Then, in November of

1934, Fitts found himself under investigation for alleged financial misdeeds. Among the papers unearthed was gardener Clifton Davis's semi-hysterical assertion that his employer had been murdered.

Davis had named no names and offered no proof. Fitts, at the suggestion of Louis B. Mayer, had unwisely brushed off these accusations and never bothered to investigate. The District Attorney was well known for this kind of accommodation; author Sidney Kirkpatrick has pieced together evidence indicating that Fitts helped to cover up the 1922 murder of William Desmond Taylor. It was decided that Davis's charges had to be looked into, to determine if he was just a crackpot or knew something that MGM was trying to hide. Mayer had been foolish to request special treatment, and when the supposed cover-up was revealed, it looked very bad for Jean.

The original jurors reassembled, Jean was hauled in for questioning, and the various players in the two-year-old drama relived the events of September 1932.

It took only one week for the grand jury to decide that Clifton Davis was, indeed, a crackpot of major proportions. There were absolutely no grounds for his accusation, and jury foreman Widenham stated that Jean was beyond the remotest hint of doubt or suspicion. Bern's death was finally and conclusively ruled a suicide.

Jean herself was worn out and angry. "I did not talk about the case before and I see no reason for discussing it now," she snapped at reporters when leaving the grand jury hearings. "If it would do any good, and any new information could be obtained, that would be different. My personal wish is that some day the matter will be dropped for all time."

To some extent, the matter *was* dropped. Of course, any fan magazine biography of Jean Harlow gave ample space to her tragic second marriage. She never completely shed the cloud Paul had cast over her. To this day, the three-month marriage looms disproportionately in her life. In his book, *The Stars,* respected film historian Richard Schickel goes so far as to misstate that "Harlow's only marriage ended in a month, with her husband's suicide."

William Powell, Joan Crawford, and Franchot Tone were set to film *Reckless,* a musical drama based (loosely enough to avoid a lawsuit) on the life of Libby Holman, a popular musical revue star on Broadway, who had married tobacco heir Zachary Smith Reynolds in 1932. On July 6 of that year, Reynolds was found dead of a gunshot wound. Although the death was ruled a suicide, Holman's career and life were shattered. On the same day the Bern investigation was finally closed, Crawford was pulled from *Reckless* and Jean replaced her. She was delighted to be working with Powell, even though MGM was obviously trying to cash in on their romance. That sort of exploitation represented Mayer's seal of approval, which in itself was a relief. It was very important for the studio to approve of these affairs. Joan Crawford recalled "at least five actresses at Metro who stopped seeing men they were terribly in love with, just because Louis B. told them to . . . because the actor involved was under contract to another studio, or he was a nobody." Jean had always been politic in her choices: a top MGM producer, a top MGM cameraman, and now a top MGM star. The romances might not have worked out in the long run, but at least Mayer smiled upon them while they lasted.

But Jean was horrified to be cast as a woman whose husband shoots himself. Bern's death was still fresh in the minds of the public. Reynolds himself had died the same summer, and the two were often featured in side-by-side headlines. Jean just wanted to get on with her life and put Paul Bern in the past, but now she would be forced to relive his death on the soundstage and in theaters all over the world. It was perhaps the most appallingly tasteless and heartless casting in the history of film.

Worse, *Reckless* was to be a musical. Joan Crawford was an accomplished singer and dancer, and the score (including some of Jerome Kern and Oscar Hammerstein's less memorable songs) and choreography were arranged especially to suit Crawford's talents. Jean had never sung or danced professionally in her life, discounting the few bars in *Hold Your Man* and her impolite shimmy in *The Beast of the City*. Much of shooting time for *Reckless* was given over to voice lessons and to rehearsals with MGM dance instructor Edward Prinz.

It didn't take long to discover that Jean was not cut out to be a musical star. While she could carry a tune, her voice wasn't strong or supple enough to give a sustained performance, and learning the choreography would have pushed the film too far over schedule. It was decided to dub her voice with that of contract player Virginia Verrill. The dancing proved more of a problem. For the first time in films, the dance sequences were dubbed as well. The camera focused on Jean's upper torso in a three-quarter shot and panned down to a swirl of skirts, coming out on the other side to show the legs of a professional dancer. While not a terribly convincing effect, it served its purpose in sparing Jean the more elaborate dance routines. She did, however, execute one nifty cartwheel, which was included in a rehearsal sequence.

Actor and singer Allan Jones made his film debut in *Reckless*. During one dance scene, director Victor Fleming hit on an idea to deflect attention from Jean's lack of musical training: get someone to sing a catchy tune, and if Jean flubbed a step, simply pan the camera over to the singer. Jones was rushed into the part and given the song *Everything's Been Done Before*—the only decent tune in the film. As this was his first on-camera experience, he was terrified. Jean and her mother tried to buck him up: "You're a stage actor," Jean told him. "Ignore the camera and pretend you're onstage at all times and you'll be fine."

Early in 1935 Jean was ordered to sing the film's title song on the radio as a publicity tie-in. Although she had long since overcome her paralyzing stagefright and was used to appearing on radio, Jean was terrified at the thought of *singing* on-air. She knew full well that the studio's decision to dub her voice on film testified to her lack of vocal ability. Why, then, was she forced to go on the air and risk making a fool of herself?

The performance was limited to singing one verse of "Reckless," with a soft guitar accompaniment (full orchestration would have drowned her out, which in fact would have been fine with her). Jean's voice had improved considerably since *Hold Your Man;* although thin and wavering slightly, it was perfectly serviceable, and she got through the performance in one piece, her dignity intact. It wasn't much of a song and never became a hit, but the lyrics of *Reckless* provide a painfully accurate description of Jean's own romantic history:

When I'm in love, I'm reckless,
Each time in love, I'm more reckless!
I waste no weeping on lost romances,
I pay my losses and I take new chances.
I'm reckless—so what if I
Keep seeking my fool's paradise?
I waste no weeping; I just keep hoping
For one who's hoping for me.

It was fortunate that she had William Powell on the set for emotional support, as *Reckless* was proving to be an exhausting experience. She also had the company of contract player Rosalind Russell, then in her second year at MGM. Russell got along well with Jean, although she was put off by Mama Jean's attempts to push the two of them together. She consoled Jean when the affair with Powell proved frustrating, and commiserated when her lack of musical training made filming more difficult. Jean found various ways of relieving this frustration. During a visit to the Club View Drive house, Russell noticed that the white bearskin rug in the living room was missing most of its teeth. "I kicked 'em in," Jean explained.

In her autobiography, Russell recalled meeting Jean for the first time. "I remember sitting under a hair dryer in a beauty parlor one day, and sitting next to me was a child, also under a dryer. She was wearing shorts, and her little baby legs, perfectly formed, rested against the back of her chair while the nails were being manicured. My word, I thought, a ten- or eleven-year old having that bright red polish put on, and suddenly the hood of the dryer went back and the child stood up and it was Jean. She was probably twenty-three at the time, but without any makeup and no eyebrows, she looked exactly like a little kid."

Russell delicately refrained from naming William Powell, but mentioned that Jean was "madly in love with a man who wouldn't marry her, and she spent the last nine months of her life drinking too much. I went into a lot of bars to try and get her out." Russell, like many people, contradicted herself by stating elsewhere that Jean did *not* drink, that "I never saw her drunk." The truth, no doubt, lies somewhere between the two statements.

Jean and Powell had what would later be termed an open relationship. Both dated other people and went for relatively long periods without seeing each other. Powell was not a social animal, and Jean frequently attended parties without him. Shortly before *Reckless* began filming, she went solo to a Halloween party given by Nicholas Schenck and Adolph Zukor. The party had a Gay Nineties theme, and Jean dressed as a bathing beauty. She also went stag to the prestigious Mayfair Ball in 1935.

In *Reckless* the tragic story of Libby Holman was thinly veiled as the life of Broadway star Mona Leslie. Mona marries alcoholic, spineless playboy Bob Harrison (played, of course, by poor Franchot Tone), to the dismay of her smitten theatrical manager, Ned Riley (Powell) and Harrison's fiancée (Russell). Mona is severely snubbed by Harrison's horsey-set family and friends, and Harrison himself admits the marriage was a mistake. After making a whining, self-pitying nuisance of himself, he commits suicide, leaving a pregnant Mona suspected of murder and fighting for her career and baby. She finally wins over a hostile audience with a plea that must have been very painful for Jean to deliver: "All I did was marry a sweet, unhappy boy . . . hoping somehow to make him happy—I didn't; I couldn't. His unhappiness was too deep—so deep, he died of it." The audience cheers her as Ned Riley whispers a marriage proposal from backstage and the curtain falls.

Incidentally, Libby Holman's end was not as happy as Mona Leslie's. Her career never really recovered, she became involved in several unhappy relationships (including doomed actors Phillips Holmes and Montgomery Clift), her son died in a mountain-climbing accident, and Holman herself ended up a possible suicide in 1971.

Reckless opened to mixed critical reaction in April, Jean's musical abilities impressing no one unduly. "Transforming an excellent comedienne into an unconvincing song-and-dance artist does not impress these untutored eyes as a miracle of horse sense," said the *New York Times* critic. In the *New York Herald Tribune* Richard Watts, Jr., said that Jean's "sincere, straight forward and generally alluring performance" was the only thing the film had going for it, and Regina Crewe in the *New York American* felt Jean carried the show ably, "even when she is presumed to sing." (Those dubbed numbers couldn't have fooled a five-year-old, let alone a New York critic.)

For what it's worth, Jean looked lovely in *Reckless.* She'd dieted and danced off the puppy fat of *The Girl from Missouri* and appeared slim and stunning. The braided coiffure she wore in one number was so attractive that RKO copied it for Ginger Rogers in *Top Hat* that same year. *Reckless* had much higher production standards than her previous film; Adrian outdid himself with stylish costumes; the sets and camera work were impressive. And so was Jean's performance, within the limitations of a mediocre script. Powell and Russell brought out a quiet intelligence in her acting. She seemed years older. Her Mona is not a brassy showgirl, but a warmly sympathetic woman. Jean handled the few comic moments with her usual aplomb, but more interesting is the assurance she brings to her dramatic scenes. Powell and Harlow weren't as electric onscreen as were Gable and Harlow, but there is an obvious warmth between the two. Tone looks understandably grumpy in his role, but Russell is a delight. *Reckless* wasn't a high point in Jean's career, but it was a step up from *The Girl from Missouri* and proved a valuable learning experience for her.

Around the same time that Jean gained a lover in William Powell, she gained a new best friend. Howard Strickling had assigned one of his assistants, Kay Mulvey, to Jean's publicity. The women became instant pals. Jean fell in love with Mulvey's young son, Dick, and spent what free time she could playing babysitter. Dick Mulvey gave Jean an outlet for her maternal energy. She'd always spoken of her desire for children, but wasn't worried yet; after all, she had plenty of child-bearing years ahead of her. In the meantime, she accompanied Kay and her son to their beach house and romped about in the surf, teaching the boy her personal recipe for a sand castle (an egg or two in the damp sand helped hold it together).

She also made the acquaintance of MGM's latest freshman, dancer Eleanor Powell. "I was amazed at the people who came on the set and watched me practice," she said in later years. "It was as though they'd never seen any dancing before." Jean, Joan Crawford, and even Garbo would sit fascinated, watching Powell tap frantically and practice her famous whirlwind spins. Jean got dizzy just watching, and must have recalled her recent experience in *Reckless* with some embarrassment.

Another young MGM player Jean befriended was Irish-born Maureen O'Sullivan, who today regrets that overwork and lack of free time prevented the two from becoming closer. O'Sullivan has been a staunch defender of Jean in recent years, standing up publicly for her friend and challenging anyone who speaks ill of her. The two became acquainted when they shared a suite of rooms at a Lake Arrowhead resort. "She was a fresh air fiend," recalls O'Sullivan. "She never wore a nightgown, and worried about what the maids would say in the morning." O'Sullivan obligingly loaned Jean one of her own nightgowns, which was convincingly tossed across the bed every morning so as not to shock the servants.

By mid-1935, Jean was one of Hollywood's most popular actresses, socially as well as at the box office. With or without Powell, she was invited to large balls and intimate dinners. She'd gathered about her an extensive but close group of friends, including Mulvey, the Hamps, the Wilsons, Cedric Gibbons, and Dolores Del Rio. She also socialized with her costars and directors. Marion Davies, one of the film capital's best-loved citizens, invited Jean and Powell to many of the elaborate parties she hosted with William Randolph Hearst.

Davies recalled Jean waiting on Powell "hand and foot" and assumed marriage was just a matter of time. She also experienced Jean's stubborn impatience with Hearst's Old World stuffiness. Jean wore her favorite dinner dress to one Davies–Hearst party—a filmy white chiffon, which she wore without underwear. As Davies recalled, "W. R. said, 'Will you please tell Miss Harlow to go back to her room and get dressed?' 'But,' I said, 'she has an evening gown on.' He said, 'To me it looks like a nightgown.' So I said to her, 'Do you realize your dress is a little . . .' 'So what?' 'Well, Mr. Hearst doesn't like it. Couldn't you change and put on something else?' 'All right,' she said. She went back

At Marion Davies's 1935 Bavarian party with (left to right) Gloria Swanson, hostess Davies, and an uncostumed Constance Bennett (Bettmann/UPI)

China Seas *poster art (1935)*

▼

up, then came down in a coat, which she wore all during dinner. She wouldn't change her dress."

In 1930 Crosbie Garstin wrote a rousing, masculine adventure novel called *China Seas.* MGM bought the rights and promptly filed it away as unfilmable. *China Seas* was the story of Alan Gaskall and his wanderings through the Orient as captain of a disreputable cargo ship. The book contained flashes of excitement and innovation, but was hardly the stuff of an MGM film (for one thing, the captain ends up ditching his nice English fiancée for a Chinese opium merchant). Nonetheless, Irving Thalberg latched onto *China Seas* as his "big" film for 1935. Thalberg was growing weary of his reputation for producing artistically prestigious, high-brow films for effete intellectuals. *China Seas,* he decided, would be a slam-bang adventure, full of sex, thrills, and laughs. It would be his baby, and Thalberg intended to oversee every phase of production (except, of course, the fact that it would be colorized in 1990).

Garstin's novel was dusted off and handed over to a bevy of screenwriters, who eliminated characters, added characters, changed episodes, and generally twisted the book beyond recognition. In desperation, Thalberg gave the project to John Lee Mahin and James Kevin McGuinness, who were horrified at what they read. Much of the script had been lifted word for word from Mark Twain and Somerset

Maugham. "And there was a well-known English novel of the time that [the writers] had taken a whole speech from," recalled Mahin. "Granted, nothing's new, but Jesus, you don't just take whole lines of dialogue!"

Mahin and McGuinness reworked the script into a short and snappy tale of Captain Gaskall, two women vying for his attention, and one rascally pirate. The rest of the book's involved subplots were either eliminated or reduced to background noise. Clark Gable was cast as Gaskall, Rosalind Russell and Jean as the feminine interest, and Wallace Beery as the disreputable Jamesey McArdle. This was the first time Jean had been teamed with both Gable and Beery since *The Secret Six* back in 1931, and the press played up the happy reunion; Jean and Clark huddled in the corner with cast members Russell, Robert Benchley, and Hattie McDaniel, while Beery huffed and puffed in his dressing room. On the set he was on his best behavior, as his four-year-old daughter Carol Ann was making her acting debut in the film. But his personality had alienated too many people for too long. During Beery's on-the-set birthday party, the cast got together and decorated a wooden cake for him, which was appreciated not one bit. To apologize, they had the prop department make a cotton-wool cake that also failed to amuse. Jean and Clark's practical joking took on an edge with Beery, whom they didn't much care about offending.

China Seas started filming in late April and took about two months to complete. Jean was once again playing a shady lady. Dolly Portland ("China Doll, the gal that drives men mad!") was a thinly disguised prostitute, plying the China seas and madly in love with Gaskall. She meets her match in Sybil Barclay (Russell), Gaskall's widowed ex-sweetheart. Spurned and rejected, Dolly throws in her lot with McArdle, guiding his Chinese pirate cohorts in their depredations. Realizing that Dolly had tried to warn him and had only turned on him out of scorned love, Gaskall agrees to testify on her behalf at her trial. McArdle kills himself, Sybil graciously bows out, and it's assumed that Dolly and her captain will live happily ever after when her jail sentence is up. (Jean had, after all, waited for Clark in *Hold Your Man.*)

An enormous amount of money was poured into *China Seas,* and when released in July it became one of the year's biggest hits. Thalberg had hit upon the box-office bait he'd wanted: the film had adventure, sex, humor, a brilliant cast (right down to the bit players), and Mahin and McGuinness had hammered out a fast-paced, witty script. One scene in particular, a dinner-table showdown among the fiery Dolly, Sybil, and the icy Yu-Lan (played by Chinese actress Soo Yong), stands out as a perfect coordination of cast, director, and screenwriters.

The filming wasn't entirely without trauma. Thalberg made a total pest of himself, hovering around the set, making the cast and crew self-conscious; Gable had just separated from his wife. Even the technical crew was jittery. During a typhoon sequence, the special effects man mistimed the release of a fifty-ton wave of water, sending it crashing directly onto Clark and Jean's stunt doubles, Chick Collins and Loretta Rush, who were swept off their feet and narrowly missed getting entangled in live electrical cables. Even today, those waves look uncomfortably realistic.

China Seas opened to unanimous raves. "As for the principals," said Regina Crewe in the *New York American,* "none of the three has ever been better." *Liberty* magazine fell all over itself with superlatives, including "triumphant," "thoroughly engrossing," and "highly exciting." André Sennwald in the *New York Times* described the film as "muscularly entertaining" and heartily congratulated the cast (although dismissing accomplished actress Hattie McDaniel with "there is a happy bit of comedy by the Negro actress who plays Miss Harlow's maid").

The film was Jean's first major, unqualified hit since *Bombshell* and put her right back on top of the entertainment world. The summer of 1935 saw her the most popular actress in Hollywood. Many of her competitors were undergoing temporary slumps: Joan Crawford, Garbo, Dietrich, Katharine Hepburn, and Norma Shearer found their careers bogged down that year (although all subsequently recovered with a vengeance).

As *China Seas* went into release, Jean was picked above these other ladies for an impressive honor: a cover story in *Time* magazine. Today, all one needs to make the cover of *Time* or *Newsweek* is a single hit film and a good press agent, but in 1935 this was a considerable coup both for Jean and her studio. Since its inception in 1923, *Time* had featured few women on its cover—mostly opera stars and a mere six actresses (all stage stars such as Eleanora Duse, Ethel Barrymore, and Katherine Cornell). Only cover girl Ina Claire had made some splash in films, but even she was still known primarily as a stage performer. On August 19, *Time* readers were confronted with a black-and-white glamour still of Jean Harlow from *Dinner at Eight,* framed by a Grecian border and captioned "fine feathers make fine fans." The article consisted of a brief biography (most of which entailed a review of *China Seas*) and no further photos of Jean. The uncredited writer produced an intelligent, sympathetic, and relatively factual overview of Jean's life and work, falling prey to only a few of Marino Bello's imaginative stories.

The writer not only hailed Jean as "the foremost U.S. embodiment of sex appeal," but, to her relief, described her as "ingratiating," genuinely intelligent, and serious about her career. The article could easily have veered into a condescending diatribe on Jean's on-screen image, but instead noted that "it distresses her sometimes to find that, however invaluable her sense of the comic may be on the screen, she rarely gets credit for it elsewhere. Last week at a party, when she made what she considered a bright remark, the person to whom she was speaking asked, 'Who did you hear say that?' Jean Harlow paused bitterly before making another remark which was both brighter and indubitably her own: 'My God, must I always wear a low-cut dress to be important?' "

The *Time* article was cause for much rejoicing at MGM and at home. Powell was impressed, Mama Jean beside herself with pride, and Jean felt she now had some leverage in her upcoming contract renegotiations with a grateful and happy Louis B. Mayer. Already Jean was making a list of her requests. She was unhappy with her appearance in *China Seas,* although the film as a whole pleased her. The fact that Dolly Portland was clearly a prostitute made Jean uneasy, especially when compared to the "refeened" character played by Russell. (At one point, Gaskall refers to Sybil as a cool, clear English stream and Dolly as a muddy, yellow Asian river. Both Dolly and the actress portraying her were infuriated.) Although Adrian designed an exceptionally beautiful wardrobe for this film (Dolly was certainly the best-dressed and most fashionable hooker in Hong Kong), Jean was unhappy with her makeup and hair.

For the first time since *Red-Headed Woman,* she elected to wear a wig on-screen, leading some to wonder if seven years of bleaching had snatched Jean bald. Actually, she was very proud of her thick, wavy hair, and her stand-in Barbara Brown insists today that the only reason Jean wore this wig was to reprieve her from repeated bleachings, settings, and hot curlers. The *China Seas* wig was rather stiff and unlifelike, and topped off with three silly spit curls.

Jean had trimmed her own hair to a short bob and stopped touching up the roots. This created a minor crisis in one scene, during which Dolly Portland was to be soaked—in that same typhoon that had nearly killed the two stunt doubles. A wet wig looks lumpy and fake, so Jean's real hair had to be used. She refused to bleach her roots for a ten-second scene, so director Tay Garnett convinced a reluctant Irving Thalberg that Jean's own hair would have to pass muster. It's only visible for a few seconds on-screen and is plainly shorter (with darker roots) than the wig. A towel is immediately wrapped around Dolly's head, ostensibly to keep her warm, but actually hiding the tell-tale hair from moviegoers. Jean had saved herself an unnecessary bleaching, and had won round one.

The publicity photos for *China Seas* also proved a sore point. Jean's makeup in the film was much harsher than usual: heavy dark lipstick, white pancake foundation, nearly inch-long eyelashes; even her eyebrows were more than customarily bizarre. On-screen she looked not so much like a "china doll" as a deranged Kewpie. When the studio stills came back, she exploded. Through some unfortunate trickery of lighting or makeup, Jean looked like a pig. Her face appeared flat and badly lit, her makeup outrageous, and the wig highly unrealistic.

Despite these complaints, Jean was on the top of the MGM heap. The studio finally tore down The Bordello and built dressing rooms more befitting their stars. The women's quarters included six deluxe star

Between assignments, spring 1935: The hairstyle is from the just-completed Reckless, *the gown from the upcoming* China Seas.

▼

dressing rooms for their current queens: Myrna Loy and Greta Garbo had the top two (with a third left available for visiting stars), and Jean, Joan Crawford, and Jeanette MacDonald were given first-floor suites. MGM's head gardener planted window boxes outside each room with the stars' favorite flowers. This was just the sort of pampering that made it the most luxurious of the major studios.

One of the film-star duties Jean greatly enjoyed was her photo sessions, despite her dissatisfaction with the *China Seas* shots. Most performers had to be dragged into the photo shoots. This was understandable, as they were required by contract to give up one of their vacation days every two months for publicity pictures. At MGM, only Joan Crawford shared Jean's enjoyment of these sessions, experimenting with different looks, lighting, and costumes. Garbo put her foot down and agreed to exactly one day, no more, per picture for photos. Not even Norma Shearer was able to get away with *that* kind of attitude.

There were always, always photographs to take, even if one weren't working in a film: portraits to be used for newspapers and fan magazines (as well as for distribution to Jean's own fans); character portraits in costume for films just completed or in planning; production stills recreating scenes from her current film on the set; and publicity stills with costars. Jean was also required to pose for advertisements, luxuriously straightening her stockings, smoothing cold cream on her face, or puffing away on a sponsor's cigarettes.

Most stars had approval of their stills, but Jean generally left this duty to her mother. Once or twice, though, she snapped out at an unflattering photo. "No need for proofs—I don't know *why* they sent them," "I don't know why these are still here—I can't stand them," and "I refuse to even look at pictures unless Mommie has seen them! I hate to sound mean—but you know" are a few of the notes she scribbled to the publicity department.

The best of these photographs are regarded today as works of art. Not only was lighting and composition carefully attended to, but postproduction retouching turned even the plainest starlet into a breathtaking goddess glowing with ethereal presence.

During her early MGM days, Jean worked primarily with Clarence Sinclair Bull and George Hurrell. Hurrell took some of Jean's best-known photos, preferring to light her dramatically with strong shadows "so that they designed the face instead of making it flat. . . . The definite shadows emphasized her strong features: her deepset eyes made it necessary for her to tilt her head down. Her high forehead and short chin were a serious consideration in lighting her, but the cleft in her chin was an asset." He found her as adept as a fashion model in holding difficult poses while lights and cameras were adjusted, and she "never got tense, never fought a position—I don't think she knew how to be awkward."

Jean's publicity photos attracted the censor's notice as much as her films did; they were axed for showing too much breast or too closely outlining her form. "You couldn't show cleavage," recalls photographer Laszlo Willinger. "There was a whole group of retouchers who did nothing but take the shadow out of the cleave of the breasts. In those days the stars had only one breast that stretched from shoulder to shoulder."

Posing for photographs wasn't the only duty of the film star. Jean also had her fans to deal with. The great majority were harmless, ingratiating folk taking a healthy interest in the career of their favorite performer. Jean, Clark Gable, and Joan Crawford had more fan clubs than any other stars—scores of independent clubs, all with their own newsletters, presidents, and conventions. Jean herself had been an avid film fan as a child and took a genuine interest in her clubs. Fan club member Wayne Martin found this out while visiting Hollywood in the mid-1930s. He staked out Jim's Beauty Parlor, where Jean had her hair done every Wednesday afternoon. When alerted that a group of fans was waiting for her on the hot sidewalk, Jean stepped outside to chat. As her hair was still up in pincurls, she declined any photos. Martin had brought along his camera and was rather disappointed, so he approached her again the next week as she stepped out of her lawyer's office. She remembered Martin, greeted him warmly, but it was too cloudy for any photos. Rather than brush him off, Jean arranged to meet him before a dental appointment. Martin finally got his photo.

The two kept in touch over the years, Jean always recognizing this one fan out of hundreds in the crowd. Martin recalls that "Jean took a deep interest in her fan club to the point of furnishing a mimeograph . . . for various fan club activities." This is typical of the genuine affection between Jean and her public. She realized that moviegoers, more than critics or columnists, were responsible for her success. If she could acquire and keep their loyalty, her position at MGM would become increasingly secure.

Occasionally there was trouble. Fourteen-year-old Joe Duggan logged $20 worth of long-distance phone calls from New Hampshire, trying to reach Jean. Blanche finally left his message, and Jean called, at her own expense, to chat with the boy. His parents were flattered until they received the bill for Joe's calls. After several months of legal wrangling, the phone company forgave the bill. Joe was undeterred and continued to "fight duels" in Jean's honor.

The press looked on the Joe Duggan episode as cute, but another run-in in 1935 proved more serious. Three Pi Beta Phi sorority sisters at the University of Arkansas ferreted out Jean's unlisted home phone number. They got Blanche on the phone, who told them that Miss Harlow didn't know anyone in Arkansas and didn't *want* to know anyone in Arkansas, thank you. The girls flew into a huff and contacted Fayetteville theater manager W. F. Sonneman, starting a one-sorority Harlow boycott. The matter reached the local press and, eventually, the national wire services. For the first time, Jean was accused of the kind of star fit that had gotten Garbo and Hepburn into hot water.

Jean was not amused. She told friends the girls had tried to trick her onto the phone by claiming to be a business manager *and* blood relative named Smith; she'd brushed them off. Publicity director Howard Strickling recognized a potential PR crisis and urged Jean to apologize, guilty or not. An appropriately conciliatory release was given out to the press, and Jean phoned to assure the girls that she would *never* snub a fan, that there must have been some mix-up. Pi Beta Phi was mollified, and the boycott called off. When the phone bill arrived at the University of Arkansas the following month, they discovered that Jean had apologized collect to the tune of $6.25.

EIGHT

LADY BY CHOICE

All of Jean's minor aggravations—overzealous fans, bad photography, pushy reporters—faded into insignificance when she won a major tactical battle that summer. She finally killed The Platinum Blonde. For the first time since *Red-Headed Woman,* Jean would appear on-screen in dark hair.

Her next scheduled film, *Riffraff,* was a rough-and-tumble dockside story that had gone through the hands of Anita Loos, Frances Marion, and H. W. Hannemann. Jean convinced the powers that be that her character, a tuna-cannery worker, was hardly the diamond-hard platinum-blonde type. Director J. Walter Ruben and associate producer David Lewis stood by her, and makeup chief Jack Dawn was ordered to create a medium-brown wig. "I've gotten over acting with my hair," the delighted actress told one interviewer.

Jean marched into Jim's Beauty Parlor and ordered the stylist to return her short, newly bobbed hair to its natural medium honey blonde. Then she returned to the studio for the first round of contract renegotiations. Her one-year's grace period was up, and Mayer had promised that if she were a good girl and played ball, she would be granted a few favors. The year was up, Jean was up to bat, and Mayer, to his credit, held to the agreement.

Salary wasn't even discussed. That was still a sore point, and Jean decided that her current $3,300 a week was quite sufficient under the circumstances. Her demands were more artistic than financial.

As early as 1932, Jean had been annoyed by the attention her hair caused. To many critics, she wasn't an actress, just an attractive wig-stand. The platinum crown had been a good gimmick to get her into films; then it became a burden. Now one of Jean's major demands was to appear on-screen in her natural hair color. "The color of hair has nothing to do with ability or personality," she told a syndicated reporter.

Portrait still from Libeled Lady *(1936)*

"Should I be called upon to play a gray-haired woman, I would do it without hesitation."

Jean's second, and stickier demand was about the *kind* of roles she was playing. Only a major star with a lot of pull could demand a certain type of role. Jean was finally in a position to call the shots and decided to take a tremendous gamble with her career. She'd been pained and embarrassed by her public image as a loose-living tramp. The public has always confused the performer with the role—from Theda Bara right up to the present—and Jean was no exception. She was getting touchy about the fact that, of her sixteen film roles, eleven characters had been of a distinctly shady nature.

Mayer was told that Jean wanted no more of this. From now on, she was to start getting some of the roles previously awarded to Joan Crawford, Myrna Loy, and Marion Davies. If he wanted a convenient chippie, he'd have to find a new one (in fact, MGM's next convenient chippie didn't show up until Lana Turner in the early 1940s).

Some people felt that this was an incredibly short-sighted move on Jean's part, career suicide, in effect. Fred Astaire didn't give up dancing, no matter how bored he got; Billie Burke was wise enough not to abandon her "bird-witted ladies"; and George Arliss never took up slapstick. All of these performers knew where their talents lay, and were smart enough to let well enough alone. But Jean decided to spit in the wind and see what happened.

What happened was *Riffraff,* which began filming in midsummer. As some indication of the film's tone, the characters had names like "Flytrap," "Ratsy," and "Belcher." Jean played Hattie, a poor but honest cannery worker in passionate (and inexplicable) love with Dutch Muller (Spencer Tracy), a loudmouthed, pigheaded fisherman.

Hattie and Dutch marry, over the objections of her other suitor, the owner of the tuna fleet. Dutch, a union organizer, loses his job and runs out on Hattie. She is thrown into jail after trying to steal money for her errant husband and gives birth in prison. Urged to it by Dutch, Hattie escapes in a hail of bullets, and the two are reunited. Dutch promises to return to his old waterfront job, and Hattie will serve out her prison sentence.

Neither the cast nor screenwriters could save *Riffraff.* Heavy-handed union sentiments overwhelm the plot, but it's mostly the unlikeable character of Dutch Muller that destroyed any audience sympathy. Dutch is so obnoxious, so lacking in charm, that it's impossible to fathom Hattie's affection for him.

On the other hand, the "villain," Nick Lewis (Joseph Calleia), is so pleasant and amusing that Hattie seems a total fool for rejecting him. Dutch insults Hattie, punches her, loses his job, abandons her, and suggests she risk her life to escape from jail. Not even Spencer Tracy could make this character sympathetic. And Jean, though she tried to make her

With Roger Imhof and Mickey Rooney in Riffraff *(1935)*

▼

character an intelligent and humorous woman, has the audience wondering why she can't see Dutch for the loser he is.

Despite the grim nature of the plot, the cast and crew enjoyed the late summer and early fall shooting, especially the location filming at the tuna canneries near Venice Pier. On her days off, Jean and her mother got up at 4:00 A.M. and joined the fleet for a day of fishing; the cast and crew spent cloudy days, when shooting was impossible, at Venice Pier eating hot dogs and posing for photos. During one of these excursions Jean found and adopted a baby goat. While her new pet's odor didn't bother her, by the end of two weeks Jean was becoming less enchanted with the dockside smells.

Back at MGM she kept the set hopping with her usual Victrola concerts. She was a different girl from the shy amateur Tracy had worked with in *Goldie* back in 1931. Jean was now fully his equal, a self-assured and professional actress. She was thrilled when President Roosevelt visited the set and named her the First Family's favorite actress. A firm Democrat, Jean wrote to a friend that the president "did seem so well and happy, which is wonderful."

Jean was also well and happy, especially with her new on-screen look. While her own hair grew out, she was given a shoulder-length reddish-brown wig and loved it. Howard Strickling dubbed the new shade "brownette" and began issuing press releases to make the shift from platinum blonde less painful for Jean's fans. She was sent to the makeup department for a darker shade of foundation to match her new hair, along with slightly less arched eyebrows. Jean was also assigned a new costume designer. Previously, all her MGM films had been under the direction of Adrian, a genius in his field. The gowns he designed have become classic examples of mid-1930s glamour and elegance.

But with Jean's new downplayed image, MGM assigned a young Englishwoman named Dolly Tree to her films. Tree had arrived at the studio in 1932, via Broadway and Fox Studios. Beginning in late 1935, she created some delightful suits and lounging pajamas for Jean's films, as well as day dresses, which were pleasant in their simplicity. But Dolly Tree also created some of the most god-awful evening gowns ever to appear before a camera.

Like many petite women, Jean was short-waisted and required a dress with a long, slim line. Tree's tended to be belted and bloused, making Jean appear as though she were standing in a hole. Jean's shoulders were not her best feature (she tended to slouch), and many of Tree's costumes were off-the-shoulder creations, which drew attention to this poor posture. Dolly Tree also had a penchant for huge lapels and unfortunate necklines. Sadly, Jean's high-intensity glamour faded a bit when Adrian stopped designing for her.

As part of this new sweep, Jean also chose a new still photographer for herself. She had been so unhappy with the *China Seas* shots that Mayer had three photographers (Ted Allan, Russell Ball, and Tom Evans) audition. Looking at the results, she chose Allan, whose softly lit, informal portraits appealed to her. Ted Allan took all of the publicity stills for Jean's films beginning with *Riffraff.* She still used Clarence Sinclair Bull and other free-lancers occasionally, but Allan took over Hurrell's former domain. He recalled Jean's first sitting with him, and how she tried to put him at ease in her own peculiar way.

A bit nervous, she had a couple of drinks to loosen up and relax. Allan set up a pier scene in his studio and handed Jean a fishing net to drape around herself. Suddenly, Jean decided that the net and her sweater, both the same color, would ruin the shot. Before Allan knew what was happening, she'd whipped off her clothes and stood draped in the fishnet like Venus rising from the sea: "Isn't this better?" she chirped innocently, as Allan's jaw dropped.

"She figured that if I were turned on, I'd take better pictures," he later reasoned. "I realized then that she always needed something personal—that feeling of being liked. It made her feel secure." This is one rare trait Jean did share with Marilyn Monroe; the two women liked to "break through" the camera during these sittings and develop an electricity with their photographers. Neither became romantically involved with their still cameramen (except for one youthful indiscretion on Monroe's part); both star and photographer realized that the flirtation was a professional one.

For the first time, some of Jean's photographs were in color. She never appeared in a color film (except for the faded Multi-Color sequences in *Hell's Angels*) and is thought of today as a strictly black-and-white personality. It's as difficult to picture Jean Harlow in color as it is to imagine Rudolph Valentino talking. But the development of Kodachrome film in 1935 slowly changed the look of Hollywood glamour photography—many think for the worse. Jean's image appeared in the first color rotogravure section of the *New York Daily News* in the fall of 1935. From then on, occasional color photographs of her popped up on the covers of fan magazines (replacing the previous pastel portraits and hand-tinted photos, thereby putting many artists out of work) and in movie ads and publicity stills. By this time, her hair had returned to its natural shade, so there are, sad to say, no natural color photographs of The Platinum Blonde.

Any doubts Jean might have had about her change of image were allayed by William Powell. He'd begun his own career as an oily villain, but with luck and determination had emerged as a debonair comic. Jean hoped that his luck would rub off on her, and that she could go from working-class chippie to sophisticated comedienne along the lines of Myrna Loy or Claudette Colbert.

The Powell–Harlow romance had remained in the headlines during 1935, so when Jean was spotted with a diamond ring that summer, gossip columns confidently announced an engagement. Both parties denied any such thing, Jean saying to an Associated Press reporter, "Well, we're still very good friends." Privately, Powell continued to dodge any commitment, but Jean felt that the ring was a good sign.

Jean liked her diamonds big: she took the $30,000 diamond to a jeweler's and had it reset alongside an $8 glass ruby, to the vast amusement of her friends and the undisguised horror of Powell.

Riffraff was released late in the year, after months in the editing room. The preview, in Whittier, California, was a disaster. The third reel was nearly lost in transit, and the film broke, resulting in a *Singin' in the Rain*–type fiasco of unsynchronized sound: Jean's lines came out of Spencer Tracy's mouth and vice versa, to the audience's delight.

The film utterly confused Jean's fans. The change from blonde comic to brunette tragedienne was too swift, and *Riffraff* wasn't a good enough film to compensate for the shock. English audiences were particularly horrified by the film's toughness. The *Film Pictorial*'s reviewer sneered, "You can get some idea of the theme by the fact that Dutch asks Hattie to spit at him 'for luck' when he is gambling. And she does." American critics were more taken aback at how unsuitable the role was for Jean. The *New York Times* found her new look flattering but her role disappointing: "It hardly seems fair to subject one of the screen's best comediennes to the rigors of mother love and a husband with an acute social consciousness. With so many Kay Francises around, Metro really should be able to stake off one small section of ground and post it with placards reading, 'Miss Harlow's Plot: No Children Wanted.'"

Riffraff poster art (1935)

Enough moviegoers liked the film and Jean's new look to save *Riffraff* from total disaster, although it did nothing for her career or Tracy's. Neither of them gave sterling performances, and they were pretty much put in the shade by supporting players Una Merkel, Mickey Rooney, and George Givot. Joseph Calleia, as evil love interest Nick Lewis, gave a particularly endearing performance, and the film sags whenever he is off-screen. Jean herself seems sincere and believable as Hattie, but too subdued by the outlandish plot for her own good.

This was an odd role for her, and her decision to play the working-class Martyr of the Wharfs was a dangerous one. It's all very well and good for an actress to stretch her talents, to explore her potential, but Jean was tampering with a successful career formula. She was an excellent comedienne, and her skill in wisecracking tough parts couldn't be matched by anyone in Hollywood; but as a dramatic actress she was up against the likes of Joan Crawford and Norma Shearer.

As Jean went out on a limb for her art, Mama Jean was going through her own crisis. William Powell detested Marino Bello. All of Jean's husbands had, but Powell was strong enough to do something about it. Jean had a blind spot regarding her mother: Mama Jean loved Marino, and that was good enough for The Baby. Most of Jean's friends regarded Marino as a pesky but harmless scamp, a loudmouthed comic character. William Powell saw something more dangerous. He suspected that Bello was embezzling from his stepdaughter, and that was the last straw. Jean had never had any money sense; Kay Mulvey recalled her handing her a $500 check to give to an MGM secretary trying to support her parents. This was one habit of Paul Bern's Jean had picked up, tossing money around like confetti. So, as the cash slowly drained out of her bank account, Jean didn't give it much thought. Only when Powell realized how broke she really was did the light begin to dawn.

Hollywood saw the fourteen-year Bello marriage as the ideal screwball romance of a dizzy, scatterbrained wife and an amiable blowhard husband living off their famous daughter. The Bellos were attractive, amusing, and apparently quite in love. But Jean's coworkers had long since run out of patience with Bello. Everyone loved Mama Jean; she was a wonderful hostess, effusive, silly, and endearing. But Marino hung around Jean's sets until finally ordered off, he infuriated MGM executives by injecting himself into contract negotiations, he drove off Jean's beaux and potential friends with his "career advice," and, more ominously, with his brilliant money-making schemes.

The latest of these was a Mexican silver mine. Marino and an unnamed partner managed to charm Jean and her mother out of 25 percent of Jean's income to invest in this surefire scheme. He hung around MGM and pressed mining reports and earnings projections into every hand that came his way. William Powell was nobody's fool, however, and hired a private detective to investigate Marino and the alleged mines.

What he found broke up the Bellos' paradise. There was no mine, there was no partner, there were no earnings. Marino had printed the literature out of his own imagination and was pocketing every cent he took in. Tens of thousands of dollars had vanished from Jean's accounts and were never recovered. This, plus the upkeep of the Club View Drive house, had nearly bankrupted her.

Jean was saddened and embarrassed but not terribly surprised when she discovered Marino's larceny—mostly, she was concerned for her mother. Mama Jean had never been a strong person. Mont Clair Carpenter had simply bored her, but Marino had deceived her. She was publicly revealed as a bubblehead, and this she could not forgive. Mama Jean had suspected for some time that Marino had been unfaithful to her, but there was never any real proof. In any case, he was an Italian male, and she even felt he was entitled to an affair or two, as long as they were kept secret. But stealing from her Baby and lying to her could not be overlooked. Marino Bello was tossed out, and divorce proceedings got under way late in September.

The two Jeans appeared before Judge Elliott Craig, the same man who had granted Jean her divorce from Hal Rosson the year before. Since the illegality of the silver mine scam couldn't be proven and the money was gone anyway, Mama Jean opted for charges of cruelty. In any case, neither woman was eager to have the phony mines publicized. Mama Jean testified that Marino threw constant temper tantrums, embarrassed her before guests, and caused her mental anguish. He spent lavishly on himself (twenty-three pairs of spats were mentioned) but denied her the money earned by her own daughter.

Jean and several servants backed up this testimony and painted Marino as an explosive tyrant. The divorce was granted and Mama Jean left the courtroom dazed and alone except for her precious Baby. Once again, it was the two Jeans against the world, the recently divorced twenty-four-year-old and her newly divorced mother.

While Jean tried to comfort her mother and repair the emotional damage Marino had inflicted, her lawyers stepped in to evaluate the financial damage. It was considerable. That autumn, Jean might have been on top of the world professionally, but a financial advisor Powell hired found her bank account to be a complete mess. The Club View Drive house had to go if she were to make ends meet.

"Mother and I weren't cosy there," Jean said, smiling tightly, when *Modern Screen* asked why she'd unloaded the mansion. "We didn't feel comfortable"—this, coming from a girl who had, as a child, rattled around in one huge home after another. But the explanation made sense to the public, and Jean began looking for more modest digs while putting the house up for sale. Several servants were dismissed, though the two Jeans retained Blanche Williams, of course, as well as a butler named Brown and an assistant for Blanche.

Nathan Levine, head of the low-budget Republic Pictures, bought the white palace for a measly $125,000. (The house has changed hands several times since then, but still stands overlooking the Los Angeles Country Club.) Jean rented a modest cottage at 512 North Palm Drive, in a nice section of Beverly Hills. She paid landlady Harriet Breese $400 a month for the two-story home, which was perfect for a small family. Located between Santa Monica and Sunset boulevards, the house (still standing today) was done in typical California-Spanish style, with a tiled roof and palm trees swaying in the front yard. Jean moved in in October and installed new locks on all the doors, over the vocal objections of Mrs. Breese. But the house was in a residential neighborhood and close to the street. Without the large barred gates of her previous home, Jean felt she needed *some* extra protection from overzealous fans.

The new home had no swimming pool, tennis court, or gym. But it also had no mortgage, no Marino Bello, and no need for many servants. With Powell's encouragement and Mama Jean's consent, Jean began to scale down her life-style—no new cars, no shopping sprees, and certainly no investments.

Jean had about one month to settle in before her new film started shooting. She sold and gave away her accumulated furniture, most of which wouldn't fit into the new house. She had friends over for teas and small-scale dinners. The old pool bashes and huge buffets were things of the past. She and William Powell took weekend jaunts during his days off from his current film, *The Great Ziegfeld,* with their friend Myrna Loy.

Jean and Loy had first met in 1934, when she'd first started dating Powell. They had just completed the fabulously successful *The Thin Man* and were "invited" to broadcast a radio version on Louella Parsons's show. Such invitations were a bane to the stars, but no one wanted to get on the bad side of Parsons, Jimmie Fidler, or any other columnist, so they gritted their teeth and appeared, script in hand.

Powell invited Jean along to the broadcast, as he knew *Thin Man* author Dashiell Hammett would be there, and Jean was always anxious to meet authors. After the show, Loy and her fiancé, Arthur Hornblow, Powell, Jean, and Hammett went to Hornblow's hotel room. The mystery writer proceeded to disillusion Jean by getting progressively drunker and (in Loy's words) "lunging and pawing" at Loy.

Jean didn't pick up any pearls of literary wisdom that night, but she did find a great friend in Myrna Loy, another Midwesterner who was also at the top of the ladder at MGM. After nearly ten years as a bit player, she'd shot to stardom the year before, making the first of six *Thin Man* films. She played the kind of roles Jean longed for—funny, but in a cool, sophisticated manner. "You would have thought Jean and I were in boarding school, we had so much fun," says Loy. Their relationship was marked by laughter and jokes, and Loy recalls Jean as "always very cheerful, full of fun, but she also happened to be a sensitive woman with a great deal of self-respect." Jean was thrilled when she discovered that she and Loy would be working together for the first time, with their mutual friend Clark Gable, in *Wife vs. Secretary.*

After the disappointing *Riffraff, Wife vs. Secretary* is a small revelation. Based on a Faith Baldwin novel called *Office Wife* (a much better title than the one MGM gave the film), this project was a light soap opera, but still much more intellectual and sophisticated than Jean's last film. Gable was cast as Van Stanhope, publisher of suspiciously *Vanity Fair*–type magazines (one lead article is entitled, "Are We Debutantes or Are We Mice?"). Loy played Linda, Van's contented wife. Jean was Helen Wilson, his secretary, who went by the unfortunate nickname "Whitey"—particularly inappropriate, as she wore her own honey blonde hair in this film, the first time she had ever appeared thus onscreen. "Wearing a wig under those lights is like carrying a heat-pad on top of your head," she told one reporter. The freedom from hair dye and wigs was liberating: "For the first time in my life, I lost that 'conspicuous' feeling. I felt more real than I had ever felt. . . . If I *feel* more real, I'm likely to *act* more real."

The plot of *Wife vs. Secretary* revolves around Linda's growing suspicion of an affair between her husband and Helen. This was not among

Loy's happier roles: Linda is pigheaded, disloyal, and whiney. When Van's mother (May Robson) and her society friends begin dropping leaden hints, Linda jumps to the wrong conclusion with alacrity and refuses to listen to Van's explanations. Van, for his part, shamelessly neglects the feelings of his wife as well as his employees. Gable was not at his best in drawing-room comedy, and seems more at home in his clubroom and office scenes. A young James Stewart appeared as Helen's doltish fiancé, Dave, who spends all his time griping about her job and insisting that her executive ambitions are unnatural and unfeminine—not an unusual view in 1935.

Van and Helen's relationship is all business, despite Linda's suspicions. But when Helen accompanies her boss on a secret Havana meeting and Linda calls Van's room only to hear Helen answer, that tears it. Linda moves out, filing for divorce and forcing Van and Helen to see each other in a new light. "If you want to keep a man honest," says Van, "never call him a liar." Helen corners Linda and explains that she is throwing Van into her arms—willing arms, at that. Linda, of course, returns to her husband, exchanging with her rival a look of sorrow and understanding that both actresses handled superbly. Helen leaves the couple, closing the office door behind her and walking down the empty hallway, alone into the dark. This would have been an effective fade-out, but fiancé Dave is waiting for her downstairs with open arms and, presumably, an open mind.

Helen Wilson was by far the most intelligent and adult character Jean had ever played. Indeed, Myrna Loy insists that Helen Wilson was very close to the real Jean Harlow, with her low, warm voice, amused air of indulgence, even Jean's own hair. As Van's right-hand "man," Helen is capable and businesslike, fully able to run Stanhope Publications herself—a far cry from the gold diggers and molls of the past. In 1935, many executive secretaries were men, and Helen was exceptional in her high corporate position. She wrote up contracts, handled research and development, advised her boss on mergers and acquisitions, interviewed prospective employees, decorated the office, and did her own typing. Jean greatly enjoyed playing this Superwoman and endowed her not only with brains and humor, but sex appeal—too much sex appeal to please censor Joseph Breen, who ordered the reshooting of a scene in Helen's large and luxurious apartment. According to Breen, the apartment was too large for a secretary and would lead audiences to think that Van "kept" her. Director Clarence Brown snorted in disgust and simply cut the scene from the film.

Dolly Tree designed an exquisite tailored wardrobe for Helen Wilson. Except for one satin evening gown, Jean wore simple office dresses and suits. The suits in particular were stylish, with broad shoulders, nipped-in waists, and peplums that foreshadowed the styles of the 1940s.

With Clark Gable, May Robson, and Myrna Loy in Wife vs. Secretary *(1936)*

▼

The *Wife vs. Secretary* set was a happy one, with Carole Lombard and William Powell dropping by to visit between scenes. Jean's old friend John Lee Mahin wrote the script with Norman Krasna and Alice Duer Miller, and Cedric Gibbons was again in charge of art direction. James Stewart, in his fourth film, was completely awestruck by Jean and she did her best to put him at ease. One of their love scenes, taking place in Dave's car, required four retakes. Jean gave the kisses more enthusiasm than Stewart had expected, which he recalled with a blush of pleasure years later.

Jean loved her character and signaled her happiness to the front office, which was lining up the following year's projects for her. *Wife vs. Secretary* took a leisurely two months to shoot, after which Jean and Powell took off to celebrate the new year. The film opened in mid-February, again to mixed reviews. Jean was reassured when her personal notices were good, but had hoped that this film would get a more enthusiastic reception.

Fans were again confused by seeing the Blonde Bombshell in a dramatic role. Frank Nugent in the *New York Times* applauded Jean and felt the film was "richly produced, competently directed . . . and well-played," but had reservations about "the nimbus of nobility around [Jean's] now brunette head." She and Loy so underplayed their roles that Nugent also got the impression "that the two girls secretly were of the opinion that Mr. Gable was no bargain." Richard Watts, Jr., found

As Helen Wilson in Wife vs. Secretary, *Jean's only fully realized dramatic role*

▼

Wife vs. Secretary lackluster, but allowed that "the one joy of the film is Miss Harlow. Once more she gets no chance to demonstrate her talents as one of the distinguished comediennes of our time, but always she is so straightforward and human and pleasant to observe that she is of inordinate value to a film that certainly does require her gifts."

The film did moderately well at the box office, and, like Crawford's *Rain,* has slowly gathered an enthusiastic audience. Many fans today feel Helen Wilson is Jean's best performance. For all the unlikely plot twists, *Wife vs. Secretary* offers a fairly serious look at sexual politics and the problems of working women in the 1930s. It's clear that Helen deserves more than a secretarial position, but it's just as clear that she's regarded as no more than a decorative accessory. Her fiancé burbles happily about his $75 a week salary, but looks upon Helen's job as a foolish indulgence. Even Linda Stanhope, who states that "people aren't willing to believe that looks go with brains," wants her dismissed just for being too attractive. It's clear that Helen would never prosper at Stanhope Publications, and one is left pondering her fate at the film's end. Helen, more than most of Jean's characters, lingers in the mind long after one has left the theater.

MGM had a number of projects set for Jean in 1936, and she spent the first few months in consultation, the photo studio, and costume fittings. She was pleased that both comedy and drama were on the agenda and happily agreed to whatever Irving Thalberg had planned for her. She trusted Thalberg more than Mayer. He seemed more in tune with performers' desires and was willing to listen and even bend the rules occasionally.

As Jean's fame continued to rise, she appeared in fewer magazine advertisements—those were a way of introducing starlets to the reading public, not exploiting established stars—but early in 1936, *Harper's Bazaar* readers were startled to see a nude Jean Harlow posing languidly in an ad for Campana Cleanser. Mayer had a fit, Jean laughed her head off, and MGM's legal department went into high gear. Jean assured Mayer that the photo was not of her, not even an old reprint of a Hesser shot. When a blowup was examined by Clarence Sinclair Bull, it was obvious that the model was not Jean Harlow: "Miss Harlow has much larger breasts," Bull solemnly assured an MGM board meeting. Mayer was advised not to sue Campana, as their ad department "may seek to obtain some free publicity and bring the whole matter to the attention of the public." MGM let the incident drop, but became paranoid about reporter and fan-writer access to Jean. A new publicity man named Larry Barbier was assigned to her, and much more red tape had to be cut to arrange a Jean Harlow interview.

Jean's next film was an unfortunate departure from anything she'd done before. *Suzy* was a World War I spy melodrama. Based on a novel by Herbert Gorman, the script was a bizarre, convoluted affair. Not surprisingly, proposed costar Cary Grant (on loan from Paramount) refused point-blank to have anything to do with it. The script had passed through many hands, including those of husband-wife team Alan Campbell and Dorothy Parker. Even the brilliant Parker could do nothing with *Suzy*.

Eventually, writer Lenore Coffee was recruited both to rewrite the script and sweet-talk Grant into playing his assigned role. "I was often called in on people who were having trouble," she recalled. "Cary was one of the handsomest men you've ever seen in your life—very chocolate brown eyes, handsome beyond belief, marvelous personality. But he looked rigid: he wasn't going to play the part. So I said, 'Mr. Grant, this is Saturday. Do you have plans for the afternoon? . . . I will get someone to give us a room. You will have a script, and I will have a script. We will go through it one page at a time, and you will tell me what you won't do under any conditions and what you might do, and I'll make suggestions."

She and Grant locked themselves in and rewrote whatever wasn't agreeable to the actor. By the end of the day, Grant happily agreed to do *Suzy*. He would have been better advised to follow his initial impulse.

Grant's input didn't help the plot any. During the course of the film, Suzy Trent, an American chorus girl in 1914 London, meets and marries poor but charming inventor Terry Moore (Franchot Tone). When Moore is shot by German spy Madame Eyrelle (Benita Hume), the terrified Suzy flees to France, where she meets and marries—with heartless speed—aviator Andre Charville (Grant). Charville's father takes the girl to his heart, although Charville reveals himself to be unfaithful to wife and country. Suzy's first husband resurfaces, not dead after all (one expects him to say "it was just a flesh wound, dearest"), and, amazingly enough, Madame Eyrelle shows up and shoots Suzy's second husband, thoughtfully saving the girl from bigamy. Moore completes a daring aerial raid and places Charville's body in the plane, sparing the dead man's good name. He and a chastened Suzy are reunited as Charville is honored posthumously.

All this is written and played with deadpan sincerity. Neither Coffee nor Parker could untwist that plot, and director George Fitzmaurice was at a loss. Dolly Tree made no attempt to recreate the styles of the period, and Jean is arrayed in a series of unremarkable costumes, all of clearly 1936 vintage. Her hair is styled in a curly, chin-length bob, which made her face appear unflatteringly pudgy. Nevertheless, Jean dragged her Victrola out of her dressing room, playing records between takes, and Fitzmaurice, in a wan attempt to instill enthusiasm, would joke, "Let's make this one for the statuette," when he wanted a good take. No one believed *Suzy* was remotely Oscar material, but all laughed weakly. Columnist Sidney Skolsky found Jean remarkably chipper. "She will tell you that it is her ambition to become an actress," he said admiringly. "The majority of them believe that they *are* actresses." Electrician Tommy Watts recalled that Jean didn't let the film's poor quality dampen her spirits or prevent her from shooting craps with the crew. "I was rolling and threw a deuce down," Watts said years later, "and the next thing I hear is this lady's voice behind me saying, 'you're faded.' I spun around and, sure enough, it's Harlow. She grabbed the dice and made three straight passes. Won about ten bucks. Then she walked off laughing."

But no amount of good will or team spirit could turn *Suzy* into a decent film. It was undoubtedly Jean's worst MGM vehicle. The film took most of April and May to complete, and after the first preview Jean and Inez Courtney were called back to reshoot a prologue. Jean's character seemed so simple-minded that a brief introductory scene was in-

With Cary Grant in the dismal Suzy *(1936)*

cluded, showing Suzy giving money to a chorus girl (to prove how generous she is) and telling Courtney that she wants to stay in London to marry into royalty (presumably to show that, although a gold digger, she's a high-minded one). *Suzy* opened on June 26 to a very limp reception from press and fans alike.

The *New York Times* reviewer found himself more entranced by a goat, which made a brief appearance, than with the human participants. Like the goat, the film "plunges across the screen, creates some mild excitement and careens out again, leaving us with a few esthetic bruises and a feeling that a little fresh air would do no harm." He compared Jean's performance to her "unsophisticated *Hell's Angels* days" and felt the film "may be numbered among her least." Bland Johaneson in the *New York Daily Mirror* felt that Jean's "bewitching and lovable" performance just managed to overcome *Suzy*'s many liabilities, while Irene

Thirer in the *New York Post* recognized that the star was "not too adept at drama—especially tragedy." Thoroughly disgusted, Richard Watts, Jr., said he would "go on screaming in my customary wilderness that it is a great shame to waste Miss Harlow in such a role. . . . nevertheless, she plays . . . with her customary honest simplicity."

Nor has time improved *Suzy.* Franchot Tone seems tired and bored, his hilariously inept Irish accent waxing and waning from scene to scene. Grant sparkles charmingly, and, thanks to his intervention, his character is the only one in the film with any life and color. Jean herself seems to rely on sheer wistfulness to get her through. She's given little chance to show any humor or wit, mainly reacting to Suzy's unfortunate circumstances. She clicks neither with Tone nor Grant, although her scenes with Lewis Stone show a certain warmth and maturity. It's a particular shame that she and Cary Grant, an excellent light comedian, were wasted in this mess of a drama.

Even *Suzy*'s score, by the usually talented William Axt, was badly done. Jean lip-synchs one catchy ballad ("Did I Remember?"), but the background music is silly and obtrusive. When Papa Charville describes his son's childhood, a tinkling children's tune suddenly blares in the background, and "La Marsellaise" overwhelms the soundtrack everytime a soldier appears on-screen. Brief reminders of Jean's more successful films resurface depressingly: the shooting death of husband Tone (from *Reckless*), a character gasping at Jean's "reading a book" (from *Dinner at Eight*), Jean bursting into tears at a piano (from *Hold Your Man*). Even some of the aerial scenes were grafted directly from a negative of *Hell's Angels.*

More disturbing to Jean's fans was the perception that their blonde bombshell was turning into a wimp. In an early scene, a producer tells Suzy Trent that she will have to "be nice" to him in order to keep her job. The old Jean would have turned on him spitting and screeching like a wildcat, putting him in his place with a few scathing insults. Suzy simply shrugs and leaves the room.

Irving Thalberg saw that Jean was heading for a slump. All stars encounter this problem. There were so many stars and so few good films at MGM that everyone—Garbo, Crawford, Gable—found themselves in occasional duds. The trick was to counteract one or two unremarkable films (in Jean's case, her last *three*) with a hit.

In early June, Jean was put into another comedy. She didn't cause a fuss about it, after her recent dramatic disasters. *Wife vs. Secretary* had proven her a capable actress, but hadn't cut much mustard at the box office. Jean badly needed a hit, and she was actually relieved to be getting back into her home territory again. She *knew* she could play comedy, so this next film was almost like a vacation—not only a vacation, but a treat. She was costarring with Powell and her friends Myrna Loy and Spencer Tracy in a screwball comedy called *Libeled Lady.*

The screwball comedy was a genre of film that had its golden years in the 1930s and has rarely been done well since. Loy was one of its queens, along with Carole Lombard, Claudette Colbert, and Irene Dunne. It's tough to come up with an accurate definition of a screwball comedy; the dictionary's "crazily eccentric or whimsical" doesn't quite fit. The films generally involved wealthy eccentrics pitted against working-class or simply level-headed opponents. Powell and Lombard's *My Man Godfrey* was a classic of the type, as was *It Happened One Night.* Jean never became known as a screwball comedienne simply because she rarely played heiresses. *Platinum Blonde* was an early screwballer, and *Bombshell* might fit the bill as well, but *Libeled Lady* was Jean's first classic, unadulterated screwball comedy. Myrna Loy, of course, played the heiress, and Jean her blue-collar rival.

Jean would have loved to switch roles, but she could no more play the cool, elegant Connie Allenbury than Loy could have played hot-headed Gladys Benton. The fact that Jean wound up with Tracy while Loy married Powell didn't please her either, but she was happy enough to be working with Powell. She got him *off*-camera, and that was good enough.

Libeled Lady began filming in mid-June, with old friend Jack Conway (*Red-Headed Woman*) directing. The plot was even more complicated and unlikely than *Suzy*'s had been, but this time was put to good comic effect. When the *New York Evening Star* accuses heiress Connie

With perennial fiancé William Powell (left) and Spencer Tracy in Libeled Lady *(1936) (Academy of Motion Picture Arts and Sciences)*

▼

Allenbury (Loy) of being a husband stealer, she files a $5 million libel suit. In order to *prove* her a husband-stealer, managing editor Warren Haggerty (Tracy) convinces conman Bill Chandler (Powell) and Haggerty's fiancée, Gladys Benton (Jean), to wed and let Connie break up their marriage.

Of course, all kinds of complications arise: Chandler falls for Connie, Gladys falls for Chandler, Haggerty and Gladys alternately fight like wildcats and make up. At the whirlwind climax (which rests on such deathless lines as "Three years ago, all Yucatan divorces were declared illegal!"), the two couples sort themselves out: Chandler and Connie, Haggerty and Gladys.

Jean was top-billed over the other three stars, and many of the film's best moments were thrown her way. Audiences knew the old Jean was back when she first entered, striding furiously through the *Star*'s newsroom in her wedding gown (obviously braless) and throwing a major temper tantrum. The film was a high-budget, top-drawer production from beginning to end. The screenplay was brilliant, and Dolly Tree created some effective costumes for Jean: a silver-and-black outfit with picture hat, and a beautifully gaudy fur-trimmed suit for the film's climax; unfortunately, she also designed two eye-poppingly hideous flower-trimmed gowns for Jean and Myrna Loy.

During the filming, Harlean Carpenter McGrew Bern Rosson officially became Jean Harlow. On June 1, she filed a petition to adopt her stage name legally. Jean was literally getting her house in order, settling into Palm Drive with Mama Jean, and straightening out her legal and financial affairs. This last was made easier with a $5,000 bonus from MGM—perhaps an apology for her last three films. She knew she was still one of the studio's top draws and Hollywood's biggest stars, but this bonus was a welcome pat on the back.

William Powell was having a good effect on Jean, easing her into adulthood. Friends noticed her calming down somewhat, partying less and taking more interest in politics and world events. The summer of 1936 was quite a season for Jean's education: King Edward VIII was romancing Wallis Simpson (a joke about this scandal was even thrown into *Libeled Lady*. When Gladys's first husband, Mr. Simpson, is brought into the plot, Warren snorts at her, "That 'Mrs. Simpson' gets me, Gladdy"); the Spanish Civil War was raging, and many American intellectuals naively threw themselves into the battle; the Berlin–Rome Axis formed, a harbinger of World War II; and Roosevelt was running for a second term. Jean had always been a Democrat, and Roosevelt a Harlow fan, so with the 1936 elections under way, she began actively campaigning. The very Republican Mayer asked Jean to keep her campaigning out of studio publicity and interviews.

Libeled Lady finished shooting on the first of September; two weeks later, Irving Thalberg died of a long-standing heart condition.

Breakfasting with Irving Thalberg in the MGM commissary (Bettmann/UPI)

Thalberg, still a young man, had been the creative master behind MGM, and his death threw many into a panic. He'd also been genuinely loved by his employees, who weren't happy about being abandoned to the dubious sympathies of Mayer. Jean was both saddened and alarmed; Thalberg had already lined up her next few films, so she knew her career was safe for a year or two. But could she trust Mayer to guide her through the 1940s? Both of her angels—Bern and now Thalberg—were gone, and Jean wondered fretfully what the future held.

The present was suitably rosy. *Libeled Lady* opened in October and became one of the biggest hits of the year. It was even nominated for an Academy Award, competing with *Romeo and Juliet, San Francisco, A Tale of Two Cities,* and Powell's *The Great Ziegfeld* (which won). This was Jean's only brush with an Academy Award, not surprising for a comic actress, since Oscars rarely went to comediennes.

The press and public went wild over *Libeled Lady.* The *New York Times* called the cast "as perfect a light comedy foursome as you will encounter anywhere" and raved over the "zestful script, which has a generous spicing of witty lines and a fund of comic situations. . . . we are . . . pathetically grateful to Metro for restoring Miss Harlow to her proper mètier." Leo Mishkin in the *New York Telegraph* was also happy that "Miss Harlow, Heaven be praised, is again a luminous comedienne," and Howard Barnes in the *New York Herald Tribune* found her scenes "gems of brash comedy and she vitalizes the material throughout."

The entire cast did themselves proud. Powell and Loy's subtle performances blended well with the pyrotechnics of Jean and Tracy; and Walter Connelly (along with Eugene Pallette, one of Hollywood's reliable comic millionaires) was superb as Connie's father. As in *Dinner at*

Eight, even the bit parts were well cast: Hattie McDaniel was brought in (unbilled) simply to utilize her matchless grin. A black-gowned extra in one shipboard scene also gave her on-screen moment the old college try: no matter where the camera pointed, this determined girl kept her best side defiantly visible. If director Conway noticed, he was good natured enough not to interfere with her moment in the sun.

With this great success behind her and two new comedies awaiting, Jean took off on a San Francisco vacation with Powell and Loy. Her friends were making *After the Thin Man,* and Jean accompanied them on their location filming, her first visit ever to the city by the Bay. The stars stayed at the St. Francis Hotel—site of the notorious Fatty Arbuckle debacle in 1921—where the room clerk, having seen too many *Thin Man* films, was under the impression that Powell and Loy were actually married. Loy and Jean took the bridal suite reserved for "William and Myrna Powell," and Powell slept downstairs in a single. "We couldn't be obvious about the situation with the press on our heels," said Loy, "but Jean was marvelous. Bill complained bitterly, let me tell you, angling to get upstairs."

What was to have been a romantic getaway for Jean and Powell turned into Girl's Night Out. While the ousted lover fumed downstairs, Jean and Loy sat up nights "talking and sipping gin, sometimes laughing, sometimes discussing more serious things." Jean told Loy of her great love for Paul Bern, and how saddened she was that the brief, happy marriage was twisted into something filthy by the press. She discussed her frustration over Powell, and her desire for marriage and children. As much as she loved William Powell, Jean was wondering if they weren't wasting each other's time. If he didn't want to get married, perhaps she should end the relationship and find someone who did.

Irving Shulman's 1964 biography depicted this innocent trip as a sex-and-drug orgy: "the weekend was an alcoholic haze of people, bars, noise, music, booze, groping hands and creaking beds. She remembered once even on the floor of a closet . . . in the back seats of speeding cars." Shulman also mistakenly put the trip in late 1932. Powell called Shulman's account "unbelievably scurrilous fiction," and Loy wrote that "it makes me wild when I think about the rubbish that's printed! . . . She was with me or Bill, for God's sake, and when we worked she hung around the set." Shulman's acknowledged source was Arthur Landau, whom Jean had barely seen since 1932 and to whom she would hardly have described sexual orgies.

After that vacation, Jean and Powell took off on a private holiday. They both loved swimming and found a lakeside cabin. To Powell's concern, Jean developed a severe sunburn. Loy had noticed that Jean's complexion had looked gray in San Francisco and tried to get her to see a doctor, but Jean laughed it off. She felt fine, she said, but promised to see Loy's doctor friend. She never kept the appointment.

Showing off her new sapphire ring (Bettmann/UPI)

Jean had always avoided sunburn before, but for some reason she was more susceptible that fall, and this case was so bad that she had to return home and lie wrapped in ointments until she healed. The press dubbed it her "$100,000 sunburn," for the costly delays Jean's filming schedule incurred as a result. She felt perfect again within a month and put the episode out of her mind.

That Christmas, Jean received another ring from William Powell—not, he made it quite clear, an engagement ring. The obvious confusion of her friends and fans was shared by Jean herself. If a man buys a woman a car, a hat, or a bracelet, it can be put off to friendship, but a ring means only one thing. That Powell would present her with the traditional token of engagement not once but twice, then pooh-pooh any talk of marriage, bewildered Jean. Since the demure diamond of last year, Powell had homed in on Jean's taste in jewels. This new ring was the biggest, gaudiest 150-carat sapphire ever seen in Hollywood. It cost $20,000 and was the size of a golf ball. Jean adored it and even insisted on wearing it in her publicity photos and in her next scheduled film. Myrna Loy thought the stone hilariously vulgar, but Jean displayed it proudly and almost defiantly.

In its year-end issue, *Modern Screen* asked psychic Dareos to predict what 1937 had in store for Hollywood's stars. "Jean Harlow was never born to see happiness in marriage, neither was Bill Powell," he wrote. "Yet with their intelligence, courage and love, they can work against the destiny that faces them."

NINE

NIGHT MUST FALL

MGM was grooming young Robert Taylor for stardom and gave him the same treatment they'd given Clark Gable, throwing him into films opposite every popular actress in Hollywood. Thus far, he'd acted with Garbo, Janet Gaynor, Joan Crawford, and—on loan-out—with Barbara Stanwyck (an assignment that developed into off-screen romance). Now it was Jean Harlow's turn. Their first 1937 film was to be a light comedy called *Personal Property*. But first the two were paired in a radio production of a 1907 stage hit, *Madame Sans-Gene*. On December 14, Jean and Taylor appeared on Cecil B. DeMille's *Lux Radio Theatre of the Air* in a considerably shortened version of this comedy, which involved a feisty laundress in Revolutionary France. Jean played Catherine Hubscher, the "Madame" of the title, Taylor her soldier-lover LeFebvre, and Claude Rains the young Napoleon. After the Revolution and the installation of Napoleon as emperor, Catherine and LeFebvre (now a duke) marry and enter the Napoleonic court, Catherine becoming a kind of early-nineteenth-century Kitty Packard. She eventually manages to overcome the disdain of Napoleon's sisters and settles happily into her new social standing.

Despite a silly script and dated plot, the stars acquitted themselves well and wisely did not attempt foreign accents. Catherine was a nice change for Jean, and she, Taylor, and Rains seem to have genuinely enjoyed chewing the scenery for DeMille.

Just as *Personal Property* began filming, on January 4, Jean and Taylor were invited by newly reelected President Roosevelt to his annual Birthday Ball in Washington, which took place on January 30, leaving little time for filming. Although Mayer was disgusted by Roosevelt's victory, he could hardly complain about this bonanza of free publicity for his stars, so he gave his consent—provided *Personal Property* had wrapped in time.

Portrait still, 1937

▼

Rehearsing a radio performance of Madame Sans-Gene, *1936— left to right: Robert Taylor, Jean, Claude Rains, C. Henry Gordon (Bettmann/UPI)*

Jean found that her recent sunburn had sapped her strength, and she had trouble bouncing back into the filming routine. "Jean was as strong as a young ox," recalled one of her coworkers. "She climbed over boats and sets like a cat. She had to be physically strong to take the punishment she did in her pictures." Assuming she was out of shape from neglecting her swimming and tennis, Jean dug in her heels and tried to regain her momentum: she had a tough three weeks ahead if she were going to make that late January date in Washington.

Personal Property had already been filmed by MGM in 1931 as *The Man in Possession,* from the Broadway play by H. M. Harwood. A frothy drawing-room comedy set in England, the earlier version had starred Robert Montgomery in Robert Taylor's role and Irene Purcell in Jean's. Jean's friend Woody Van Dyke was called in to direct this latest production.

Jean played Crystal Wetherby, an American who marries a wealthy Englishman, only to find herself broke after his death. Ne'er-do-well Robert Dabney (Taylor) is assigned by the bailiff to guard Crystal's personal property until she pays her debts; unknown to her, Robert is the brother of her stuffy fiancé, Claude (Reginald Owen). Crystal and Robert eventually fall in love, and, of course, the elder brother takes flight when he discovers his fiancée's financial situation.

Nebraska-born Robert Taylor was about as British as apple pie, completely miscast in a role that cried for the comedic talents of a Cary Grant or David Niven. He was inept at light comedy and helplessly babbled his lines with no idea of timing or flair. Jean, attempting to act refined and sophisticated as Crystal Wetherby, came off as merely bored and distracted.

On the Personal Property *set with (left to right) hairdresser Peggy McDonald, companion Blanche Williams, and cameraman William Daniels, January 1937 (Bettmann/UPI)*

This is what happens when a film is rushed through production. "One-Take" Van Dyke didn't have time to coach his cast or delve into character; some cast members even stumbled over their lines. Jean had a minor coughing fit during one scene, but no retakes were ordered. The cast worked late into the night and weekends; nerves were soon frayed. At one point, Jean lost her precious sapphire ring, which she'd handed to a makcup man during a dishwashing scene. After an all-night search, it was found safely resting in an ashtray; the next's day's filming was faced after only an hour or two of sleep.

The script, by Hugh Mills and Ernest Vajda, was uneven. When the cast was given good material, they came through wonderfully. Jean was delightful clomping upstairs in heavy boots, trying to convince Taylor that her "husband" had returned. A mid-film dinner party proved a comic masterpiece, in part thanks to character actors Barnett Parker (as an unintelligible British guest) and Cora Witherspoon (doing an amazing impersonation of actress Alice Brady).

But Jean was hardly at her best in cool-blooded English comedy. Van Dyke desperately tried to get a decent performance out of the young, inexperienced Robert Taylor, resorting to any lengths for laughs. At one point, Taylor is given a ridiculous Bavarian hat to wear, for no other reason than as a last-ditch attempt to *look* funny. ("Will you take off that silly-looking hat!" Crystal understandably snaps.) He completely ruins another scene, which could have been quite amusing, imitating a dog while Crystal tries to talk on the phone to her fiancé. Taylor's dog routine is painfully uninspired, and the bit falls flat.

But, all things considered, *Personal Property* turned out to be a pleasant, good-natured little comedy, painless to sit through and in-

With Robert Taylor in Personal Property *(1937)*

▼

stantly forgotten. The breakneck filming was completed on January 21 and the film released in early March to kind but unenthusiastic reviews. "Miss Harlow—sweeping or flouncing through expensive sets in that eternal negligée of hers—is positively the indignant lady of a Peter Arno drawing," said the *New York Times.* Irene Thirer in the *New York Post* found Jean's performance "flip and amusing," and Regina Crewe in the *New York American* said that the star "jumps right into character and gets everything out of it that was ever written in" (which, of course, was not much: "Both Mr. Taylor and Miss Harlow have enjoyed roles better suited to their talent," she adds).

As soon as *Personal Property* had wrapped, Jean and Taylor stuffed their suitcases full of evening clothes from the film and hopped onto an eastbound train (Jean accompanied by her mother, Blanche, a studio hairdresser, and publicity man Larry Barbier). Also crammed into the sleeper car were twenty-one pieces of luggage and five-gallon bottles of spring water for washing Jean's hair.

MGM wanted all the mileage they could get out of this trip, so the stars made several whistle-stops along the way and were handed a list of publicity events to attend in Washington. In the last few days of January, Jean and Taylor appeared at twenty-two events, greeting the March of Dimes chairman, dashing to a press conference at Annapolis Naval Academy, stopping in Alexandria, Virginia, and Mount Vernon, as well as attending parties in the District of Columbia. J. Edgar Hoover kept files on nearly everyone he met, and he seemed particularly proud of his Hollywood acquaintances. According to Jean's recently declassified FBI file, she was even treated to a machine-gun demonstration by a star-struck J. Edgar himself. Her reaction was not recorded for posterity.

On the 29th, Jean appeared on the steps of the U.S. Capitol with a bevy of eager politicians, including eccentric North Carolina Senator Reynolds. The portly, aging Reynolds had somehow acquired a reputation as a ladies' man and was anxious to be seen with the nation's leading sex symbol. A *Life* photographer asked for a photo of the senator and actress embracing: "Absolutely no," snapped Barbier. "I didn't think it would be the right kind of publicity for Jean."

To Jean's utter amazement, the exuberant senator dashed forward, grabbed her, and planted a kiss smack on her mouth as the cameras flashed away. Coming up for air, Reynolds good-naturedly complained that Jean's kiss couldn't compare to a North Carolina kiss, and Jean in turn cracked, "If that's the best a senator can do, I'm glad I didn't get to the Cabinet!"

"Mother Jean, figuring I was in on the stunt, threw me a look and shouted, 'you're fired!'" recalled Barbier. "I spent the whole afternoon running around trying to get that picture killed. . . . Sunday morning my boss, Howard Strickling, called from the studio and said, 'Louis B. Mayer thinks the picture . . . is the greatest public relations that ever happened to Hollywood!'"

On the night of January 30, Jean and Taylor appeared at all seven hotels hosting Birthday Balls. Before the main event, the stars were ushered into Roosevelt's "fireside chat" room and introduced to the president and first lady. Jean, looking haggard and exhausted, sat

With Eleanor Roosevelt at the president's Birthday Ball, January 30, 1937

on Mrs. Roosevelt's left during dinner, nearly speechless with admiration. Eleanor Roosevelt, a dedicated film fan, seemed more animated than Jean.

The next day, the stars and their entourage packed up and hopped onto the connecting train back to Hollywood. By then, the whole party had come down with a violent case of influenza. The trip westward was a long agony for Jean, whose symptoms worsened with every mile. By the time the train reached Pennsylvania, Mama Jean had to hire a private nurse to look after her ailing daughter. Mama Jean herself suffered some flu symptoms, but Jean's condition was far more worrisome. Fortunately, the women had a separate sleeping compartment, so their neighbors weren't aware of the star's condition. Robert Taylor sympathetically poked his head in from time to time, but Jean was barely able to acknowledge his kindness. The flu is bad enough under the best of circumstances, but Jean was traveling on a train with no doctor and no real medication; the rocking of the cars was a constant source of misery. Unable to read or converse from nausea and cramps, she lay in her compartment trying to get up enough strength to eat.

She spent February at home recuperating. Mama Jean's parents picked that month for their first-ever visit to the West Coast, and Jean tried her best to show the Harlows the town. Unfortunately, she also gave her grandmother a good case of her flu. By mid-month, Jean was well enough to accompany William Powell to Palm Springs, where she hoped the sun would bake all the infection out of her system. Her next film was awaiting, and MGM impatiently requested her presence on the set.

She squeezed in several interviews during that time, telling Louella Parsons, "I've been worn out since that . . . trip to Washington. It seems that everything tires me. I guess I'm just run down." In a chirpier mood, she told *Modern Screen*'s Carolyn Hoyt, "I have achieved, of late, a degree of peace. I feel, now, at peace with myself and with my world. I have attained this state of being by forcing myself to realize that all I can do is done in the best way I know—and that that is that."

Saratoga was scheduled to begin costume and wardrobe tests in March. The picture was a romantic racetrack comedy, and Jean was to appear for the sixth time on-screen with Clark Gable. The script was by Anita Loos and Robert Hopkins, and Jean's reliable old friend Jack Conway was assigned to direct. The cast line-up was impressive: Walter Pidgeon, Frank Morgan, Una Merkel, Lionel Barrymore, Hattie McDaniel, Margaret ("Wicked Witch of the West") Hamilton, and Cliff "Ukelele Ike" Edwards (known to later audiences as the voice of Jiminy Cricket).

While the production was being firmed up, Jean overcame her fear of hospitals long enough to visit Spencer Tracy, who was in Good Samaritan having a throat tumor removed. The operation, which might have ended his career, was hushed up by his studio. Jean appeared at the actor's bedside early the morning of his surgery, wished him good luck, and hightailed it out of the hospital as quickly as she could. Jean was feeling none too well herself. She'd been having some difficulty with her teeth, and had put off seeing a dentist until the pain was nearly unbearable. By mid-March, all four of her wisdom teeth had grown in and were impacted; there was nothing to do but extract them. Jean knew this and, like most people, put it off till the last possible moment. She entered the hospital and the teeth were pulled.

Pulling teeth was no great danger even in the 1930s, but Jean developed blood poisoning. On March 30, she was ordered back into the hospital for observation. There wasn't much that could be done for blood poisoning in those days, as antibiotics were only in their infancy, but Jean was given painkillers for the throbbing in her jaws, and her condition was carefully monitored. By early April she was well on her way to recovery, and MGM was champing at the bit. *Saratoga* was already behind schedule, and Jean had two more pictures (one of them a loan-out at Fox) waiting.

Joan Blondell later recalled the reaction at Warner Bros. when she fell ill filming *Back in Circulation* that same year. Blondell was too seriously ill to leave the hospital, "so they made a deal with the doctor to take me by stretcher to my house up on Lookout Mountain, and they had the set designer come in and make it look like the bedroom Pat [O'Brien] and I had done a scene in . . . and changed the end of the story so that I was sick in bed and that I'd marry Pat or something." That was the similarly sympathetic attitude Jean faced as she tried to recover her health while *Saratoga* sat and waited.

In its May 3 issue, *Life* magazine did a cover story called "Portrait of Hollywood." It included profiles of the city, major stars, and bit players, and street scenes and photos of "royalty"—Chaplin, Mae West, Gary Cooper, Sylvia Sidney, Dietrich, Lombard, Shearer, and Claudette Colbert. On the cover was a photo of Jean Harlow taken around the time of *Reckless,* showing her strolling through the backlot at sundown, smiling back over her shoulder at the cameraman. She was the queen of Hollywood that spring and was even considering a stage career; Charles Washburn had approached her about a Los Angeles theatrical production. The prospect terrified her, but she agreed to consider it for her next vacation.

Clark Gable was going through his own traumas that spring. He had divorced Ria Langham and was openly romancing Carole Lombard when a half-deranged cockney woman slapped him with a paternity suit. Gable was hauled into court on the charge, at a time when sexual misconduct was no laughing matter. Gable was easily acquitted, but endured weeks of having his name dragged through the courts and the press (including the Hollywood issue of *Life*). When *Saratoga* finally be-

Shooting Saratoga, *May 15, 1937*

▼

gan filming on April 22, it was an exhausted and weary Jean and an unusually thin and haggard Gable who faced the cameras.

"I am working in a picture called *Saratoga,* all about horse racing," Jean wrote to Louis Samuelson, a New York fan of long standing. "I am jittery because I have horses on all sides of me and surrounding me, practically all day long, and I am scared to death of them. But I hope to survive."

Jean was cast as Carol Clayton, heiress of a horse-breeding farm; Gable played bookie Duke Bradley, and Pidgeon was Carol's stuffy fiancé, Hartley Madison. The film was essentially a love triangle complicated by plot twists: Carol is flat broke and trying to save her farm; Duke Bradley wants to gyp her rich fiancé out of the money, but Carol refuses to be indebted to him and tries to earn it herself. Carol eventually falls in love with Bradley against her better judgment, she "honestly" wins the money in a horserace, and Hartley manfully steps aside to let True Love take its course.

Still from Saratoga *with Clark Gable*

▼

Carol Clayton was another of Jean's high-toned characters; traveling through Europe, she's become more refined than either Duke Bradley or Jean's fans would like: "Take that crown off yer head!" he snarls when she starts spouting lines like, "I don't know how to parry wisecracks with you. I fear I've been away . . . too long." Although the film's racetrack plot was far too involved and confusing for its own good, the script was much more sprightly than that of *Personal Property,* and Conway directed his talented cast well. *Saratoga* had an almost 1940s flavor to it, with Jean's wavy, shoulder-length hair, modern costumes, and even the "hepcat jive" flavor of the title song, performed by Four Hits and a Miss.

Jean continued, tired and worn-out, into early May, but with clever makeup and Ray June's expert camerawork, she looked lovelier than ever. Although her appetite had been falling off steadily, she'd put on a little weight. It appeared to be water weight rather than fat, and her friends, assuming it was That Time of Month, politely ignored it.

As winter gave way to spring, Jean again confronted William Powell about their relationship, suggesting that he either marry her or let her date other men. She began dining out with New York publisher Donald Friede, who was negotiating with the Orsatti brothers for rights to *Today Is Tonight.* Powell himself was spotted dining alone at a nightclub, and gossip began flying about the break-up ("Bill Powell and Jean Harlow are singing 'Let's call the whole thing off,'" crowed one fan magazine). The fact that Friede looked suspiciously familiar (middle-aged and balding) helped fuel rumors. But after three years, Jean and Powell were in each other's blood. Two weeks of not speaking were all they could stand, and soon they were back to where they had started: she wanted to get married and he didn't. They couldn't live with each other and couldn't live without each other, so the couple simply tried to come to terms with their differences. When columnist Harrison Carroll grilled Jean about her dates with Friede and Powell's solo appearances, she tried to explain, "that is nothing for people who have been going together for three years. I'm giving you the lowdown: Bill and I are just the same as ever. That is, unless he is putting something over on me."

She told Louella Parsons that "I suppose he is right. Marriage hasn't panned out for either of us in the past. And two movie people with careers perhaps shouldn't marry." But Powell continued sending flowers to the *Saratoga* set and in mid-May sent Jean an anniversary cake. She shared it with the cast and crew, beaming with happiness.

She was her usual cheerful self on the set, but still didn't feel quite right. Parsons noticed that "Jean . . . couldn't seem to get warm enough and kept asking Blanche for someone's coat . . . and sought her portable dressing room couch between scenes, to rest." One morning hairdresser Jeanette Landry came to do Jean's hair and found her lying down, completely washed out. "I told her I was tired, too, so she sat down on the floor and insisted that I sit in the chair. . . . She told me she would be glad to . . . run away with Bill Powell into a world where nobody knew either of them. 'I'm so much in love with him, I'd be happy to leave everything for him,' she told me."

Jean began spending nights in her dressing room. The thought of driving all the way home exhausted her. Around May 20, she was shoot-

Jean's first scene in Saratoga: *Carol Clayton phones home*

ing a scene with Walter Pidgeon when, he recalled, "she suddenly doubled up in my arms and said, 'I have a terrible pain.' I called to Jack Conway, 'Baby's got a pain.' He told her to go have lunch in her dressing room and rest." Mama Jean insisted that Jean stay home the next day and called Dr. E. C. Fishbaugh, who diagnosed the flu and a slight gall bladder infection—nothing to worry about.

Dr. Fishbaugh, who was not associated with MGM, was not, perhaps, the best physician to call in; when actress Fay Wray consulted him about her husband's severe alcoholism, Fishbaugh recommended sleeping pills as a cure. Even in the 1930s, Wray realized this was a dangerously unprofessional recommendation and avoided Fishbaugh thereafter. Actually, Jean's symptoms didn't seem all that troubling: fatigue, slight nausea, water weight, and abdominal pain. The pain could be blamed on her gall bladder, and her fatigue and general fogginess to exhaustion from a cold. It's not certain if Fishbaugh even knew of her recent sunburn, flu attack, and blood poisoning. Jean soon felt well enough to return to work.

Although she found it hard to concentrate and keep her energy level up, she continued giving interviews, dining out with both Powell and Friede, and kidding around on the set. Gable had also cheered up somewhat, playing a "six-year anniversary" joke. When Duke Bradley was called upon to give Carol a chaste peck on the cheek in one scene, Gable instead swept Jean into a passionate, prolonged embrace, to the appreciative cheers and whistles of the crew.

On Saturday, May 29, Mama Jean started out on a Catalina fishing trip, first seeing The Baby off to the studio. "She complained of feeling miserable and in pain," Mama Jean recalled, "but she insisted on working 'as long as I can stay on my feet.'" Not thinking anything was seriously wrong, Mama Jean went ahead with her plans, telling Blanche to keep her apprised of Jean's health.

Jean was working in a mock-up of a train compartment that day: her character, suffering from a bad cold, is finally about to confess her love to Duke Bradley. Jean, Gable, and Hattie McDaniel shot several takes, but Jean was obviously sicker than her character ("Hey, you've got a fever. You all right? You had me scared there for a minute!" a concerned Duke tells Carol). For the first time, Jean looked seriously ill. Her eyes were red and swollen, and she had difficulty putting any pep and feeling into her lines. After several uninspired takes, she stood and adjusted her fur negligée as Gable repositioned himself by her side. Jean leaned weakly against her costar, who noticed that she'd broken into a cold sweat. He lowered her onto the sofa and she whispered, "I feel terrible. Get me back to my dressing room." As assistant director "Red" Golden helped her off the set, she said, "Red, please call Bill. I'm terribly sick." Powell rushed over from the set of *Double Wedding* and had a studio chauffeur take Jean and Blanche Williams home.

When Powell checked in on Sunday morning, Jean still didn't feel any better. Blanche summoned Mama Jean home from Catalina, and Dr. Fishbaugh was again called in. He carefully examined Jean and decided, to the best of his knowledge, that she was suffering from the flu complicated by a gall bladder inflammation. No one, not even Jean herself, realized that her kidneys had been slowly failing for nine months and that this final infection had crippled them fatally.

Kidney disease strikes up to 400,000 Americans yearly. Today, antibiotics, dialysis, and even transplant have cut the death rate to 25 percent even in the most serious cases of acute renal failure. But effective antibiotics weren't developed until World War II, and hemodialysis and transplants weren't practical until the 1960s. There was no power on Earth to heal seriously failing kidneys in 1937.

A still (posed earlier) from the last scene Jean was able to complete in Saratoga *(with Clark Gable)*

▼

Jean's autumn sun poisoning had been the first warning signal. As the kidneys lose their power to break down certain hormones, the skin tone often darkens (the grayness Myrna Loy noticed) and leaves the patient susceptible to sunburn.

Kidneys can fail slowly, "silently," giving few clues that poisons are building up in the body, weakening the entire system. As in AIDS, this weakness leaves one open to every opportunistic infection that comes along. That was why simple impacted wisdom teeth led to serious blood poisoning, and Jean fell prey to several flu viruses. She was unable to shake one off before the next felled her.

As Jean slowly but steadily weakened, the uremic poisons built up, giving her a slightly bloated look and feeling. She probably had to urinate often, but couldn't rid her body of the toxins. Jean's appetite decreased as her mouth and digestive system were affected, and she no doubt had a lot more aches and pains than she let on. It's certain that she was tired and lethargic during the day and may not have been able to sleep well at night. As the poisons entered her brain and nervous system, Jean felt as though she were living behind a fuzzy curtain. It became difficult for her to concentrate on her part and even to remember her lines. This must have been horribly frustrating and frightening, although she probably blamed it on her lack of sleep.

Then came the gall bladder infection. Her gall bladder might have been attacked by poisons floating through her system; or this final infection might have been the knock-out blow to her kidneys. Whatever the cause, the outcome was certain. By the end of May, Jean's kidneys ceased to function. It was a sign of her youthful strength and resilience that she lasted as long as she did.

Jean fought back with great vitality. Dr. Fishbaugh stopped by daily; Mama Jean and Blanche constantly hovered around her bedside, and William Powell came by three times that week after work. By June 2, Jean was unable to keep down any nourishment, even liquids. Dr. Fishbaugh tried glucose injections to keep up her strength, and by Thursday morning, June 3, she was feeling stronger. "Miss Harlow just had a cold, was resting comfortably today and feeling much better," Dr. Fishbaugh told an Associated Press reporter. Mama Jean added, "This Baby of mine is quite improved. Her doctor says she is out of danger."

On Friday morning Jean was able to walk around the room and take some food; Powell stopped by, but her *Saratoga* costars assumed she'd be back on the set Monday morning and didn't bother to visit.

William Powell came to the Palm Drive house on Sunday evening, June 6, to see how Jean was feeling. "I thought she looked wan, but that was all. . . . no one was very concerned. She startled me when she said, 'you look fuzzy.' 'I don't really?' I joked. But I was suddenly worried. I held up my hand. 'How many fingers can you see?' I asked her. She couldn't see any. . . . I knew something was wrong."

Blanche Williams telephoned for Dr. Fishbaugh, who rushed to Jean's bedside. By the time he arrived, Powell was gently shaking her, but Jean had quietly slipped into a deep slumber. Fishbaugh listened to her labored breathing and called an ambulance. He finally realized that there was more wrong than a gall bladder infection or a cold.

Jean arrived at Good Samaritan Hospital in downtown Los Angeles at 6:30 that evening, and Dr. Fishbaugh called in resident Leland Chapman to assist him. Jean was checked into room 826, the "celebrity suite." In her extremity, Mama Jean had summoned Marino Bello back to her side, as well as Jean's great-aunt Jetta, and cousin Donald accompanied by Blanche Williams. Actor Warner Baxter drove a shaken William Powell to the hospital. They stood helpless by Jean's bedside all through Sunday night. She'd fallen into a coma and was put into an oxygen tent.

On Monday morning, June 7, the still-comatose Jean began having difficulty breathing and suffered several minor, almost imperceptible seizures as the poisons took over her major organs. The Los Angeles Fire Department was called in with emergency respiration equipment not then available at Good Samaritan. "We knew Jean Harlow and we did everything that years of training, experience in hundreds of cases and daily life-saving drills have taught us," said Fire Captain Warren Blake. "We made the trip to the hospital in record time. From the first it appeared a hopeless task."

At 11:37 Monday morning, a swelling of Jean's pericardium caused her heart to stop beating. The doctors tried for three minutes to revive her, but she didn't respond. Dr. Fishbaugh stepped back and told the assembled group that Jean was dead.

Mama Jean collapsed and was quickly sedated. Blanche, Jetta, and cousin Donald drove numbly back to Palm Drive, and Warner Baxter somehow got a sobbing, hysterical William Powell home. A Good Samaritan official contacted MGM shortly after noon, just as most films were breaking for lunch.

Walter Pidgeon recalled sitting on the *Saratoga* set with Gable, Anita Loos, and Jack Conway, who was "called to a phone about ten or fifteen feet away. He came back and said, 'Oh, my God, Baby's gone.'" Gable rushed home, snapping at reporters, "I am too overcome by grief to make any comment." Harold Rosson, back on the MGM lot, simply disappeared from his set at midday, without even telling anyone what was wrong. News quickly spread. Writer Harry Ruskin said years later that "the day The Baby died there wasn't one sound in the commissary for three hours. Not one goddam sound."

Last snapshot: on a date with publisher Donald Friede, May 23, 1937

TEN

LIBELED LADY

Portrait still from Jean's final studio sitting

▼

The death of Jean Harlow hit the front page of every newspaper on Tuesday morning with a mixture of genuine grief and inaccuracy. Jean's illness had been so underestimated and misinterpreted that all kinds of bizarre rumors sprang up.

The most popular (later perpetuated by Irving Shulman) had a starry-eyed Christian Scientist Mama Jean imprisoning her daughter, praying over her, and denying her medical treatment: "The air is filled with evil vibrations!" she supposedly ranted. "Evil is struggling to stay inside Jean. . . . She's just pretending, to make a fool of me. I hate her!" This is, of course, sheer nonsense, though for years the Church of Christ, Scientist, has found itself in the position of defending Mama Jean, who was not, in fact, a Christian Scientist; although a Christian Science service was read at Jean's funeral, Mama Jean declared, "I have no creed, no denominational religion." Indeed, it was she who *insisted* on medical help when Jean caught the flu in February of 1937. Kay Mulvey stated that Jean "was such a little trouper that she made little" of her illness, but that "had she [Mama Jean] known that she needed a doctor that soon, she would have had one." Far from being held prisoner that week, Jean had the constant attention of Dr. Fishbaugh and Blanche Williams, as well as regular visits from Powell. Medical bulletins detailed exactly what treatments she was receiving, and bedside prayer was not among them.

Shulman also hinted strongly that the alleged 1932 beating from Paul Bern damaged Jean's kidneys so badly that they failed five years later. This is medically impossible. Any beating that severe would have killed or crippled Jean outright, not left her perfectly healthy only to fell her five years later. Still, this story was given the seal of veracity by its appearance in print, and it promptly entered into legend.

Kidney disease was barely understood in 1937, and Dr. Fishbaugh's press releases were somewhat vague. His statement that the cause of death was a "cerebral odema" simply shows his shaky grasp of medicine. While a cerebral edema (swelling of the brain) is often a side effect of severe kidney disease, it is rarely if ever fatal in itself. What finally killed Jean was the failure of her major organs, the heart and respiratory system in particular.

The public loves a good rumor, and Jean's demise was no exception. Many people didn't even realize she'd been ill, so her sudden death gave rise to all sorts of wild speculation. To this day, many people in Great Britain believe Jean died of a botched abortion. Brain poisoning from hair dye was a popular theory, as were alcoholism, over-dieting, sunburn, and various venereal diseases.

Actress Evelyn Brent said in the 1970s that "ghastly stories . . . came out about Jean Harlow, that she drank herself to death or whatever." Brent herself felt that "it was sun poisoning, and she had been warned not to go into the sun." Film historian Homer Dickens solemnly wrote to a friend, "Jean died of syphillis of the eyes which can only be contracted one way: by blowing a man with syphillis!" But the constant medical bulletins, hospital reports, and interviews with friends point to a textbook case of kidney disease. No cover-up could account for symptoms well-documented as far back as the fall of 1936.

Jean's death was particularly shocking and saddening. She had represented youth and life. Garbo had died so often in films that her fans almost resented her rosy health; Marie Dressler's death had been heartbreaking but not unexpected. Fans felt they had lost more than a popular actress. Jean had been their kid sister, the girl down the block. "The passing of Jean Harlow," wrote one British editorialist, "means more emotionally to a multitude of readers than the death of President Roosevelt, or Stanley Baldwin, Adolph Hitler, or all the combined armies of reds and anti-reds."

In hindsight, friends and coworkers began recalling weird foreshadowings of doom. Clarence Sinclair Bull insisted that, after his last photo session with Jean, "she kissed me good-bye and said she would never be back again." Makeup artist Violet Denoyer told a reporter that "Jean looked at me strangely one morning—the same day she was taken ill. . . . 'You know, Violet,' she told me, 'I have a feeling I'm going away from here and never coming back.'" Her body barely cold, Jean was already entering Hollywood mythology.

Jean's remains were taken to Pierce Brothers Mortuary, where her hair was styled and face made up for the viewing. Mama Jean, in her few lucid moments, had finally agreed to this ritual in order to forestall rumors that The Baby was somehow disfigured in death. The white satin wedding gown from *Libeled Lady* was chosen for her last dress and her

Mont Clair and Maude Carpenter arrive in California for Jean's funeral, June 1937 (Bettmann/UPI).

body placed on a chaise in the Tennyson Room. A self-appointed honor guard of MGM grips and lighting assistants stood by Jean through the night, telling mortuary attendants that "The Baby didn't like to be alone in the dark."

On Wednesday, June 9, MGM closed its doors for Jean's funeral. At the Wee Kirk o' the Heather in Glendale, she lay in a silver and bronze coffin, looking "as though she were asleep. . . . She looked so natural it was frightening." Mama Jean had a last-minute change of mind regarding wardobe; Jean was now attired in a pink mousseline-de-soie negligée from *Saratoga.* In one hand was a white gardenia and a note reading, "Goodnight, my dearest darling," in William Powell's handwriting. Over $15,000 worth of flowers filled the small church, but it was Powell's single gardenia that stayed in the mind.

The church held only two hundred fifty mourners, but thousands of friends, coworkers, and hysterical fans crowded around the gates, pressing for entrance, plucking flowers from left-over bouquets, and snapping photographs. Mama Jean was half-carried in by the Beverly Hills police chief; a sobbing, nearly hysterical William Powell was assisted by his mother. Marino Bello, Mont Clair and Maude Carpenter, and Harold Rosson attended alongside such luminaries as Louis B. Mayer, a shaken Clark Gable and Carole Lombard (who was appalled at the crowds and asked Gable to spare *her* any such circus), the Marx Brothers, Carey and Carmelita Wilson, Billie Burke, Joan Crawford, Myrna Loy—more than enough to satisfy the morbid stargazers outside (fiery Mexican actress Lupe Velez was, embarrassingly, turned away at the door). Indeed, the event seemed to have been staged with publicity in mind. Many members of the Harlow and Carpenter families were pointedly *not* invited and bear a grudge to this day.

Jeanette MacDonald sang "Indian Love Call," Nelson Eddy followed with "Ah, Sweet Mystery of Life," and Genevieve Smith read a Christian Science eulogy. Jean's stand-in, Barbara Brown, was overcome and had to be led sobbing from the ceremony.

Jean's coffin was carried to a waiting hearse by Clark Gable, Eddie Mannix, Ray June, Hunt Stromberg, Jack Conway, and Woody Van Dyke. As soon as the coast was clear, crowds burst into the church and stripped bare the thousands of dollars' worth of floral offerings.

The following Saturday, Jean was interred at Forest Lawn Cemetery in Glendale. Visitors to Forest Lawn are directed reluctantly to the Great Mausoleum. Strolling past the Dolly Sisters, Gable and Lombard, Marie Dressler, and Theda Bara, one encounters the Jean Harlow Room, barred from the public by a gate, a guard, and a security camera. Jean rests in one of three drawers in a small room of multicolored marble, purchased by William Powell for $25,000. A reproduction of Jean's signature graces her silver name plate. The two other drawers were reserved for Mama Jean and Powell.

When Jean's will was probated later that summer, it became apparent that she'd learned little about money management in her final years. Despite her considerable salary, the estate totalled a mere $41,000. Landlady Harriett Breese sued for $10,000 worth of damages to the Palm Drive house, claiming that it was "frightfully dirty" and that the new locks had wrecked the doors. There was also the $400-a-month lease, which still had ten months to run.

Jean's will, written in September 1935, left her estate to Mama Jean. In the event of her mother's death, everything would go to her grandparents or cousin Donald Roberson. Neither Mont Clair Carpenter, William Powell, nor her ex-husbands were mentioned. Jean left very little property: three cars, some jewelry. "She did not have as much clothing as *I* have," explained Mama Jean.

Her friends were requested to rummage through the house and take away any memento they wished. Mont Clair chose a pair of Jean's shoes and her good-luck rabbit's foot; Kay Mulvey kept her friend's "dancing girl/piggie" charm bracelet. William Powell and Mama Jean divided up the remaining items. The fate of the enormous sapphire is a mystery.

MGM's schedule was disrupted by Jean's death; no star had ever had the temerity to die in the midst of a major production. In addition to deciding what to do with *Saratoga,* her next two films had to be swiftly recast. Fox had planned to borrow her for their romantic period drama *In Old Chicago,* costarring Tyrone Power and Don Ameche; in return, MGM

Clark Gable and Carole Lombard brave the photographers at Jean's funeral, June 9, 1937 (Bettmann/UPI).

would have gotten Shirley Temple for *The Wizard of Oz.* Jean's death caused the deal to fall through, and the two studios had to use homegrown players in these films—Judy Garland played Dorothy, and Alice Faye was Belle Fawcett. The careers of both gained from this arrangement, and Jean would have been ill at ease in the bustles and ruffles of nineteenth-century Chicago anyway. (The film was probably a test to see how she looked in period costume; like every other actress in Hollywood, Jean had been under consideration for the long-projected *Gone With the Wind.*)

The next shuffle was truly heartbreaking. Jean had been set to costar with Cary Grant and W. C. Fields in the classic comedy *Topper.* It would have been her biggest hit since *Libeled Lady,* a delightful screwball romp about two madcap ghosts (Jean and Grant) who reform their business partner (Fields, in a role eventually played by Roland Young) and his stuffy wife (the incomparable Billie Burke). Jean was replaced by Constance Bennett, who, while quite effective in the role, was a touch too arch and brittle. Jean would have brought a gleeful mischievousness to Marion Kerby that might have finally earned her an Oscar nomination.

The rest of Jean's planned films were filed away for possible future use: *Tell It to the Marines* (with Robert Taylor and Spencer Tracy), *The Best-Dressed Woman in Paris, Maiden Voyage, U.S. Smith,* and *The Four Marys. Maisie* was bumped to a low-budget production and given to contract player Ann Sothern.

But there was still the unfinished *Saratoga* to deal with. The situation was touchy, and Mayer was at a loss. When Clarine Seymour died during the filming of *Way Down East* (1920), her scenes were reshot with another actress. Mayer thought this was the best way to go and cast contract starlet Virginia Grey as Carol Clayton. In later years, numerous performers died in the midst of filming; the final productions of James Dean, Kay Kendall, Vic Morrow, Robert Walker, and Natalie Wood all managed to reach the screen posthumously. Low-budget director Edward Wood, Jr., wasn't discouraged one bit when Bela Lugosi died after filming some thirty seconds of the hilarious *Plan Nine from Outer Space.* He merely hired a "double" to hide behind a cape.

When Grey was announced as her replacement, Jean's fans and the press let out such a howl of indignation that Mayer realized he would somehow have to salvage her *Saratoga* footage. Jean had been about three-quarters through production when she took ill, and enough usable film existed to piece together the plot. Carol was written out of a few scenes by means of transparent excuses ("She's got a slight headache; she's staying in her room," "She's busy with our guests," "She knew *you* were here; she wouldn't come in") and her lines given to other characters. But there were five important scenes the character couldn't be written out of, and Mayer decided to use doubles to replace Jean in these. Auditions and screen tests were held for Harlow lookalikes. Geraldine Dvorak, whose nose and chin resembled Jean's, played several close-up scenes (with her back to the camera or her face hidden by hats or binoculars). Dancer Mary Dees, whose figure and coloring were right, doubled in long shots, wearing costumes previously designed for Jean. Paula Winslowe dubbed some sixteen lines, doing a very indifferent Harlow imitation. Dees was promptly offered vaudeville tours as Jean Harlow's Death Double, but had the taste and decency to turn them down.

Saratoga was rushed through filming and post-production, to open while Jean's death was still fresh in the public mind. On July 23 it premiered nationwide, the eeriest film experience up to its time. To this day, *Saratoga*'s faults and merits are forgotten as audiences crowd close

Saratoga *poster art (1937)*

▼

to the screen playing "spot the double" and looking eagerly for traces of the star's illness.

The *New York Times* noted that the film's complex plot had been made more confusing by the cut-and-paste production, "an unstable thing, a framework of cross-purposed motivation balanced on a mightily small point. . . . It was not, moreover, Miss Harlow's best work, judged by the standard she set for herself." The *Motion Picture Herald* was more sympathetic (or emotional): "Jean Harlow takes her final curtain call as the least boisterous and most attractive heroine of her career." *Time* amazingly thought *Saratoga* "Jean Harlow's best picture as well as her last."

All reviewers eulogized Jean, demurring slightly at having to criticize her performance. Marguerite Tazelaar in the *New York Herald Tribune* was saddened by the sight of the late star "striving gallantly to inject into her performance characteristic vigor and vibrancy. . . . Her few brief glimpses of natural brilliance as a comedienne . . . only seem to intensify the shadow hovering over her spirit and subduing it. *Saratoga* is, in a way, an obituary of a lovely person and a talented actress."

It is, indeed, impossible to view *Saratoga* with detachment. The film drags at points, but is buoyed by clever writing, a marvelous cast, and several effective scenes. Helping things along are a catchy sing-

Weeks after this unsettling scene from Saratoga *(with George Zucco), Jean was buried in this same negligée.*

along aboard a train, a cameo appearance by Margaret Hamilton, and a scene wherein Carol tries to disguise Duke's presence under her sofa by calmly puffing on his cigar as though she's smoked them all her life. Jean's deadpan comedy in this last bit was top-notch.

But some moments send a shudder up the spine. Lionel Barrymore (who goes through the film doing a terrible Lionel Barrymore imitation) strolls through a horse graveyard muttering sadly, "Every one of them champions." Carol's father dies in her arms of a heart attack. Carol's maid warns that her health will suffer, working so hard. And, most ironic, Duke tries to convince Carol that she's too ill to see her fiancé. A doctor (George Zucco) examines her earnestly as Carol fumes, "This is absolutely ridiculous, doctor, I *told* you there's nothing the matter with me!" To make things even worse, Jean is wearing the negligée in which she was buried weeks later.

As time passed, Jean Harlow faded from the public consciousness. MGM began promoting youngsters Judy Garland and Lana Turner, as well as new imports Greer Garson and Hedy Lamarr. Elsewhere in Hollywood, Rita Hayworth, Betty Grable, and Veronica Lake prepared to take the Sex Symbol into the war years. From time to time, Jean resurfaced, never completely out of view. A character in Tennessee Williams's *Camino Real* fantasizes about planting "Jean Harlow fields," to grow a crop of perfect women. Blues singer Leadbelly wrote "Harlow," a song that played upon the myth and mystery of Jean's death:

Send for the doctor, the doctor come
Mother says, "Doctor, can you save me one?"
Doctor says, "Well, I believe I will go,
Need me tomorrow, you can let me know"

A more commercial (and much sillier) tribute was published by songwriters Nat Simon and Dick Sanford, who had previously tried to eulogize Enrico Caruso, Will Rogers, and Rudolph Valentino. Their latest effort, "There's a Platinum Star in Heaven Tonight," never made the Hit Parade, but should have won some kind of bad-taste award:

There's a platinum star in heaven tonight
That is destined to shine on for years.
And this platinum star in heaven tonight
Smiles while the world is in tears.
Why did the angels take her away?
She was so young, so lovely and gay.
There's a platinum star with a heart made of gold,
And it's shining in heaven tonight.

Marino Bello managed to make a new life for himself without the support of his stepdaughter. Bello remarried and went into public relations (a field he was seemingly born for); he remained in the Los Angeles area, dying of cancer and heart disease in 1953.

Mont Clair Carpenter retired from dentistry in 1951 and moved to Joplin, Missouri, with his wife. He remained proud of his daughter and granted what few interviews were requested. Mama Jean had been so voluble over the years that not many people had even heard of Mont Clair. He spent his time reading and hiking, and considered writing a book—not about his famous daughter, but his Civil War veteran father ("If this goes over, then I might write about Harlean"). Mont Clair died at the age of ninety-six; the man who had been born the year after Custer's Last Stand lived until May 1, 1974.

Mama Jean found herself strapped for money after her daughter's estate was settled. On the advice of some very wily lawyers, she approached MGM and demanded some kind of remuneration for her "services" over the years. After a few months, Jean Bello was issued a seven-year contract at a salary of $137 a week as a "talent and literary scout and a reader." The job description was merely a smokescreen, as the terms of the contract plainly stated that she was not required to put in a single day's work. The contract "in effect constitutes an agreement to pay Mrs. Bello some $50,000 over the course of seven years without any assurance of receiving services therefore." In addition, MGM purchased the manuscript of *Today Is Tonight* from Mama Jean for $5,000. She claimed in this agreement to have written the book herself, although this was patently untrue.

Why would MGM agree to these things? Surely not out of the goodness of their hearts. This is the studio that threw John Gilbert to the dogs and ruined the careers of Mae Murray and William Haines without shedding a tear. The most probable explanation is that Mayer wanted to buy Mama Jean's silence. She could very well have gone to the press or even the courts charging that MGM had worked her Baby to death, maliciously and criminally. Of course, this wasn't true. Jean's illness was such that little short of a miracle could have saved her. But this wasn't known in 1937, and even if it had been, Mama Jean could have given the studio some very unfavorable and damaging publicity.

She diligently saved her salary, moving into a smaller house and relying on the kindness of friends. Many were willing to help her out for Jean's sake, so she never went hungry. After her parents died in the 1940s, Mama Jean moved to Palm Desert and ran an antique store, cluttered with mementos of her famous daughter. She succumbed to heart disease in the summer of 1958, dying in the same hospital that Jean had, and was buried in the crypt next to her daughter.

Mama Jean never really got over her Baby's death. In 1938 she wrote a rambling, heartbreaking article called "A Year without My Jean." "Some days are harder to bear than others, of course," she said. "One such day came to me five weeks ago . . . so bowed down beneath my sorrow that I felt I simply could not raise my head above it . . . *and she came to me.* She came to me and took me in her arms and just held me there. I can't say for how long. I just know that I felt such a sense of joyousness and brightness and light as had not been mine since she went away. . . . I have not lost, and will not lose, that sense of uplift she brought me with her own hands, when she held me in her arms."

When William Powell left the screen for a year following Jean's death, the romantically minded laid it to a broken heart. Actually, Powell was critically ill himself with rectal cancer. Such a diagnosis might have ended his career, though, so he let the "broken heart" theory pass. At that point, Powell needed all the public sympathy he could get. The whole world (thanks to Louella Parsons and her fellow gossips) knew that he had denied Jean the wedding she'd wanted for so long. Carole Lombard expressed the popular opinion when she wrote to Kay Mulvey, "I shall always consider Bill a friend, but even if I searched my mind from end to end I would not be able to understand why he did what he did to Jean."

His heart mended and guilt abated, Powell married starlet Diana "Mousey" Lewis in 1940, a marriage that lasted for life. Mousey delicately suggested that Powell stop placing weekly flowers at Jean's tomb, and steered any interviews away from the subject of her late rival. Jean's ghost was not welcome in their new home. Powell recovered from his bout with cancer, and his career continued successfully for decades, with hits such as *Life with Father* (1947) and *Mr. Roberts* (1955). He and Mousey retired to Palm Springs for a life of "solitude and quiet and a few sincere friends." After his death at the age of ninety-one in 1984, Mrs. Powell handled the funeral arrangements. The third crypt in the Jean Harlow Room at Forest Lawn remains empty, and probably will for all time.

Over the years, several abortive attempts were made to film Jean's life: Marilyn Monroe, Jayne Mansfield, and Natalie Wood were considered for such projects in the 1950s, but nothing ever came of them ("I am the perfect Harlow," squealed Jayne. "But no, they can't see me playing the dramatic side of Harlow's life"). Jean was remembered fondly, and whenever a star died young, her name was invoked as a sad precedent. Her films played on television and in the occasional revival house, and Jean Harlow remained a happy, warm memory for decades. It wasn't until the 1960s that ex-novelist Irving Shulman and Jean's ex-agent dragged her name through the mud.

When the first film-star biographies began appearing, the often still-living subjects were depicted as angels descended from the heavens. All traces of temperament, scandal, and career reversal vanished, to be replaced by glowing quotes from press releases, dear friends, and fan magazines. The stars emerged as sweet, noble, and virtuous mannequins, less believable and interesting than their worst film roles.

Today, the trend has reversed with a fury. Joan Crawford becomes a child abuser, Errol Flynn a Nazi spy, John Lennon a psychopath, and Marilyn Monroe is variously murdered by the Kennedys, the FBI, and/or the Mafia. This trend in biography began in 1964, when a minor novelist named Irving Shulman published an unprecedented character assassination of Jean Harlow.

Shulman had the luck to meet up with Arthur Landau. The aging agent was in severe debt, plagued by medical expenses, and had been trying to peddle the life story of his famous ex-client. The two men teamed up and sold an idea to Bernard Geis Associates for $20,000. The result, published in the summer of 1964, was an astonishing "intimate biography" (Shulman's own term) consisting of page after page of factual errors and shameless lies. The book became an instant best-seller on the strength of its frequent use of obscenity and explicit sexual scenes. It also did mortal damage to the reputation of Jean Harlow.

Shulman claimed to have consulted Landau, who was "much closer to Jean than any member of her family," and many unnamed sources. Reading the book, one wonders if he actually did any research at all, it is so crammed with wild inaccuracies. Shulman's grasp of simple facts such as Jean's real name ("Carpentier" in his book), birthplace (Kansas instead of Missouri), ancestry, childhood (entirely eliminating her early years in Los Angeles), and living quarters is shaky, to say the least. He completely misstates the circumstances of her adolescence and first marriage. According to Shulman, she and McGrew never lived together; with a stroke of the pen he wipes out a four-year marriage. Shulman has Jean and Robert Taylor attending Roosevelt's Birthday Ball in 1933 (when Taylor was not even employed at MGM), and his comments on Jean's film roles suggest that he'd not even seen her on-screen. He has her doing the Charleston in *The Saturday Night Kid,* wearing a black lace negligée in *Hell's Angels,* and doing her own singing and dancing in *Reckless.* But lack of research was the least of this biographer's sins.

With Landau's permission, Shulman turned Jean Harlow into a talentless, foulmouthed tramp; Mama Jean an evil, brainless religious fanatic; and Paul Bern a violent sadist. The author's views on Hollywood and its stars were quite clear. "The book represents all the accumulated garbage that makes up the Hollywood myth, the Hollywood legend," he told reporter Ann Marsters. "Oh, how they cling to the fiction that tries to make princes and princesses of their wonderful, glittering people!" As if his hatred for film stars were not already apparent, Shulman declares on the very first page of his book that "actors and actresses were mimes, walking conceits with enormous egos inflated to smother deeply rooted acid doubts of their ability." It is as if Shulman were looking for a victim, and the conveniently dead Jean got in the way.

He scripted ludicrous, stilted, and obscene dialogue for his characters, ingenuously invoking Lytton Strachey's theory of fictionalized biography. "The line between biographical fiction and fictional biography is very fine indeed," Shulman said on the "Today" show. Fine indeed. Shulman succeeded in erasing it entirely, generating stories that, once in print, were implicitly believed by those too young to remember Jean Harlow. Despite documentary evidence to the contrary, these stories have entered into legend and are quoted and requoted until they have become accepted as fact. Film historians, biographers, and writers of documentaries refer to Shulman's book as a source, and the stories are repeated until they acquire the appearance of truth. Yet they are all easily disproven.

Shulman has Jean willfully hacking off her hair after Paul Bern's death, in a rage of rebellion; according to the book, she wore wigs for the rest of her life. This is denied by Jean's stand-in Barbara Brown, who insists that she wore wigs in only three films, and then only to protect her hair from constant setting. A careful examination of her films and candid snapshots reveals what is obviously Jean's own, healthy hair.

Nor did Shulman ever explain why the hair failed to grow back after its 1932 trimming; no one's hair takes five years to grow five inches.

He quotes violent, constant quarrels between Jean and her mother, depicting them as shrieking enemies. Apparently nothing could have been further from the truth. "There was a great and sincere love between Jean and her mother," insisted Kay Mulvey. Howard Strickling added, "Jean loved her mother so much, I believe she would have committed murder for her." Shulman had Jean engaging in sex orgies; he gave her a drug and alcohol habit that would shock today's public. Her friends asserted that Jean was, if anything, undersexed, never used drugs, and rarely touched liquor. "Anyone who thinks it [Shulman's biography] tells the truth about Jean Harlow is being taken in," snapped Robert Taylor. "I don't understand how anyone could do something like this to such a warm, generous human being."

The two stories that gained greatest circulation concerned the Bern marriage and Jean's death. Shulman lingered ghoulishly over Bern's alleged impotence, depicting him as a psychologically disturbed sadist; the author entered the bedroom and imagined all sorts of pornographic high jinks. Never once does Shulman cite his sources, and even Landau himself disclaimed many of the stories. Jean's own death, already clouded by rumor, was further mythologized in Shulman's book.

Reviews of the biography were universally negative: *Variety* recognized sadly that "the book will sell, but it will also sicken." *Newsweek* called it a "protracted effusion of speculative gossip . . . a standard by which to measure shoddiness," and Hedda Hopper deemed it "a cruel, sordid book catering solely to sensationalism." *Newsweek* summed up literary opinion of the author by suggesting that readers "tiptoe into a bookstore where the security is weak, tear out the illustrations and run like hell."

The press reaction was nothing compared to that of Jean's friends. Maureen O'Sullivan, Kay Mulvey, and Adela Rogers St. Johns cornered Shulman on a segment of the "Today" show, challenging him to verify facts and name sources. He could not or would not. St. Johns crowed, "Mr. Landau knew that *I* knew the truth. He wouldn't dare to tell me the junk that's in this book!" William Powell sighed, "Thank God Jean herself cannot be hurt at all. She is sleeping very peacefully in Forest Lawn Cemetery. But the living who loved her are suffering, and it is deplorable that any writer would do this just to make a fast buck." Joan Crawford, in a rare moment of clairvoyance, fumed, "There must be some way you can write your will . . . to leave your life story to someone to protect your reputation from exploitation."

The level of Shulman's research became apparent when Mont Clair Carpenter filed a $3 million libel suit; Shulman had no idea Carpenter was still alive. Marino Bello's widow also filed suit, but libel laws hold that one cannot sue on behalf of a third party. "The dead are fair game," the judge admitted.

Arthur Landau himself, in a sudden attack of conscience, publicly disavowed the work. "I thought I would die. . . . I had no idea the book was to be written in that kind of language. . . . I saw [Shulman] only four times in three years. . . . he sent me lists of questions and I sent him the answers." Landau, however, did not return the money he'd made. In Shulman's book, Landau was depicted as Jean's guardian angel, guiding her career and private life till the day of her death. Jean is even said to have owed Landau some $30,000. This conveniently ignores the fact that Landau was fired in 1932 (the Orsatti Agency is never once mentioned), and that his assistance during her early career was negligible. Jean's only contact with him after 1932 consisted of polite postcards and frequent loans of money to the failing businessman. "The only agents we ever saw were the Orsatti brothers," asserted Howard Strickling. "The only time I ever saw Landau at Metro was recently, when I told him he was a filthy liar, and to get out, or I'd throw him out."

The only positive result of the book was a renewed interest in Jean Harlow, dead for nearly a generation. The long-planned biographies were finally filmed, although they were too awful even to be funny. The 1981 Joan Crawford biopic *Mommie Dearest* was hilarious enough to become an instant camp classic ("NO WIRE HANGERS!"), but the two *Harlows* of 1965 rarely turn up even on late-night television.

The first-released was a cheap "Electronovision" film made by the low-budget Magna Pictures. It was rushed through production to beat its rival to theaters in the spring of 1965. The film starred Carol Lynley as Jean, Ginger Rogers as her mother, and the evil-looking Hurd Hatfield as Paul Bern. While not based directly on the Shulman book, this film repeated so many nonsensical legends that it ultimately bore no resemblance to the truth. It was so shoddily made and badly acted (with the exception of Rogers, in her last film role to date), that it promptly died at the box office. "The cheap, lustreless and excruciatingly dull picture spares the late actress—and the audience—nothing," said the *New York Times*.

Harlow II, a high-budget Paramount film, was released some two months later. Starring Carroll Baker as Jean, Angela Lansbury as Mama Jean, comic Red Buttons as Landau, and the inappropriately handsome Peter Lawford as Paul Bern, this second effort also flopped. Based directly on the Shulman book, it showed no interest in the truth. "We will go as far as we can and stay out of jail," one producer was quoted. With the exception of its Mama Jean (played excellently by Angela Lansbury, who bore a frightening resemblence to her character), the acting was embarrassing, as was the plot. The finale had Jean collapsing on the beach in an alcoholic daze and dying of pneumonia. "More bomb than bombshell," summed up the *New York Herald Tribune*. "Hollywood has again succeeded in reducing one of its few fascinating realities to the sleazy turgid level of its more sordid fictions."

But although Jean's reputation was tarnished, her star has continued to burn brightly to the present day. She has become an icon in American pop culture. When MGM auctioned off its costume collection in 1969, fashion discovered the "retro" look. California hippies paraded around in Adrian's satin gowns and negligées, and soon Seventh Avenue caught on. By the early 1970s, the thirties look was running rampant, and wanna-be Jean Harlows with plucked brows, blondined hair, and bias-cut dresses were seen in every city. A Jean Harlow Ball was *the* social event of the mid-1960s in Manhattan. Jean turned up in the early Andy Warhol film *Harlot* and the Michael McClure play *The Beard* (also filmed by Warhol). She was imitated by actresses Mary Vivian Pearce (*Pink Flamingos* and *Multiple Maniacs*) and Lesley Anne Warren (*Victor/Victoria*) among others. Jean's image is still popular on posters and greeting cards. A chain of Harlow & Bogart hair salons opened in Maryland. Self-named Philadelphian Rachel Harlow opened a successful nightclub and restaurant.

Jean's face continues to appear in advertisements, including recent Max Factor and Swan's Matches campaigns. She shared a French postage stamp with Marilyn Monroe, commemorating the film industry. A West Coast "Harlow" resort is advertised in gay publications. One of her famous Hurrell photos decorates the set of the popular TV show "Night Court." She's cropped up in several rock songs: Kim Carnes's "Bette Davis Eyes" and Madonna's "Vogue" pay tribute to her. And, most happily, Jean Harlow's films continue to be seen regularly in revival houses and television, particularly cable. A new generation is discovering Jean, people too young to have read the Shulman book. The president of the current Jean Harlow fan club is twenty-one years old, carrying the platinum blonde's popularity well into the twenty-first century, and beyond.

Recent ad for Swan matches

EPILOGUE

Costume still from Saratoga *(1937)*

▼

What turns would Jean's career have taken if she'd lived? Her terribly early death lends the "what-if" game endless possibilities. Her contemporaries, also born in 1911, give some indication of her unfulfilled potential. Lucille Ball, Ronald Reagan, Robert Taylor, Vincent Price, Margaret Sullivan, Ginger Rogers, Merle Oberon, and Paulette Goddard all had many productive decades ahead of them.

Jean Harlow would have been in her early thirties when World War II erupted, a shade too old (by Hollywood standards) to parade about in bathing suits à la Grable, but still young enough to provide moral support in the Hollywood Canteen and over the Voice of America. The 1950s would have been a dangerous point in Jean's career, but she might have charged gamely into the new medium of television. While the success of a Lucille Ball or Loretta Young might have eluded her, with luck, Jean could have coasted easily into middle age.

Jean would have turned eighty in 1991. One would like to think she'd enter old age with the grace and elegance of Myrna Loy or Alice Faye, although there's every possibility that she might have hardened into a lacquered caricature of herself, a beautiful ruin like Mae West or Tallulah Bankhead. Jean never got the chance. Frozen at the age of twenty-six, she remains a creature of her time, a permanent resident of the 1930s, the "tragic sex symbol" of legend.

Hollywood has always been rather broad in its definition of tragedy. The dictionary defines it as "a conflict between the protagonist and a superior force (such as destiny) and having a sorrowful or disastrous conclusion that excites pity or terror." By this definition, the overwhelming forces that hastened the unhappy ends of Judy Garland, Marilyn Monroe, and Rock Hudson qualify as tragic. The shattered careers of D. W. Griffith, Mabel Normand, and John Gilbert can also be considered genuine tragedies. But not Jean Harlow.

It's impossible to say how Jean herself would react to being called tragic, but her friends and coworkers have affectionately derided the thought. "She was just like a great big overgrown happy kid," recalls George Hurrell. Louella Parsons said of Jean, "It wasn't a part of her make-up ever to show discouragement, or to let the world see her down in the mouth. . . . Even during those last weeks when she was so much sicker than anyone dreamed, she laughed and joked and refused to complain." "She was Jake," remembers MGM publicity man Ralph Wheelwright. "I don't know quite where the name Jake came from, but I reserved it for girls I particularly liked—Mabel Normand and Marion Davies, for instance. Garbo, much as I admired—and admire—her, could never be a Jake. . . . Maybe you can see the difference." Robert Taylor recalled her as a "kind and amusing child," and Maureen O'Sullivan said, "There wasn't anyone at MGM who didn't love her, and wasn't amused by her, and didn't think her an absolute darling."

Jean Harlow was a young woman with a great deal of healthy perspective on her life. She rebounded superbly from adversity; indeed, her eternal optimism was such that she was engaged, for a fourth time, when she died.

Jean's life was a short one, but happier and more eventful than most. She is one of the few top stars who inspired such genuine devotion and affection that not one of her intimates has sought personal notoriety by blackening her name; indeed, they came rushing out by the score to defend her. An early death does not qualify one as tragic, not if one has lived life to the fullest and given and received a good deal of enjoyment. Jean Harlow's life, like the Tin Man's heart, should be judged not by how much she loved, but by how much she was loved by others.

British fan magazine, 1937

FILMOGRAPHY

MORAN OF THE MARINES
Paramount, 1928
Crew
DIRECTOR: Frank Stayer; STORY: Linton Wells; SCREENPLAY: Agnes Brand Leahy; SCENARIO: Sam Mintz and Ray Harris; TITLES: George Marion; CAMERA: Edward Cronjager; EDITOR: Otto Levering
Cast
Richard Dix, Ruth Elder, Roscoe Karns, Brooks Benedict, E. H. Calvert, Duke Martin, Tetsu Komai, Jean Harlow (unbilled extra)

FUGITIVES
Fox, 1928
Crew
PRODUCER AND DIRECTOR: William Beaudine; SCENARIO: John Stone; SUPERVISOR: Kenneth Hawks; STORY: Richard Harding Davis; TITLES: Malcolm Stuart Boylan; ASSISTANT DIRECTOR: Thomas Held; CAMERA: Chester Lyons
Cast
Madge Bellamy, Don Terry, Arthur Stone, Earle Fox, Matthew Betz, Lumsden Hare, Edith Yorke, Jean Laverty, Hap Ward, Jean Harlow (unbilled extra)

WEAK BUT WILLING
Al Christie Production, 1929 (other specifics unknown)

THIS THING CALLED LOVE
Pathé, 1929
Crew
ASSOCIATE PRODUCER: Ralph Block; DIRECTOR: Paul Stein; STORY: Edwin Burke; SCREENPLAY: Horace Jackson; CAMERA: Norbert Brodine
Cast
Edmund Lowe, Constance Bennett, Roscoe Karns, Zazu Pitts, Carmelita Geraughty, John Roche, Stuart Erwin, Ruth Taylor, Wilson Benge, Adele Watson, Jean Harlow (unbilled extra)

CLOSE HARMONY
Paramount, 1929
Crew
DIRECTORS: John Cromwell and Edward Sutherland; STORY: Elsie Janis and Gene Markey; ADAPTOR: Percy Heath; DIALOGUE: John V. A. Weaver; SONGS: Richard A. Whiting and Leo Robin; SOUND: Franklin Hansen; CAMERA: Roy Hunt; EDITOR: Tay Malarkey
Cast
Charles "Buddy" Rogers, Nancy Carroll, Harry Green, Jack Oakie, Richard "Skeets" Gallagher, Matty Roubert, Ricca Allen, Wade Boteler, Baby Mack, Oscar Smith, Greta Granstedt, Gus Partos, Jessie Stafford and His Orchestra, Jean Harlow (unbilled extra)

THE UNKISSED MAN
Hal Roach All-Star Series, 1929
Crew
DIRECTOR: Hal Roach; EDITOR: Richard Currier; TITLES: H. M. Walker; CAMERA: John McBurnie
Cast
Bryant Washburn, Jean Harlow

WHY IS A PLUMBER?
Hal Roach All-Star Series, 1929
Crew
DIRECTOR: Hal Roach; EDITOR: Richard Currier; TITLES: H. M. Walker; CAMERA: John McBurnie
Cast
Edgar Kennedy, Jean Harlow, Albert Conti, Eddie Dunn, Gertrude Sutton

THUNDERING TOUPEES
Hal Roach All-Star Series, 1929
Crew
DIRECTOR: Hal Roach; EDITOR: Richard Currier; TITLES: H. M. Walker; CAMERA: John McBurnie
Cast
Edgar Kennedy, Vivien Oakland, Jean Harlow, Eddie Dunn, Mickey Daniels

LIBERTY
Hal Roach Studios, released January 1929
Crew
DIRECTOR: Leo McCarey; TITLES: H. M. Walker; STORY: Leo McCarey
Cast
Stan Laurel, Oliver Hardy, James Finlayson, Tom Kennedy, Harry Bernard, Jean Harlow

DOUBLE WHOOPEE
Hal Roach Studios, released May 1929
Crew
DIRECTOR: Lewis R. Foster; STORY: Leo McCarey; TITLES: H. M. Walker
Cast
Stan Laurel, Oliver Hardy, Charlie Hall, Ham Kinsey, Stanley "Tiny" Sandford, Jean Harlow

BACON GRABBERS
Hal Roach Studios, released October 1929
Crew
Director: Lewis R. Foster; Story: Leo McCarey; Titles: H. M. Walker
Cast
Stan Laurel, Oliver Hardy, Edgar Kennedy, Charlie Hall, Jean Harlow, Buddy the Dog

THE LOVE PARADE
Paramount, 1929
Crew
Director: Ernst Lubistch; Story: Leon Xanrof, Jules Chancel, and Ernst Vajda; Libretto: Guy Bolton; Dialogue Director: Percy Ivins; Art Director: Hans Dreier; Songs: Victor Schertzinger and Clifford Grey; Sound: Franklin Hansen; Camera: Victor Milner; Editor: Merrill White
Cast
Maurice Chevalier, Jeannette MacDonald, Lupino Lane, Lillian Roth, Edgar Norton, Lionel Belmore, Albert Roccardi, Carlton Stockdale, Eugene Pallette, Russell Powell, E. H. Calvert, Andre Cheron, Yola D'Avril, Winter Hall, Ben Turpin, Anton Vaverka, Albert De Winton, William von Hardenburg, Margaret Fealy, Virginia Bruce, Josephine Hall, Rosalind Charles, Helene Friend, Jean Harlow (unbilled extra)

NEW YORK NIGHTS
United Artists, 1929
Crew
Producer: Joseph M. Schenck; Director: Lewis Milestone; Supervisor: John W. Considine, Jr.; Story: Hugh Stanislaus Stange; Adaptor: Jules Furthman; Song: Al Jolson, Ballard MacDonald, and Dave Dryer; Sound: Oscar Lagerstrom; Camera: Ray June; Editor: Hal Kern
Cast
Norma Talmadge, Gilbert Roland, John Wray, Lilyan Tashman, Mary Doran, Roscoe Karns, Landers Stevens, Stanley Fields, Jean Harlow (unbilled extra)

THE SATURDAY NIGHT KID
Paramount, released October 1929
Crew
Director: Edward Sutherland; Story: George Abbott and John V. A. Weaver; Screenplay: Ethel Doherty; Dialogue: Lloyd Corrigan and Edward E. Paramore, Jr.; Titles: Joseph L. Mankiewicz; Adaptor: Lloyd Corrigan; Camera: Harry Fischbeck; Editor: Jane Loring
Cast
Clara Bow, James Hall, Jean Arthur, Charles Sellon, Ethel Wales, Frank Ross, Edna May Oliver, Hyman Meyer, Eddie Dunn, Leone Lane, Jean Harlow, Getty Bird, Alice Adair, Irving Bacon, Mary Gordon, Ernie S. Adams

HELL'S ANGELS

United Artists/The Caddo Company, Inc., released November 15, 1930

Crew

PRODUCER AND DIRECTOR: Howard Hughes; STORY: Marshall Nielan and Joseph Moncure March; SCREENPLAY: Harry Behn and Howard Estabrook; DIALOGUE: Joseph Moncure March; DIALOGUE DIRECTOR: James Whale; ART DIRECTORS: Julian Booth Fleming and Carroll Clark; MUSIC: Hugo Riesenfeld; ASSISTANT DIRECTORS: Reginald Callow, William J. Scully, and Frederick Fleck; CAMERA: Gaetano Gaudio, E. Burton Steene, Harry Perry, Elmer Dyer, and Zech and Dewey Wrigley; EDITORS: Douglass Biggs, Perry Hollingsworth, and Frank Lawrence

Cast

MONTE RUTLEDGE: Ben Lyon; ROY RUTLEDGE: James Hall; HELEN: Jean Harlow; KARL ARNSTEDT: John Darrow; BARON VON KRANTZ: Lucien Prival; LT. VON BRUEN: Frank Clark; BALDY: Roy Wilson; CAPTAIN REDFIELD: Douglas Gilmore; BARONESS VON KRANTZ: Jane Winton; LADY RANDOLPH: Evelyn Hall; STAFF MAJOR: William B. Davidson; RFC SQUADRON COMMANDER: Wyndham Standing; GRETCHEN: Lena Malena; ZEPPELIN COMMANDER: Carl von Haartmann; ELLIOTT: Stephen Carr; VON SCHIEBEN: Hans Jobuy; MARRYAT: Pat Somerset; KISS BOOTH GIRL: Marian Marsh; ZEPPELIN OFFICER: F. Schumann-Heink; VON RICHTHOFEN: William von Brincken

THE SECRET SIX

Metro-Goldwyn-Mayer, released April 18, 1931

Crew

DIRECTOR: George Hill; STORY AND SCREENPLAY: Frances Marion; WARDROBE: Rene Hubert; SOUND: Robert Shirley; CAMERA: Harold Wenstrom; EDITOR: Blanche Sewell

Cast

LOUIS SCORPIO: Wallace Beery; RICHARD NEWTON: Lewis Stone; HANK ROGERS: John Mack Brown; ANNE COURTLAND: Jean Harlow; PEACHES: Marjorie Rambeau; NICK MIZOSKI: Paul Hurst; CARL LUCKNER: Clark Gable; JOHNNY FRANKS: Ralph Bellamy; SMILING JOE COLIMO: John Miljan; CHIEF DONLIN: DeWitt Jennings; DUMMY METZ: Murray Kinnell; JIMMY DELANO: Fletcher Norton; EDDIE: Louis Natheaux; JUDGE: Frank McGlynn; DISTRICT ATTORNEY: Theodore von Eltz; HOOD: Tom London

IRON MAN

Universal Pictures Corporation, released April 30, 1931

Crew

PRODUCER: Carl Laemmle, Jr.; ASSOCIATE PRODUCER: E. M. Asher; DIRECTOR: Tod Browning; STORY: W. R. Burnett; SCREENPLAY: Francis Edwards Faragoh; ART DIRECTOR: Charles D. Hall; SOUND: C. Roy Hunter; CAMERA: Percy Hilburn; SUPERVISING EDITOR: Maurice Pivar; EDITOR: Milton Carruth

Cast

KID MASON: Lew Ayres; GEORGE REGAN: Robert Armstrong; ROSE MASON: Jean Harlow; PAUL H. LEWIS: John Miljan; JEFF: Eddie Dillon; MCNEIL: Mike Donlin; RATTLER O'KEEFE: Morris Cohan; ROSE'S FRIEND: Mary Doran; GLADYS DEVERE: Mildred Van Dorn; RILEY: Ned Sparks; MANDL: Sam Blum; TRAINER: Sammy Gervon; BARTENDER: Tom Kennedy; REFEREE: Bob Perry; REPORTER: Wade Boteler; LOUISE LEWIS: Claire Whitney

THE PUBLIC ENEMY

Warner Bros., released May 15, 1931

Crew

DIRECTOR: William A. Wellman; STORY: John Bright and Kubec Glasmon; SCREENPLAY: Harvey Thew; ART DIRECTOR: Max Parker; MUSIC DIRECTOR: David Mendoza; COSTUMES: Earl Luick; MAKEUP: Perc Westmore; CAMERA: Dev Jennings; EDITOR: Ed McCormick

Cast

TOM POWERS: James Cagney; GWEN ALLEN: Jean Harlow; MATT DOYLE: Edward Woods; MAMIE: Joan Blondell; MA POWERS: Beryl Mercer; MIKE POWERS: Donald Cook; KITTY: Mae Clarke; JANE: Mia Marvin; NAILS NATHAN: Leslie Fenton; PADDY RYAN: Robert Emmett O'Connor; PUTTY NOSE: Murray Kinnell; BUGS MORAN: Ben Hendricks, Jr.; MOLLY DOYLE: Rita Flynn; DUTCH: Clark Burroughs; HACK: Snitz Edwards; MRS. DOYLE: Adela Watson; YOUNG TOMMY: Frank Coghlan, Jr.; YOUNG MATT: Frankie Darrow; OFFICER BURKE: Robert E. Homans; NAILS'S GIRL: Dorothy Gee; BARTENDER: Lee Phelps; LITTLE GIRLS: Helen Parrish, Dorothy Gray, and Nanci Price; YOUNG BUGS: Ben Hendricks III; HIT MAN: George Daly; WHITE HEADWAITER: Eddie Kane; MUG: Charles Sullivan; ASSISTANT TAILOR: Douglas Gerrard; BLACK HEADWAITER: Sam McDaniel; PAWNBROKER: William H. Strauss; DOCTOR: Landers Stevens; POOLROOM HABITUE: Bob Reeves

GOLDIE

Fox, released June 28, 1931

Crew

DIRECTOR: Benjamin Stoloff; SCREENPLAY: Gene Towne and Paul Perez; CAMERA: Ernest Palmer; WARDROBE: Dolly Tree; EDITOR: Alex Troffey; STORY: Howard Hawks and James Kevin McGuiness

Cast

BILL: Spencer Tracy; SPIKE: Warren Hymer; GOLDIE: Jean Harlow; GONZALES: Jess DeVorska; WIFE: Leila Karnelly; HUSBAND: Ivan Linow; CONSTANTINA: Lina Basquette; RUSSIAN GIRL: Eleanor Hunt; DOLORES: Maria Alba; BARKER: Eddie Kane; PICKPOCKET: George Raft

PLATINUM BLONDE

Columbia, released October 31, 1931

Crew

PRODUCER: Harry Cohn; DIRECTOR: Frank Capra; STORY: Harry E. Chandler and Douglas W. Churchill; ADAPTOR: Jo Swerling; CONTINUITY: Dorothy Howell; DIALOGUE: Robert Riskin; CAMERA: Joseph Walker; EDITOR: Gene Milford

Cast

GALLAGHER: Loretta Young; STEW SMITH: Robert Williams; ANNE SCHUYLER: Jean Harlow; MRS. SCHUYLER: Louise Closser Hale; MICHAEL SCHUYLER: Donald Dillaway; DEXTER GRAYSON: Reginald Owen; BING BAKER: Walter Catlett; CONROY: Edmund Breese; SMYTHE: Halliwell Hobbes; VIOLINIST: Claud Allister; DINNER GUEST: Bill Elliott; WAITER: Harry Semels; RADCLIFFE: Olaf Hytten; REPORTERS: Tom London, Hal Price, Eddy Chandler, and Charles Jordan; SPEAKEASY PROPRIETOR: Dick Cramer; BUTLER: Wilson Benge

THREE WISE GIRLS

Columbia, released January 11, 1932

Crew

DIRECTOR: William Beaudine; STORY: Wilson Collison; ADAPTOR: Agnes C. Johnson; DIALOGUE: Robert Riskin; CAMERA: Ted Tetzlaff; EDITOR: Jack Dennis

Cast

CASSIE BARNES: Jean Harlow; GLADYS KANE: Mae Clarke; JERRY DEXTER: Walter Byron; DOT: Marie Prevost; DEXTER'S CHAUFFEUR: Andy Devine; RUTH DEXTER: Natalie Moorehead; ARTHUR PHELPS: Jameson Thomas; MRS. BARNES: Lucy Beaumont; MRS. KANE: Katherine C. Ward; LEM: Robert Dudley; LANDLADY: Marica Harris; STORE MANAGER: Walter Miller; ANDRE: Armand Kaliz

THE BEAST OF THE CITY

Metro-Goldwyn-Mayer (A Cosmopolitan Production), released February 13, 1932

Crew

DIRECTOR: Charles Brabin; STORY: W. R. Burnett; SCREENPLAY: John Lee Mahin; CAMERA: Norbert Brodine; EDITOR: Anne Bauchens; RECORDING DIRECTOR: Douglas Shearer; ART DIRECTOR: Cedric Gibbons

Cast

JIM FITZPATRICK: Walter Huston; DAISY STEVENS: Jean Harlow; EDWARD FITZPATRICK: Wallace Ford; SAM BELMONTE: Jean Hersholt; MARY FITZPATRICK: Dorothy Peterson; MICHAELS: Tully Marshall; DISTRICT ATTORNEY: John Miljan; CHIEF OF POLICE: Emmett Corrigan; TOM: Warner Richmond; MAC: Sandy Roth; CHOLO: J. Carroll Naish; FINGERPRINT EXPERT: Edward Coppo; REPORTER: George Chandler; ABE GORMAN: Nat Pendleton; WITNESS: Arthur Hoyt; BLONDE: Julie Haydon; CORONER: Clarence Wilson; COP IN HALL: Charles Sullivan; POLICE CAPTAIN: Morgan Wallace; MICKEY FITZPATRICK: Mickey Rooney

RED-HEADED WOMAN

Metro-Goldwyn-Mayer, released June 25, 1932

Crew

PRODUCER: Paul Bern; ASSOCIATE PRODUCER: Al Lewin; DIRECTOR: Jack Conway; STORY: Katherine Brush; SCREENPLAY: Anita Loos; CAMERA: Harold G. Rosson; EDITOR: Blanche Sewell; WARDROBE: Adrian

Cast

LIL ANDREWS: Jean Harlow; BILL LEGENDRE: Chester Morris; WILLIAM LEGENDRE, SR.: Lewis Stone; IRENE LEGENDRE: Leila Hyams; SALLY: Una Merkel; GAERSATE: Henry Stephenson; AUNT JANE: May Robson; ALBERT THE CHAUFFEUR: Charles Boyer; UNCLE FRED: Harvey Clark

RED DUST

Metro-Goldwyn-Mayer, released October 22, 1932

Crew

PRODUCER AND DIRECTOR: Victor Fleming; STORY: Wilson Collison; SCREENPLAY: John Lee Mahin; CAMERA: Harold G. Rosson; WARDROBE: Adrian; EDITOR: Blanche Sewell

Cast

DENNIS CARSON: Clark Gable; VANTINE: Jean Harlow; GARY WILLIS: Gene Raymond; BARBARA WILLIS: Mary Astor; GUIDON: Donald Crisp; MCQUARG: Tully Marshall; LIMEY: Forrester Harvey; HOY: Willie Fung

HOLD YOUR MAN

Metro-Goldwyn-Mayer, released July 1, 1933

Crew

Producer and Director: Sam Wood; Story: Anita Loos; Screenplay: Anita Loos and Howard Emmett Rogers; Title Song: Arthur Freed and Nacio Herb Brown; Art Directors: Cedric Gibbons and Merrill Pye; Wardrobe: Adrian; Set Director: Edwin B. Willis; Camera: Harold G. Rosson; Editor: Frank Sullivan; Recording Director: Douglas Shearer

Cast

Ruby Adams: Jean Harlow; Eddie Hall: Clark Gable; Al Simpson: Stuart Erwin; Gypsy: Dorothy Burgess; Slim: Garry Owen; Bertha Dillon: Muriel Kirkland; Sadie Kline: Barbara Barondess; Aubrey Mitchell: Paul Hurst; Miss Tuttle: Elizabeth Patterson; Lily Mae Crippen: Theresa Harris; Maizie: Inez Courtney; Mrs. Wagner: Blanche Frederici; Miss Davis: Helen Freeman; Reverend Crippen: George Reed; Washroom Attendant: Louise Beavers; Cops: Jack Cheatham and Frank Hagney; Dancer: Jack Randall; Phil Dunn: G. Pat Collins; Neighbor: Harry Semels; Sewing Teacher: Nora Cecil; Cooking Teacher: Eva McKenzie

DINNER AT EIGHT

Metro-Goldwyn-Mayer, released August 25, 1933

Crew

Producer: David O. Selznick; Director: George Cukor; Story: George S. Kaufman and Edna Ferber; Screenplay: Frances Marion and Herman J. Mankiewicz; Additional Dialogue: Donald Ogden Stewart; Art Directors: Hobe Erwin and Fred Hope; Wardrobe: Adrian; Camera: William Daniels; Editor: Ben Lewis; Musical Score: Dr. William Axt; Recording Director: Douglas Shearer

Cast

Carlotta Vance: Marie Dressler; Larry Renault: John Barrymore; Dan Packard: Wallace Beery; Kitty Packard: Jean Harlow; Oliver Jordan: Lionel Barrymore; Max Kane: Lee Tracy; Dr. Wayne Talbot: Edmund Lowe; Millicent Jordan: Billie Burke; Paula Jordan: Madge Evans; Jo Stengel: Jean Hersholt; Lucy Talbot: Karen Morley; Hattie Loomis: Louise Closser Hale; Ernest Degraff: Phillips Holmes; Mrs. Wendel: May Robson; Ed Loomis: Grant Mitchell; Miss Alden: Phoebe Foster; Miss Copeland: Elizabeth Patterson; Tina: Hilda Vaughn; Fosdick: Harry Beresford; Hotel Manager: Edwin Maxwell; Assistant Manager: John Davidson; Eddie the Bellhop: Edward Woods; Gustave: George Baxter; Waiter: Herman Bing; Dora: Anna Duncan

BOMBSHELL [also known as *BLONDE BOMBSHELL*]

Metro-Goldwyn-Mayer, released October 11, 1933

Crew

Associate Producer: Hunt Stromberg; Director: Victor Fleming; Story: Caroline Francke and Mack Crane; Screenplay: John Lee Mahin and Jules Furthman; Wardrobe: Adrian; Art Director: Merrill Pye; Set Director: Edwin B. Willis; Camera: Harold G. Rosson; Recording Director: Douglas Shearer; Editor: Margaret Booth

Cast

Lola Burns: Jean Harlow; Space Hanlon: Lee Tracy; "Pop" Burns: Frank Morgan; Gifford Middleton: Franchot Tone; Jim Brogan: Pat O'Brien; Mac: Una Merkel; Junior Burns: Ted Healy; Marquis di Binelli: Ivan Lebedeff; Junior's Girl: Isabel Jewell; Loretta: Louise Beavers; Winters: Leonard Carey; Mrs. Middleton: Mary Forbes; Mr. Middleton: C. Aubrey Smith; Alice Cole: June Brewster

THE GIRL FROM MISSOURI

Metro-Goldwyn-Mayer, released August 3, 1934

Crew

Producer: Bernard H. Hyman; Director: Jack Conway; Screenplay: Anita Loos and John Emerson; Music: Dr. William Axt; Camera: Harold G. Rosson and Ray June; Editor: Tom Held; Wardrobe: Adrian; Recording Director: Douglas Shearer; Art Director: Cedric Gibbons; Assistant Art Directors: Arnold Gillespie and Edwin B. Willis

Cast

Eadie Chapman: Jean Harlow; T. B. Paige: Lionel Barrymore; Tom Paige, Jr.: Franchot Tone; Cousins: Lewis Stone; Kitty: Patsy Kelly; Lord Douglas: Alan Mowbray; Miss Newbery: Clara Blandick; Bert: Russell Hopton; Charles Turner: Hale Hamilton; Senator Titcombe: Henry Kolker; Lifeguard: Nat Pendleton; Wardrobe Mistress: Marion Lord; Blonde Showgirl: Carol Tevis; Butler: Desmond Roberts; Willie: Bert Roach; Second Butler: Norman Ainsley; Senator: Howard Hickman; Policemen: James Burke and Lee Phelps; Manicurist: Alice Lake; Doorman: Lane Chandler; Office Manager: Richard Tucker; Secretary: Gladys Hulette; Lieutenant: Charles C. Wilson; Cameramen: Charles Williams and Fuzzy Knight; Dancer: Dennis O'Keefe; Stateroom Extra: Larry Steers; Eadie's Stepfather: William "Stage" Boyd

RECKLESS

Metro-Goldwyn-Mayer, released April 17, 1935

Crew

Producer: David O. Selznick; Director: Victor Fleming; Story: Oliver Jeffries; Screenplay: P. J. Wolfson; Wardrobe: Adrian; Songs: Jack King, Edwin Knopf, Harold Adamson, Burtin Lane, Jerome Kern, and Oscar Hammerstein ii; Choreography: Chester Hale and Carl Randall; Camera: George Folsey; Orchestration: Victor Baravalle; Synchronization: Herbert Stothart; Art Director: Cedric Gibbons; Assistant Art Directors: Merrill Pye and Edwin B. Willis; Editor: Margaret Booth

Cast

Mona Leslie: Jean Harlow; Ned Riley: William Powell; Bob Harrison: Franchot Tone; Granny: May Robson; Smiley: Ted Healy; Blossom: Nat Pendleton; Paul Mercer: Robert Light; Jo: Rosalind Russell; Eddie: Mickey Rooney; Harrison: Henry Stephenson; Louise: Louise Henry; Dale Every: James Ellison; Ralph Watson: Leon Ames; Man Mountain Dean: Himself; Gold Dust: Farina [Allen Hoskins]; Singer: Allan Jones; Carl Randall: Himself; Nina Mae McKinney: Herself

CHINA SEAS

Metro-Goldwyn-Mayer, released July 25, 1935

Crew

Producers: Irving Thalberg and Albert Lewin; Director: Tay Garnett; Story: Crosbie Garstin; Screenplay: Jules Furthman and James Kevin McGuinness; Song: Arthur Freed and Nacio Herb Brown; Wardrobe: Adrian; Art Director: Cedric Gibbons; Assistant Art Directors: James Havens and David Townsend; Set Director: Edwin B. Willis; Camera: Ray June; Editor: William Levanway; Music: Herbert Stothart

Cast

Alan Gaskall: Clark Gable; Dolly Portland: Jean Harlow; Jamesy McArdle: Wallace Beery; Tom Davids: Lewis Stone; Sybil Barclay: Rosalind Russell; Dawson: Dudley Digges; Sir Guy Wilmerding: C. Aubrey Smith; Charlie McCaleb: Robert Benchley; Rockwell: William Henry; Mrs.

Volberg: Live Demaigret; Mrs. Timmons: Lilian Bond; Wilbur Timmons: Edward Brophy; Yu-Lan: Soo Young; Carol Ann: Carol Ann Beery; Romanoff: Akim Tamiroff; Ngah: Ivan Lebedeff; Isabel McCarthy: Hattie McDaniel; Chess Player: Donald Meek; Lady: Emily Fitzray; Kingston: Pat Flaherty; Steward: Forrester Harvey; Ship's Officer: Tom Gubbins; Bertie: Charles Irwin; Cabin Boy: Willie Fung; Policeman: Ferdinand Munier; Rickshaw Boy: Chester Gan; Pilot: John Ince

RIFFRAFF

Metro-Goldwyn-Mayer, released December 24, 1935

Crew

Associate Producer: David Lewis; Director: J. Walter Ruben; Story: Frances Marion; Screenplay: Frances Marion, Anita Loos, and H. W. Hanemann; Music: Edward Ward; Wardrobe: Dolly Tree; Art Directors: Cedric Gibbons and Stanwood Rogas; Camera: Ray June; Editor: Frank Sullivan

Cast

Hattie: Jean Harlow; Dutch Muller: Spencer Tracy; Nick Lewis: Joseph Calleia; Lil: Una Merkel; Jimmy: Mickey Rooney; Flytrap: Victor Kilian; Brains: J. Farrell MacDonald; Pops: Roger Imhof; Rosie: Juanita Quigley; Belcher: Paul Hurst; Lew: Vince Barnett; Gertie: Dorothy Appleby; Mabel: Judith Wood; Ratsy: Arthur Houseman; Bert: Wade Boteler; Al: Joe Phillips; Pete: William Newell; Speed: Al Hill; Sadie: Helen Flint; Mrs. McCall: Lillian Harmer; Lefty: Robert Perry; Markis: George Givot; Maisie: Helene Costello; Head Matron: Rafaela Ottiano; Fishermen: King Mojavea, Al Herman, Philo McCullough, Sherry Hall, Jack Byron, Stanley Price, Herman Marx, Eddie Sturgis, and John George; Moving Man: Ivor McFadden; Fishwife: Mary Wallace; Newsreel Cameraman: Wally Maher; Agitator: Marshall Ruth

WIFE VS. SECRETARY

Metro Goldwyn-Mayer, released February 19, 1936

Crew

Producer: Hunt Stromberg; Director: Clarence Brown; Story: Faith Baldwin; Screenplay: John Lee Mahin, Norman Krasna, and Alice Duer Miller; Wardrobe: Dolly Tree; Art Director: Cedric Gibbons; Music: Herbert Stothart and Edward Ward; Camera: Ray June; Editor: Frank E. Hull; Recording Director: Douglas Shearer; Assistant Art Directors: William A. Horning and Edwin B. Willis

Cast

Van Stanhope: Clark Gable; Helen Wilson: Jean Harlow; Linda Stanhope: Myrna Loy; Mimi Stanhope: May Robson; Joe: Hobart Cavanaugh; Dave: James Stewart; Underwood: George Barbier; Simpson: Gilbert Emery; Edna Wilson: Margaret Irving; Tom Wilson: William Newell; Eve Merritt: Marjorie Gateson; Taggart: Leonard Carey; Hal Harrington: Charles Trowbridge; Mr. Jenkins: John Qualen; Mary Conners: Hilda Howe; Ellen: Mary McGregor; Joan Carstairs: Gloria Holden; Finney: Tommy Dugan; Howard: Jack Mulhall; Mr. Barker: Frank Elliott; German Cook: Greta Meyer; Mrs. Barker: Aileen Pringle; Hotel Clerk: Frank Puglia; Miss Clark: Myra Marsh; Frawley: Holmes Herbert; Trent: Frederick Burton; Williams: Harold Minjir; Bakewell: Maurice Cass; Businessman: Tom Herbert; Cuban Waiter: Guy D'Ennery; Tom Axel: Niles Welch; Bridegroom: Richard Hemingway; Raoul: Paul Ellis; Battleship: Tom Rowan; Bit Players: Edward Le Saint and Helen Shipman; Herbert: Clay Clement; Policeman: Tom Mahoney; Telephone Operator: Nena Quartaro; Information Clerk: Charles Irwin; Frenchman: Andre Cheron; Ship's Officer: Eugene Borden; Postal Clerk: Hooper Atchley; Scrubwoman: Lucille Ward; Elevator Boy: Clifford James (aka Philip Trent)

SUZY

Metro-Goldwyn-Mayer, released June 26, 1936

Crew

PRODUCER: Maurice Revnes; DIRECTOR: George Fitzmaurice; STORY: Herbert Gorman; SCREENPLAY: Dorothy Parker, Alan Campbell, Horace Jackson, and Lenore Coffee; SONG: Harold Adamson and Walter Donaldson; MUSIC: Dr. William Axt; WARDROBE: Dolly Tree; CAMERA: Ray June; EDITOR: George Boemler; RECORDING DIRECTOR: Douglas Shearer; ASSISTANT ART DIRECTORS: Edwin B. Willis and Gabriel Scogramlio

Cast

SUZY TRENT: Jean Harlow; TERRY MOORE: Franchot Tone; ANDRE CHARVILLE: Cary Grant; MADAME DIANE EYRELLE: Benita Hume; BARON CHARVILLE: Lewis Stone; CAPTAIN BARSANGES: Reginald Mason; MAISIE: Inez Courtney; MRS. SCHMIDT: Greta Meyer; KNOBBY MCPHERSON: David Clyde; MRS. BOGGS: Elspeth Dudgeon; RAOUL: Tyler Brooke; PIERRE: Robert Livingston; LT. CHARBRET: Dennis Morgan; POP GASPAROL: Christian Rub; POMMOT: Ferdinand Gottschalk; GASTON: George Spelvin; PETER: Charles McNaughton; MRS. BRADLEY: Una O'Connor; COUNTERMEN: Forrester Harvey and John Rogers; ADJUTANT: Hugh Huntley; LONDON: Bob Adair; AVIATOR: Drew Demarest

LIBELED LADY

Metro-Goldwyn-Mayer, released October 7, 1936

Crew

PRODUCER: Lawrence Weingarten; DIRECTOR: Jack Conway; STORY: Wallace Sullivan; SCREENPLAY: Maurice Watkins, Howard Emmett Rogers, and George Oppenheimer; ART DIRECTORS: Cedric Gibbons and William A. Horning; SET DIRECTOR: Edwin B. Willis; MUSIC: Dr. William Axt; WARDROBE: Dolly Tree; RECORDING DIRECTOR: Douglas Shearer; CAMERA: Norbert Brodine; EDITOR: Frederick Y. Smith

Cast

GLADYS BENTON: Jean Harlow; BILL CHANDLER: William Powell; CONNIE ALLENBURY: Myrna Loy; WARREN HAGGERTY: Spencer Tracy; JAMES B. ALLENBURY: Walter Connelly; HOLLIS BANE: Charley Grapewin; MRS. BURNS-NORVELL: Cora Witherspoon; EVANS E. E. Clive; BABS BURNS-NORVELL: Bunny Laurie Beatty; CHING: Otto Yamaoka; GRAHAM: Charles Trowbridge; MAGISTRATE MCCALL: Spencer Charters; BELLHOP: George Chandler; SCRUBWOMAN: Hattie McDaniel; CONNIE'S MAID: Greta Meyer; JOE: William Benedict; HARVEY ALLEN: Hal K. Dawson; PRESS MAN: Fred Graham; EDITOR: William Stack; WASHINGTON CHRONICLE EDITOR: Selmer Jackson; DIVORCE DETECTIVE: William Newell; TAXI DRIVER: Duke York; DETECTIVE: Pat West; CLERK: Ed Stanley; PHOTOGRAPHER: Wally Maher; ALEX: Tom Mahoney; GLADYS'S MAID: Libby Taylor; SECRETARY: Myra Marsh; CABLE EDITOR: Howard Hickman; BARKERS: Charles King, Dennis O'Keefe, Jack Mulhall, and Richard Tucker; FORTUNE TELLER: Ines Palange; CHARLES ARCHIBALD: Charles Croker King; DANCERS: Jay Eaton and Ralph Brooks

PERSONAL PROPERTY

Metro-Goldwyn-Mayer, released March 19, 1937

Crew

PRODUCER: John W. Considine, Jr.; DIRECTOR: W. S. Van Dyke; STORY: H. M. Harwood; SCREENPLAY: Hugh Mills and Ernest Vajda; MUSIC: Franz Waxman; ART DIRECTORS: Cedric Gibbons and Henry McAfee; SET DIRECTOR: Edwin B. Willis; WARDROBE: Dolly Tree; RECORDING DIRECTOR: Douglas Shearer; CAMERA: William Daniels; EDITOR: Ben Lewis

Personal Property
poster art (1937)

Cast

CRYSTAL WETHERBY: Jean Harlow; ROBERT DABNEY; Robert Taylor; CLAUDE DABNEY; Reginald Owen; CLARA: Una O'Connor; MR. DABNEY: E. E. Clive; MRS. DABNEY: Henrietta Crosman; MRS. BURNS: Cora Witherspoon; ARTHUR TREVALYN: Barnett Parker; BAILIFF: Forrester Harvey; KATHERINE BURNS: Marla Shelton; LORD CARSTAIRS: Lionel Braham; POLICEMAN: William Stack; CABBIES: Jimmy Aubrey, Leyland Hodgson, and Douglas Gordon; BUSINESSMEN: Arthur Stuart Hull and Charles Requa; ELDERLY MAN: Tom Ricketts; WAITER: Billy Bevans

SARATOGA

Metro-Goldwyn-Mayer, released July 23, 1937

Crew

PRODUCER: Bernard H. Hyman; ASSOCIATE PRODUCER: John Emerson; DIRECTOR: Jack Conway; STORY AND SCREENPLAY: Anita Loos and Robert Hopkins; ART DIRECTORS: Cedric Gibbons and John Detlie; SET DIRECTORS: Edwin B. Willis; MUSIC: Edward Ward; SONGS: Walter Donaldson, Bob Wright, and Chet Forrest; WARDROBE: Dolly Tree; RECORDING DIRECTOR: Douglas Shearer; CAMERA: Ray June; EDITOR: Elmo Vernon

Cast

DUKE BRADLEY: Clark Gable; CAROL CLAYTON: Jean Harlow*; GRANDPA CLAYTON: Lionel Barrymore; HARTLEY MADISON: Walter Pidgeon; JESSE KIFFMEYER: Frank Morgan; FRITZIE O'MALLEY: Una Merkel; TIP O'BRIEN: Cliff Edwards; DR. BEARD: George Zucco; FRANK CLAYTON: Jonathan Hale; ROSETTA: Hattie McDaniel; DIXIE GORDON: Frankie Darrow; BOSWELL: Carl Stockdale; HAND-RIDING HURLEY: Henry Stone; MRS. HURLEY: Ruth Gillette; VALET: Charley Fox; AUCTIONEER: Robert Emmett Keane; MEDBURY: Edgar Dearing; KENYON: Frank McGlynn, Sr.; MAIZIE: Margaret Hamilton; HORSE OWNERS: Lionel Pape, Pat West, and John Hyams; JUDGE: Sam Flint; CLIPPER: Harrison Greene; TRAIN PASSENGERS: Irene Franklin, Bill Carey, Ernie Stanton, Franklyn Ardell, John "Skins" Miller, Hank Mann, Nick Copeland, and Bert Roach; PULLMAN STEWARD: Forbes Murray; BUTLERS: George Reed and Billy McLain; GARDENER: Si Jenks; CAMERAMEN: George Chandler and Drew Demarest; TOUR: Mel Ruick; TRAIN PORTER: Fred Toones; BIT PLAYER: Gertrude Simpson; SINGERS AT PARTY: Four Hits and a Miss

*CLOSE-UP DOUBLE: Geraldine Dvorak; LONG-SHOT DOUBLE: Mary Dees; VOCAL DOUBLE: Paula Winslowe

SOURCES

In addition to the sources listed below, I obtained information from personal interviews with Allan Jones, Irene Mayer Selznick, and Gilbert Roland; birth, death, and marriage certificates; hospital records; contracts, memos, and press books in MGM's files; the FBI files; war records; the Los Angeles Department of Building Safety; and private letters of Miss Harlow, her family, and friends made available to me by the Carpenter family and fans of Jean Harlow.

BOOKS

Blum, Daniel. *A Pictorial History of the Talkies.* New York: Putnam, 1973.

Davies, Marion. *The Times We Had.* New York: Bobbs-Merrill Co., 1975.

Davis, Bette. *The Lonely Life.* New York: Putnam, 1962.

Davis, Dentner. *Jean Harlow, Hollywood Comet.* London: Constable House, 1937.

Dressler, Marie. *My Own Story.* Boston: Little, Brown & Co., 1934.

Fountain, Leatrice Joy. *Dark Star.* New York: St. Martin's Press, 1985.

Gardner, Gerald. *The Censorship Papers.* New York: Dodd, Mead & Co., 1987.

Green, Harvey. *The Light of the Home.* New York: Pantheon Books, 1983.

Harlow, Jean. *Today Is Tonight.* New York: Grove Press, 1965.

Kobal, John. *The Art of the Great Hollywood Portrait Photographers.* New York: Harrison House, 1980.

———. *People Will Talk.* New York: Knopf, 1985.

Keats, John. *Howard Hughes.* New York: Random House, 1966.

Lamparski, Richard. *Whatever Happened to . . . ?* New York: Crown Publishers, 1973.

Loos, Anita. *A Cast of Thousands.* New York: Grosset & Dunlap, 1977.

———. *Fate Keeps on Happening.* New York: Dodd, Mead & Co., 1984.

Loy, Myrna. *Being and Becoming.* New York: Knopf, 1987.

Lyon, Ben. *Life with the Lyons.* London: Oldham's Press, 1953.

McGilligan, Pat. *Backstory.* Berkeley: University of California Press, 1986.

Marx, Samuel. *Mayer and Thalberg, the Make-Believe Saints.* New York: Random House, 1975.

Moore, Colleen. *Silent Star.* New York: Doubleday, 1968.

Morella, Joe, and Edward Z. Epstein. *Gable and Lombard and Powell and Harlow.* New York: Dell, 1975.

Newquist, Roy. *Conversations with Crawford.* Secaucus, N.J.: Citadel Press, 1980.

Parish, James Robert. *The Hollywood Beauties.* Carlstadt, N.J.: Rainbow Books, 1978.

Pascal, John. *The Jean Harlow Story.* Popular Library, 1965.

Russell, Rosalind. *Life Is a Banquet.* New York: Random House, 1977.

Schessler, Ken. *This Is Hollywood.* La Verne, Calif.: Ken Schessler Publishing Co., 1989.

Schickel, Richard. *The Stars.* New York: Bonanza Books, 1962.

Tornebene, Lynn. *Long Live the King.* New York: Putnam, 1976.

Vieira, Mark A. *Hollywood Portraits.* New York: Portland House, 1988.

Walker, Alexander. *The Celluloid Sacrifice.* New York: Pelican Books, 1968.

Weathercock (1921 Yearbook). Kansas City, Mo.: Miss Barstow's School, 1921.

Wray, Fay. *On the Other Hand.* New York: St. Martin's Press, 1989.

NEWSPAPERS AND PERIODICALS

Chicago American, Chicago Daily Mirror, Film Pictorial Review (UK), *Films in Review, Hollywood Reporter, Hollywood Studio Magazine, Kansas City* (Missouri) *Star, Liberty, Life, Look, Los Angeles Record, Modern Screen, Motion Picture Herald, New Movie Magazine, New York American, New York Daily Mirror, New York Daily News, New York Evening Journal, New York Herald Tribune, New York Post, New York Telegraph, New York Times, New York World Telegram, Newsweek, Photoplay, Screen Book, Time, Vanity Fair, Variety.*

ACKNOWLEDGMENTS

Writing and researching a biography is a lot like being a private detective, only without the gun fights and car chases. The following people and institutions proved to be invaluable in my investigations, providing information, resources, and encouragement:

Julian Bach and Susan Merritt (Julian Bach Literary Agency), David L. Baldwin, David Blazak, Barbara Brown Martin, Curtis F. Brown, Diana Brown and Susan Fisher (Turner Entertainment/MGM), Children's Mercy Hospital (Kansas City, Mo., Randye Cohen, Dr. Arturo Constantiner (Hemodialysis Unit, Beekman Hospital), Olivia De Havilland, Glen Distefano, Harold W. Golden, Barbara Hall and Val Almendarez, Allan Jones, Mrs. Thurston Krebs, Fred L. Lee, Gregory Mank, Kathleen Manwaring (Syracuse University Press), Gloria Maxwell (Kansas City Public Library), Barbara Naimark (Good Samaritan Hospital), Judy Nathanson, National Personnel Records Center, Maureen O'Sullivan, the late Eddie Quillan, Esther Ralston, Gilbert Roland, Ann Schlosser (USC), the late Irene Mayer Selznick, Nathan Talbot (Committee on Publication for New York/Christian Science Church), Sandra Tubin and Christopher Dietrich (Mitchell, Silberberg & Knupp), Mary Wilson (Bedford County Pioneer Library), Mickey Woolard and Marj Finley (University of Kansas School of Dentistry), Lauren Wright, Barbara Wynn (Barstow's School), J. Kim Ziebel (Lake Forest Academy/Ferry Hall).

And especially Alan Axelrod, my editor; The New York Public Library at Lincoln Center (the country's most valuable film and theater research center); Catherine Childs, the best assistant a biographer ever had; and Walter J. Wiener, Jr., who knows more about Jean Harlow than Jean Harlow did herself.

PHOTO CREDITS

The photographers and the sources of photographic material other than those indicated in the captions are as follows: Academy of Motion Picture Arts and Sciences: pp. 124 (bottom right), 191; Courtesy of Gene Andrewski: p. 47; Avery Collection: p. 124 (bottom left); Courtesy of David L. Baldwin: p. 211; Bettmann/UPI: pp. 17, 21, 24, 69 (right), 80 (both), 83, 88, 93 (both), 111, 115, 137, 141, 146, 159, 166, 193, 195, 198–99, 215, 217; Bison Archives: pp. 96, 106, 120; Courtesy of Eddie Brandt's Saturday Matinee: pp. 73, 78; Courtesy of Catherine Childs: front cover, pp. 5, 51, 60, 69 (left), 86, 124 (top), 174, 219; Courtesy of Glen Distefano: pp. 186, 230; The Kobal Collection: pp. 42, 227; Courtesy of The Memory Shop: p. 134; Courtesy of Movie Star News: pp. 15 (left), 39 (all), 40–41, 46, 66, 72; Courtesy of Jerry Ohlinger's Movie Material Store: pp. 91, 99, 167, 171, 180, 185, 212, 241; Courtesy of Quality First: pp. 2, 8, 12, 30, 35, 45, 48, 53–54, 67, 76, 100, 112, 121, 125, 127, 132, 138, 155, 177, 189, 200; Courtesy of Walter J. Wiener, Jr.: pp. 1, 15 (right), 129 (left and right), 195–96, 204–5, 207, 209, 220, 228, back cover (also British cigarette cards on pp. 11, 13, 49, 61, 87, 113, 135, 175, 197, 213, 229); World Wide Photos: p. 201.

INDEX

Page numbers in *italics* refer to illustrations.

Adrian, 90, 127, 148, 165, 170, 178, 227
After the Thin Man, 194
Age of Larceny, The, 143
Alger, Horatio, 76
Algiers, 90
Allan, Ted, 178
All Quiet on the Western Front, 50, 57, 65
Anger, Kenneth, 43–44
Arbuckle, Fatty, 110, 150, 194
Arliss, George, 176
Armstrong, Robert, 65, 66
Arthur, Jean, 45, *45*
Asphalt Jungle, The, 158
Astaire, Fred, 176
Asther, Nils, 131, 142
Astor, Mary, 98, 101
As You Desire Me, 38
Athletic Girl and the Burglar, The, 150
Axt, William, 190
Ayres, Lew, 65, 66

Baby Face, 92
Back in Circulation, 203
Bacon Grabbers, 28, 233
Baer, Max, 122–23, 131, 147
Baker, Carroll, 226
Ball, Russell, 178
Bankhead, Tallulah, 62, 110
Bara, Theda, 77, 150, 176, 216
Barbier, Larry, 187, 200, 201
Barnard, Dr. Harold, 114
Barnes, Howard, 193
Barrymore, John, 11, 83–84, 123, 126
Barrymore, Lionel, 110, 123, 126, 154, 202, 220
Barthlemess, Richard, 158
Baxter, Warner, 158, 210, 211
Beard, The, 227
Beast of the City, The, 77–79, 84, 162, 236
Beau Chumps, 40
Beaudine, William, 73
Beau Geste, 158
Beebe, Lucius, 90
Beery, Wallace, 64–65, 83, 123, *124,* 125, 126, 140, 168
Bello, Marino (Jean's stepfather), *96,* 104, 106, *111, 137,* 215; Bern and, 96, 106, 110; as business manager for Jean, 79–80, 142–44, 145; financial dependence on Jean of, 41, 53, 80, 81, 102, 137, 148, 181, 221; Jean's conflicts with, 137, 139, 148; Mama Jean and, 23–25, 26, 28, 180–82, 210; Powell and, 180–81; remarriage of, 221, 225; Rosson and, 136, 143, 148
Benchley, Robert, 168
Bennett, Constance, *39, 166,* 218
Bern, Henry, 107, 109
Bern, Paul (Jean's second husband), *88, 93, 96;* background of, 92; death of, 104–9, 111, 113–14, 160–61, 162; Jean's engagement to, 92, 95; Jean's friendship with, 63, 74, 82, 87–89, 136; Jean's marriage to, 96–97, 102, 194; Millette and, 93–95, 103, 108, 110; "Pygmalion complex" of, 87, 102; Shulman's claims about, 213, 225; support of Jean's career by, 75, 77, 79, 84; wills of, 110, 111
Best-Dressed Woman in Paris, The, 218
Big Parade, The, 57
Blonde Baby (story; Collison), 73
Blonde Bombshell. See Bombshell
blonde hair, popularity of, 37, 38, *39,* 68, 78, 175
Blondell, Joan, *39,* 68, 116, 203
Bombshell, 131–33, *132,* 135, 137, 139–40, 141, 142, 169, 191, 237
Booth, Frederick, 122
Born to be Kissed, 149
Bow, Clara, 29, *45, 46,* 63, 76, 84; as a blonde, 38; gambling debts of, 118; home life of, 129, 131; roles of, 45, 92, 152
Boyer, Charles, 90, *91*
Brabin, Charles, 77, 78
Brats, 40
Breen, Joseph, 153, 184
Breese, Harriet, 182, 216
Brent, Evelyn, 214
Brown, Barbara, 96, 149, 170, 216, 224
Brown, Clarence, 184
Brown, John Mack, 64
Brown, Nacio Herb, 120
Brown, Stanley, 89, 128–29, 154
Browning, Tod, 65
Bruce, Virginia, 96
Brush, Katherine, 84, 90
Bull, Clarence Sinclair, 77, 82, 99, 100, 172, 178, 187, 214
Buntz, Russell, 82
Burgess, Dorothy, 119
Burke, Billie, 123, 126, 176, 215, 218
Buttons, Red, 226
Byron, Walter, 74

Caddo Company, 49, 52, 56, 61, 63, 68, 71, 74, 75, 79, 234
Cagney, James, 67, *67,* 68
Calleia, Joseph, 176, 180
Call Her Savage, 92, 152
Camino Real (play; Williams), 220
Campbell, Alan, 187
Capra, Frank, 70, 71, 72, 74–75
Carmichael, John, 88, 104–5
Carmichael, Winifred, 88, 104–5
Carpenter, Abraham (Jean's grandfather), 13, 14, 130
Carpenter, Dianna Beale (Jean's grandmother), 14, 130
Carpenter, George, 13
Carpenter, Harlean. *See* Harlow, Jean
Carpenter, Jean. *See* Harlow, Jean Poe
Carpenter, Maude Seth (Jean's stepmother), 25, 215, *215,* 221
Carpenter, Mont Clair (Jean's father), 13, 14, 15–16, 20, 22, 24, 36, 53, 129, 136, 181, 215, *215,* 216, 221, 225
Carroll, Harrison, 206
Carroll, Nancy, 36
Catlett, Walter, 72
censorship, 91, 149–54, 184
Central Casting, 33, 34, 36, 43, 45
Chadsey, Jetta Roberson (Jean's great aunt), 15, *96,* 129, 210, 211
Chaplin, Charlie, 11, 23, 47, 95
Chevalier, Maurice, 36–37
China Seas, 167, 167–70, 171, 238–39
Christian Scientists, 213, 216
Christie, Al, 36, 231
City Lights, 47
Clarke, Mae, 67, 73, 74
Clift, Montgomery, 164
Close Harmony, 36, 232
Club View Drive house (Harlow-Bello home), 82, *83,* 92, 97, 102, 105, 136, 139, 143, 163, 181, 182
Coffee, Lenore, 187–88
Colbert, Claudette, 68
Collins, Chick, 169
Collison, Wilson, 73, 98
Colman, Ronald, 158
Columbia Studios, 63, 70–71, 72, 75, 235, 236
Connelly, Walter, 193
Conway, Jack, 84, 89, 148, 149, 191, 194, 202, 206, 207, 211, 216
Coolidge, Calvin, 83–84
Cooper, Gary, 31, 71, 203
Cosmopolitan studio, 64, 145, 236
Courtney, Inez, 188–89
Craig, Judge Elliott, 157, 181
Crane, Mack, 131
Crawford, Joan, 62, 68, 82, 84, 110, 131, 215, 226; Bern and, 87, 109; as a blonde, 38, *39;* Jean awarded roles

of, 161, 162, 176; MGM credo and, 83, 148; movie roles of, 98, 123, 186; photo sessions and, 171
Crellin, Yvonne, 158
Crewe, Regina, 164, 169, 200
Cukor, George, 125–26

Daniels, Bebe, 46
Daniels, William, *199*
Davenport, Dorothy, 151
Davies, Marion, 37, *39,* 75, 84, 87, 166, *166,* 230
Davis, Bette, 11, 38, 57, 142, 148
Davis, Clifford, 156
Davis, Clifton, 88, 104, 105, 161
Dawn, Jack, 175
Day of the Locust, The (book; West), 56
Dees, Mary, 218
De Havilland, Olivia, 143
Delehanty, Thornton, 68
Del Rio, Dolores, 114, 166
Delta Queen (ship), 107
DeMille, Cecil B., 133, 197
Denoyer, Violet, 214
Devine, Andy, 73
Dickens, Homer, 214
Dietrich, Marlene, 76, *146,* 152
Dietrich, Noah, 58
Dinner at Eight, 123, *124, 125,* 125–28, *127,* 132, 139, 154, 169, 190, 193, 237
Dix, Richard, 34
Double Wedding, 208
Double Whoopee, 38, 40–41, *41,* 52, 151, 232
Dracula, 65
Dressler, Marie, 84, 110, 123, 125–26, 128, 140, 148, 214, 216
Duggan, Joe, 173
Dvorak, Geraldine, 218

Eadie Was a Lady, 149
Eagels, Jeanne, 98, 116
Easton Drive house (Bern home), 87–88, 95–96, 104–5, *106,* 113, 130
Eddy, Nelson, 216
Edwards, Cliff, 202
Egli, Joe, 33, 36
Elder, Ruth, 34
Emerson, John, 149
Erwin, Hobe, 127
Erwin, Stuart, 119
Evans, Madge, 123, 126
Evans, Tom, 178
Everything's Been Done Before, 162
extra work, necessities for, 36

Fairbanks, Douglas, Jr., 23, 82, 103
Fashions of 1934, 38
Faye, Alice, 38, *39,* 217
Ferber, Edna, 123
Ferry Hall (school), 25–27, 28, 43
Feyder, Jacques, 98
Fidler, Jimmie, 183
Fields, W. C., 150, 217–18
Film Pictorial (magazine), 179
Fishbaugh, Dr. E. C., 207, 208, 210, 211, 213, 214
Fitts, Buron, 109, 160–61
Fitzmaurice, George, 188
Fleming, Victor, 98, 101, 110, 131, 162
Flying Down to Rio, 152
Ford, Wallace, 77, *78*
Four Marys, The, 218
Fox Studios, 32, 33, 63, 68, 150, 216, 235
Francis, Kay, 179
Francke, Caroline, 131
Frankenstein, 50, 65
Freaks, 66
Freed, Arthur, 120
Freeman, E. A., 135–36
Friede, Donald, 206, 208, *211*
Fugitives, 36, 231
Furthman, Jules, 131

Gable, Clark, 98, *100,* 104, 106, 119–22, *120, 121,* 123, 130, 143, 183–84, *185,* 203, *204,* 205, *209,* 216; Jean and, 64, 100–101, 110, 116, 119, 208, 211; at Jean's funeral, 215, *217;* Lombard and, 160, 203
Gallagher, 71. *See also Platinum Blonde*
Garbo, Greta, 75, 81, 84, 92, 99, 123, 214, 230; as a blonde, 38, *39;* rebelliousness of, 83, 100, 142, 171
Garden of Allah, The, 158
Garland, Judy, 11, 129, 143, 217
Garnett, Tay, 170
Garrison, Harold, 88, 104, 105
Garstin, Crosbie, 167
Gentlemen Prefer Blondes (book; Loos), 84, 149
Geraughty, Carmelita, 103, 137, 144, 147, *155,* 155–56, 215
Gibbons, Cedric, 114, 136, 166
Gilbert, John, 81, 95, 96, 98, 102, 107, 142, 222
Gilmore, Douglas, *54*
Girl from Missouri, The, 148–49, 154–55, 156–57, 158, 165, 238
Girl in Every Port, A, 69
Givot, George, 180
Glyn, Elinor, 26
Goldbach, Willis, *111*
Golden, Red, 208
Goldie, 69, 69–70, 72, 153, 177, 235
Goldwyn studio, 93. *See also* Metro-Goldwyn-Mayer
Gone With the Wind, 217
Gordon, C. Henry, *198*
Gorman, Herbert, 187
Goudal, Jetta, 130
Go West, Young Man, 38
Grable, Betty, *39*
Grand Hotel, 87, 123, 152
Grant, Cary, 187–88, *189,* 190, 217
Grauman's Chinese Theatre, 56, 87, *138,* 139
Great Ziegfeld, The, 183, 193
Grey, Virginia, 218
Grieve, Harold, 130
Griffith, Corinne, 43
Grove Press, 145

Haines, William, 110, 222
Hale, Louise Closser, 71
Hall, Evelyn, *53*
Hall, James, 45, 46, 49, 50, 52, *53, 54,* 55, 57
Hall, Mordaunt, 57, 65, 68, 78
Hamilton, Margaret, 202, 220
Hammett, Dashiell, 183
Hamp, Johnny, 114, 166
Hamp, Ruth, 114, 145, 166
Hannemann, H. W., 175
Hardy, Oliver, 38, 40, *41*
Harlow, Ellen Williams (Jean's grandmother), 14, 16, 18, 129, 202
Harlow, Jean (née Harlean Carpenter), *8, 27, 47, 69, 80, 111, 129, 138, 146, 155, 171, 195, 198, 201, 211, 230;* in advertisements, 76, *76,* 187, 227, *227;* background of, 13–14; in *The Beast of the City,* 77–79, *78;* Bern's death and, 106–11, 114, 160–61; Bern's engagement to, 92, *93,* 95; Bern's friendship with, 63, 74, 82, 87–89, *88,* 136; Bern's marriage to, *96,* 96–97, 102, 194; biography of, 96–97, 108, 109, 194, 213, 223–26; in *Bombshell,* 130–33, *132,* 135, 139–40; childhood of, *12,* 13, *15,* 16, *17,* 18–28, *21, 24;* in *China Seas,* 168–70; on cigarette cards, *1, 9, 11, 13, 31, 49, 61, 87, 113, 135, 175, 197, 213, 229;* clothing style of, *8,* 11, 83; contract disputes of, 79–80, 142–45; death of, 211, 213–14; in *Dinner at Eight,* 123, *124, 125,* 125–28, *127;* early movies of, *35,* 38, *40,* 40–41, *41,* 45–47, *46;* as an extra, 33–37; eyebrow style of, 76–77, 177; family's disapproval of career of, 36, 43, 44–45; funeral of, *215,* 215–16, *217;* Gable and, 64, 100–101, 110, 116, 119, *120,* 208, 211; gambling skill of, 119, 188; in *The Girl from Missouri,* 148–49, 154–55, 156–57; in *Goldie,* 69–70; hair color of, 13, 37–38, 170, 175–76, 177; in *Hell's Angels,* 52–53, *53, 54,* 55–59; Hesser photos of, *42,* 43–44, 58; in *Hold Your Man,* 119–22, *120, 121;* illnesses of, 140–41, 194–95, 198, 202, 203, 206–11; in *Iron Man,* 65–66, *66;* in *Libeled Lady, 4,* 190–93, *191;* McGrew and, 28–29, *29,* 32, 43, 44, 58; Mama Jean and, 19, 22, 28, 29, 35, 113, 136–37, 157, 172, 201, 207, 210; Mayer and, 10, 77, *80,* 161–62, 170, 175–76, 201; Mayer's conflicts with, 79–80, 81, 82, 83–84, 96, 140, 141, 143–44, 148, 187, 192–93; menagerie of, 16, 19, 114, *115;* movies about, 226–27; novel by, 145–47, 206, 222; in *Personal Property,* 197–200, *199, 200;* in *Platinum Blonde,* 71–72, *72;* portrait stills of, *6, 30, 48, 60, 87, 112, 124, 134, 174, 196, 204, 212, 228;* Powell and, 158–60, *159,* 163–64, 165, 179, 183, 192, 194–95, 206, 208, 210; in *The Public Enemy, 67,* 67–68; in *Reckless,* 161–65; in *Red Dust,* 98–101, *100,*

116–17; in *Red-Headed Woman, 2,* 84–85, 89–91, *91;* in *Riffraff,* 176–77, 179–80; Rosson's divorce from, 157–58; Rosson's friendship with, 85, 117, 123, 135; Rosson's marital difficulties with, 140, 143, 144, 147–48, 155–56; Rosson's marriage to, 135–36, *137,* 139, *141;* salary of, 34, 53, 80–81, 140, 175; in *Saratoga, 204, 205,* 205–6, 207, *207,* 208, *209,* 218–20, *220, 228;* in *The Secret Six,* 63–65; sense of humor of, 10–11, 83–84; singing difficulties of, 89, 120, 162–63, 190; in *Suzy,* 188–90, *189;* Thalberg and, 77, 84, 85, 96, 103, 105–6, 116, 142, 187, 193, *193;* in *Three Wise Girls,* 72–74, *73;* in *Wife vs. Secretary,* 183–87, *185, 186;* will of, 216

Harlow, Jean Poe (Jean's mother), *15, 96,* 106, *137,* 208; acting-career attempts of, 22, 23, 25, 26, 34, 38, 140; Bello and, 23–25, 26, 28, 180–82, 210; Carpenter and, 13, 15–16, 20, 22; Christian Scientists and, 213; death of, 222; family background of, 14–15; financial dependence on Jean of, 41, 53, 80, 81, 102, 137, 148; as hostess, 10–11, 92, 97, 136; hysterical tendencies of, 15, 106, 107, 181; Jean's death and, 211, 213, 214, 215, 216, 222; MGM and, 221–22; protectiveness over Jean of, 19, 22, 28, 29, 35, 113, 136–37, 157, 172, 201, 207, 210; travels with Jean of, 58, 63, 118, 160, 200–202

Harlow, S. D. (Jean's grandfather), 14, 16, 18, 36, 41, 43, 44–45, 53, 129, 202

Harlow (film biography), 226

Harper's Bazaar (magazine), 187

Harrison, Paul, 152

Harwood, H. M., 198

Hatfield, Hurd, 226

Hays, Will, 151

Hays Office, 91, 151–53

Hearst, William Randolph, 75, 145, 166

Hell's Angels, 46, 49–59, *51, 53, 54,* 61, 63, 64, 65, 70, 74, 79, 85, 96, 128, 179, 189, 190, 224, 234

Hendry, Whitey, 105

Hepburn, Katharine, 11, 31, 83

Hesser, Edwin Bower, 43, 44, 187

Hill, George, 64, 65

Hobbes, Halliwell, 71

Hold Your Man, 119–22, *121,* 126, 131, 148, 162, 163, 168, 190, 237

Holliday, Judy, 125

Hollywood Babylon (book; Anger), 43–44

Hollywood Revue of 1933, The, 130

Holman, Libby, 161, 164

Holmes, Phillips, 127, 164

Hoover, J. Edgar, 201

Hope, Fred, 127

Hopkins, Robert, 202

Hopper, Hedda, 225

Hornblow, Arthur, 183

How Bridget Served the Salad Undressed, 150

Hoyt, Carolyn, 33, 68, 202

Hughes, Howard, 46, 49, 50, 52, 53, 55, 58, 61, 62, 63, 65, 67, 68, 70, 74

Human Wreckage, 151

Hume, Benita, 188

100% Pure, 149

Hurrell, George, 172, 178, 230

Hurst, Paul, *121*

Huston, Walter, 77, *80*

Hymer, Warren, *69*

I Am a Fugitive from a Chain Gang, 67

Imhof, Roger, *177*

In Old Chicago, 216

Invisible Man, The, 50

Iron Man, 65–66, *66,* 70, 72, 234

It Happened One Night, 191

Jazz Singer, The, 31

Jeritza, Marie, 23

Johaneson, Bland, 57, 70, 90, 128, 189

Jones, Buck, 23

Jones, Dr. Edward, 107, 108

Joy, Leatrice, 95

June, Ray, 155, 206, 216

Karloff, Boris, 11

Kaufman, George S., 123

Kelly, Patsy, 149

kidney disease, 208–10, 214

King Kong, 65, 74

Kirkpatrick, Sidney, 161

Kramer, William, 82

Krasna, Norman, 185

LaMarr, Barbara, 87, 109, 113

Landau, Arthur, 38, 52, 61, 63, 70, 74, 79, 95, 97, 194, 223, 224, 225, 226

Landry, Jeanette, 206

Lane, Leone, *45,* 46

Lane, Lola, 38

Langham, Ria, 100, 203

Lansbury, Angela, 226

Last Command, The, 158

Laurel, Stan, 38, 40, *41*

Lawford, Peter, 226

Leadbelly, 221

Lee, Lucille, 32

Leigh, Vivien, 57

Levine, Nathan, 182

Levy, Paul Bern. *See* Bern, Paul

Lewin, Al, 87

Lewis, David, 175

Lewis, Diana, 222–23

Libeled Lady, 4, 174, 191–94, *191,* 214, 217, 240

Liberty (film), 38, 232

Liberty (magazine), 113, 169

Liechtenstein, Prince Ferdinand, 102

Life (magazine), 203

Life with Father, 223

Lightner, Winnie, 120

Lingeman, Richard, 146

Literary Digest (magazine), 61

Little Caesar, 67

Living in a Big Way, 140, 141, 143, 148

Lloyd, Harold, 79

Lombard, Carole: as a blonde, 38, *39;* Gable and, 203; at Jean's funeral, 216, *217;* Powell and, 159, 160, 185, 222

Loos, Anita, 38, 55, 84–85, 91, 103, 119, 120–21, 149, 175, 202, 211

Louise, Anita, 38

Love, Bessie, 43

Love Parade, The, 36, 151, 233

Lowe, Edmund, 123

Loy, Myrna, 171, 185, *185,* 190–92, 193; Jean and, 183, 184, 194, 195, 209, 215; Powell and, 158, 183, 194

Lubistch, Ernest, 36, 151

Lulu Belle, 130

Lux Radio Theatre of the Air, 197

Lynley, Carol, 226

Lyon, Ben, 46, 49, 50, 52, *53, 54,* 55, 57

McClure, Michael, 227

McCrea, Joel, 23

McDaniel, Hattie, 168, 169, 194, 202, 208

MacDonald, Jeanette, 36–37, 171, 216

McDonald, Peggy, *199*

McGrew, Charles Fremont, II (Jean's first husband), 27–29, *29,* 32, 36, 43, 44, 47, 58, 80, 82, 136, 224

McGuinness, James Kevin, 167–68

Madame Sans-Gene, 197, *198*

Mahin, John Lee, 98, 101–2, 123, 130–31, 167–68, 185

Maiden Voyage, 218

Maisie, 218

Mamoulien, Rouben, *146*

Man in Possession, The, 198

Mankiewicz, Herman J., 126

Mannix, Eddie, 216

Mansfield, Jayne, 223

March, Joseph Moncure, 49, 50, 52–53, 55

Marion, Frances, 126, 175

Marked Woman, 148

Marsters, Ann, 224

Martin, Wayne, 172–73

Marx Brothers, 215

Masquerade, 38

Mata Hari, 92

Maugham, Somerset, 98

Mayer, Irene. *See* Selznick, Irene Mayer

Mayer, Louis B., 9, 75, 215, 218, 222; Bern's death and, 105, 107, 108, 109–10; Jean and, 10, 77, *80,* 161–62, 170, 175–76, 201; Jean's conflicts with, 79–80, 81, 82, 83–84, 96, 140, 141, 143–44, 148, 187, 192–93

Merkel, Una, 85, 90, 180, 202

Metro-Goldwyn-Mayer (MGM), 75, 101, 105, 119, 123, 220, 234, 236–41; censorship and, 91, 92; Jean and, 63, 75–77, 97, 103, 129–31, 148, 161–62, 170–71, 187, 230; Jean's

contract with, 79–82, 142–45; Jean's death and, 211, 216–17; Mama Jean and, 221–22
Metro studio, 94. *See also* Metro-Goldwyn-Mayer
Miller, Alice Duer, 185
Millette, Dorothy Roddy, *93,* 93–95, 103, 107, 108, 109, 110, 111
Million Dollar Legs, 150
Mills, Hugh, 199
Minter, Mary Miles, 150
Mishkin, Leo, 193
Mr. Roberts, 223
Modern Screen (magazine), 14, 61, 195, 202
Mommie Dearest, 148, 226
Monroe, Marilyn, 11, 43, 117, 125, 129, 178, 223
Montgomery, Robert, 198
Moore, Colleen, 79, 81, 95, 97, 102
Mooring, W. H., 145
Moran of the Marines, 34, *35,* 36, 231
Morgan, Frank, 131, *132,* 202
Morris, Chester, 85, 90
Morrison, Adaline, 26
Motion Picture Herald, 219
Multi-Color, 50, 56, 178
Multiple Maniacs, 227
Mulvey, Dick, 165
Mulvey, Kay, 10, 165, 166, 213, 216, 222, 225
Murray, Mae, 23, 37, 222
My Little Chickadee, 150
My Man Godfrey, 191

Nance, Frank, 106–7, 109
Negri, Pola, 110
Neilan, Marshall ("Mickey"), 49, 79
Newsweek (magazine), 44, 169, 225
New York American, 164, 169, 200
New York Daily Mirror, 57, 70, 72, 90, 128, 189
New York Daily News, 66, 70, 78, 90
New York Evening Star, 191
New York Herald Tribune, 66, 72, 90, 116, 128, 164, 193, 219, 226
New York Nights, 46, 233
New York Post, 68, 79, 190, 200
New York Telegraph, 193
New York Times, 57, 65, 66, 68, 74, 79, 116, 122, 128, 139, 146, 156, 164, 169, 179, 185, 189, 193, 200, 219, 226
Night Life, 130
Nissen, Greta, 49, 50, 52
Nixon, Marion, 97
Nora, 130
Normand, Mabel, 87, 109, 150, 230
Novarro, Ramon, 92
Nugent, Frank, 185

O'Brien, Pat, 131, 133, 203
Office Wife (book; Baldwin), 183
Oliver, Edna Mae, 45
Orsatti, Vic, 117
Orsatti Agency, 79, 143, 145, 206, 226
Osornio, Dr. Servando, 118
O'Sullivan, Maureen, 158, 165, 225, 230
Owen, Garry, *121*
Owen, Reginald, 198

Pallette, Eugene, 193
Paradise, 143
Paramount Studios, 34, 36, 45, 63, 81, 93, 133, 187, 226
Parker, Barnett, 199
Parker, Dorothy, 187, 188
Parsons, Louella, 156, 183, 202, 206, 222, 230
Pathé studio, 95, 231
Patterson, Elizabeth, 38
Pearce, Mary Vivian, 227
Personal Property, 197–200, *199, 200,* 205, 240–41, *241*
Pettit, Theodore, 110
Photoplay (magazine), 14, 61, 65, 143–44, 156–57
Piazza, Ben, 74–75
Pickford, Mary, 82
Pidgeon, Walter, 202, 205, 207, 211
Pierce Brothers Mortuary, 214
Pink Flamingos, 227
Platinum Blonde, 71–72, *72,* 73, 74, 75, 132, 191, 235
Powell, Eleanor, 165
Powell, William, 161, 185, *191, 193,* 202, 225; background of, 158; Bello and, 180–81; Jean and, 158–60, *159,* 163–64, 165, 179, 183, 192, 194–95, 206, 208, 210; Jean's death and, 211, 215, 216, 222; marriage of, 222–23
Presenting Lily Mars, 143
Prevost, Marie, *73,* 73–74
Prize Fighter and the Lady, The, 122, 123
Production Code, 149–54
Public Enemy, The, 60, 67, 67–68, 69, 70, 72, 127
Purcell, Irene, 198

Quarberg, Lincoln, 56, 61, 62–63
Queer People, 74

Rain, 98, 116, 152, 186
Rains, Claude, 197, *198*
Rambeau, Marjorie, 64
Rand, Sally, 109
Rankin, Ruth, 143–44
Ray, Charles, 23
Raymond, Gene, 38, 98, 101
Reckless, 158, 161–65, 190, 203, 224, 238
Red Dust, 98–101, *99, 100,* 103, 110, 113, 116–17, 130, 131, 152, 236
Red Gables (S. D. Harlow estate), 18
Red-Headed Woman, 2, 84–85, 89–92, *91,* 98, 101, 116–17, 152, 236
Red-Headed Woman in Paris, 131
Redondo, John, 135
Reid, Wallace, 150–51
Reynolds, Zachary Smith, 161, 162
Richman, Harry, 63
Riffraff, 175, 176–80, *177, 180,* 183, 239
Ring, Robert R., 116
Riskin, Robert, 73
Ritz Bar, The, 130
RKO studio, 67, 74
Roach, Hal, 38, 40, 41, 43, 52, 56
Roberson, Donald (Jean's cousin), *96,* 129, 210, 211, 216
Roberti, Lyda, 38, *39,* 78
Robson, May, 184, *185*
Rogers, Charles "Buddy," 36
Rogers, Ginger, 165, 226
Rogers, Howard Emmett, 119
Rogers, Will, 81, 83
Roland, Gilbert, 46, 47, 55
Romeo and Juliet, 193
Romola, 158
Rooney, Mickey, 77, *177,* 180
Roosevelt, Eleanor, *201,* 202
Roosevelt, Franklin Delano, 117, 177, 192, 197, 201, 224
Rosson, Arthur, 133
Rosson, Gladys, 133
Rosson, Harold (Jean's third husband), 119, 133, *137, 141,* 211, 215; Bello and, 136, 143, 148; as cameraman, 133, 135, 140, 149, 155, 158; Jean's divorce from, 157–58; Jean's friendship with, 85, 117, 123, 135; Jean's marriage to, 135–36, 139; marital difficulties of, 140, 143, 144, 147–48, 155–56
Rosson, Richard, 133
Ruben, J. Walter, 175
Rubin, Robert, 74–75
Rush, Loretta, 169
Ruskin, Harry, 211
Russell, Allen, 135
Russell, Rosalind, 163–64, 165, 168

St. Johns, Adela Rogers, 43, 95, 113, 225
Samuelson, Louis, 205
Sanford, Dick, 221
San Francisco, 193
Saratoga, 202–3, *204, 205,* 205–7, *207, 209,* 211, 215, 216, 218–20, *219, 220,* 241
Saturday Night Kid, The, 45, 45–46, *46,* 52, 224, 233
Scarface, 67
Scarlet Empress, The, 152
Schenck, Nicholas, 164
Schickel, Richard, 161
Screen Book (magazine), 156
Sebring, Jay, 113
Secret Six, The, 63–65, 70, 234
Selznick, David O., 96, 103, 105
Selznick, Irene Mayer, 22, 23, 92, 96, 108–9
Sennwald, André, 66, 156, 169
Seymour, Clarine, 218
Shearer, Norma, 75, 84, 96, 98, 100, 103, 105–6, 142, 171
She Done Him Wrong, 150
Short, Bobby, 41
Show Boat, 50
Shulman, Irving, 97, 108, 109, 194, 213, 223–26
Silberberg, Mendel, 79
Simon, Nat, 221
Singin' in the Rain, 158, 179
Skolsky, Sidney, 188

Smith, Genevieve, 216
Sonneman, W. F., 173
Sothern, Ann, 218
Stanwyck, Barbara, 92, 197
Stars, The (book; Schickel), 161
Stephenson, Henry, 90
Sternberg, Josef von, *146*
Stewart, James, 184, 185
Stone, Lewis, 64, 90, 190
Strickling, Howard, 76, 105, 117, 122, 165, 173, 177, 201, 225, 226
Stromberg, Hunt, 98, 216
Sunset Boulevard, 33
Suzy, 187–90, *189,* 191, 240
Swanson, Gloria, 23, 43, 64, 98, 133, *166*
Sweet, Blanche, 37

Tabor, Horace, 14
Tale of Two Cities, A, 193
Talmadge, Norma, 46
Tarkington, Booth, 143
Taylor, Robert, 197, *198,* 198–200, *200,* 218, 224, 225, 230
Taylor, William Desmond, 150, 161
Tazelaar, Marguerite, 219
Tell It to the Marines, 218
Temple, Shirley, 217
Thalberg, Irving, 75, 79, 95, 130, 131, 167, 168, 170, 192–93; Jean and, 77, 84, 85, 96, 103, 105–6, 116, 142, 187, 193, *193*
Thin Man, The, 158, 183
Thirer, Irene, 66, 70, 90, 189–90, 200
This Modern Age, 38
This Thing Called Love, 36, 231
Thomas, Jameson, 74
Thomas, Olive, 150
Three Wise Girls, 72–74, *73,* 236
Thundering Toupees, 38, 232
Time (magazine), 116, 117, 169–70, 219
Today Is Tonight (book; Harlow), 145–47, 206, 222
"Today" show, 225
Todd, Thelma, 43, 52
Tone, Franchot, 131, 133, 135, 154, 161, 164, 165, 188, 190
Top Hat, 165
Topper, 217–18
Tracy, Lee, 123, 131, 132–33
Tracy, Spencer, 69, 176, 177, 179, 190, *191,* 192, 193, 202–3, 218
Tree, Dolly, 70, 178, 184, 188, 192
Tucker, Sophie, 62
Turner, Florence, 9–10

United Artists, 46, 47, 49, 233, 234
Universal studio, 63, 65, 234
Unkissed Man, The, 38, *40,* 232
U.S. Smith, 218

Vajda, Ernest, 199
Van Dyke, Woodbridge Strong ("Woody"), 9–10, 136, 198, 199, 216
Vanity Fair (magazine), 118, 225
Variety (magazine), 57, 74
Vaughn, Hilda, 127, *127*
Velez, Lupe, 215
Verrill, Virginia, 162
Victor/Victoria, 227
Viva Villa!, 140
Vorkapich, Slavka, 104

Walker, Alexander, 68
Warhol, Andy, 227
Warner Bros., 31, 63, 67, 142, 148, 235
Warren, Lesley Anne, 227
Washburn, Bryant, *40*
Washburn, Charles, 203
Watts, Richard, Jr., 66, 68, 72, 116, 128, 139, 157, 164, 185–86, 190
Watts, Tommy, 188
Way Down East, 218
Weak But Willing, 36, 231
Weissmuller, Johnny, 143
West, Mae, 38, 62, 68, 81, 150, 152
West, Nathaniel, 56
Whale, James, 50, 52, 55–56, 57, 64
What Price Glory, 69
Wheeler, Ralph, 230
Why Is a Plumber?, 38, 232
Widden, Jay, 122
Widenham, William, 109, 161
Wife vs. Secretary, 183–87, *185, 186,* 190, 239
Williams, Blanche, 61–62, 63, 65, 80, 97, 106, 113, 139, 149, 156, 172, 182, *199,* 200, 206, 208, 210, 211, 213
Williams, Robert, 71, 72, *72,* 74, 132
Williams, Tennessee, 220
Willinger, Laszlo, 172
Wilson, Carey, 87, 95, 102, 103, 107, 116, 136, 144–45, *155,* 155–56, 166, 215
Winslowe, Paula, 218
Witherspoon, Cora, 199
Wizard of Oz, The, 158, 217
Wood, Natalie, 223
Wood, Sam, 119, 121
Woods, Edward, *67,* 127
Woolwine, Thomas, 110
Wray, Fay, 207

Yong, Soo, 168
Young, Loretta, 71
Young, Roland, 218

Zucco, George, 220, *220*
Zukor, Adolph, 164